W9-BKQ-073

NEW SCHOOLS
for a NEW
CENTURY

A Leader's Guide to
High School Reform

NEW SCHOOLS
for a NEW
CENTURY

A Leader's Guide to
High School Reform

Kenneth J. Tewel

St. Lucie Press
Delray Beach, Florida

Printed and bound in the U.S.A. Printed on acid-free paper.
10 9 8 7 6 5 4 3 2 1

Library of Congress Cataloging-in-Publication Data

Tewel, Kenneth J.
    New schools for a new century : a leader's guide to high school
reform / by Kenneth J. Tewel
        p.   cm.
    Includes bibliographical references and index.
    ISBN 1-884015-38-7 (alk. paper)
    1. High schools—United States.   2. Educational change—United
States.   3. School management and organization—United States.
4. Educational leadership—United States.   I. Title.
LB1607.5.T49   1995   94-46301
373.73—dc20   CIP

    Direct all inquiries to St. Lucie Press, Inc., 100 E. Linton Blvd., Suite 403B, Delray Beach, Florida 33483.

Phone: (407) 274-9906
Fax: (407) 274-9927

S^{t}L

Published by
St. Lucie Press
100 E. Linton Blvd., Suite 403B
Delray Beach, FL 33483

Dedication

for
DAVID GROSS
November 22, 1956–August 17, 1992

He died as he lived:
With courage, integrity, wisdom, and compassion

Without him, this book would not have been written

Table of Contents

Preface

This book started out as an examination of the leader's role as a catalyst for high school reform; however, it soon became much more. The need for a book that emphasized the leader's role in making change *long-lasting* hit me smack in the face in April 1994 when I visited Franklin K. Lane High School in Brooklyn, New York, after an absence of thirteen years. My return visit took place almost eighteen years to the day since I first sat down at my kitchen table, opened a large official-looking envelope from the New York City Schools Chancellor, and received notification that I had been appointed principal of the system's most troubled and violent high school, a position that I left five years later for a high-level job at central headquarters.

After leaving Lane, I declined invitations to attend student and teacher activities and refrained from visiting with friends and colleagues who remained at the school, believing that the new principal could not take charge with me hanging around. What's more, everyone knows that visits from former principals are as attractive a prospect to a new leader as a man coming home and finding his wife's former husband's shoes under the bed.

In 1994, however, I decided it was time to go back. I had completed the first draft of this book, and I wanted to verify the facts and conclusions in the Lane chapters. Essentially, I wanted to make certain that the memory and perception of what had occurred at the school was aligned with the reality experienced by others. I got more than I bargained for.

The return visit was an agonizing, sobering, and troubling experience that raised fundamental questions about the nature of high schools, the type of leadership needed to change them, and my own responsibility for the distressing situation I found at the school. It wasn't as if I hadn't been warned beforehand by one of the teachers: "Stay away, Ken. Live with your memories. Don't come to the school." At the time, before my visit, I didn't know what she meant.

From afar, 400 feet across the plaza on Jamaica Avenue, the building looked the same: majestic and regal. The copper dome atop the school's central tower still dominated the skyline of the entire neighborhood, and the stately Greek columns adorning the main entrance evoked images of stability and permanence; the building itself commanded respect. However, upon more careful inspection, the school did not resemble the one I left in 1981—the school that had won fame as a model of school turnaround from the U.S. Congress, the New York State Legislature, and the Ford

Foundation in its City High School Recognition Program, among others. It resembled, instead, the one I had arrived at five years earlier, the school known more for violence, student disruption, and faculty protests than for learning.

An assistant principal I had never met approached me as I reached the second floor corridor. "Don't wander around alone," she suggested. "There's likely to be an incident." I had heard those same words before, on my first day at the school in 1976. They had been worried about my safety in the building then as well.

Life at Lane these days does not tender a pretty picture for teachers or students. I found teachers' mailboxes in the general office stuffed with a multi-page newsletter that was obviously one of a series. This issue, labeled #4, dealt, as did the others, with attacks on teachers, lawlessness in the building, and anger at the school administration for inaction. The front page contained a lengthy list of the names of teachers who had been physically assaulted or abused by students during the previous six months. All four issues of the newsletter, when read carefully, revealed an almost single-minded preoccupation—an obsession, perhaps—with safety and security issues. Nothing else matters if people do not feel safe.

Powerlessness and despair are the dominant themes in the newsletter and throughout the school. No one I spoke with suggested that teachers shared responsibility for the dismal situation in the building, no one proposed that they could play a leadership role in making things better, and no one had any ideas for improvement. People have lost hope of setting things right again. What's needed, they say without smiling, is a "bomb" or a "roto-rooter," something that gets at everything clogging the institution's arteries.

Everyone I spoke with focused almost immediately on the deplorable situation in the halls; they were filled with kids at all times, they said. Kids were loitering, making noise, and disturbing classrooms by banging on doors. They were a general nuisance to anyone trying to focus on teaching and learning. It was all the fault of the administration, particularly the principal, staff members asserted. They were emphatic about this. It was the administration's job to get the kids out of the halls and to punish those who wouldn't cooperate. It was the administration's job to get the place under control so that teachers could teach. Well, frankly, I saw the offending kids that the teachers were talking about. Most had official hall passes signed by staff members. Most were in the halls with the full approval of their teachers, many of whom I observed sitting at their desks while their classes did busywork from a photocopied sheet or a workbook. Yet most people were so busy pointing fingers at others that they were unable to observe what actually was going on around them.

Teachers I spoke with identified the cause of the deterioration in school tone and in the instructional program as lack of strength, rather than lack of interest, among school administrators. "Looseness became an epidemic," was how one teacher described it. Over the years, slowly at first, then more quickly as time passed, the school had declined, they explained. By the time of my return visit, nothing remained of the school's reform efforts nor of the student and community activities that had filled the building late into the night, activities that generated a spirit that made the place "glisten and shine" as the kids used to sing to their favorite rock melodies. In those days, they referred to Lane as "their other family." The school emblem, chosen and designed by the students, had been two clasped hands, one black and one white, with the inscription "we stick together" written across them. Living as well as wearing the motto on shirts, jackets, and buttons was important to the students in those days, as Paul Stero, a former student, recently reminded me.

Now all of that is gone. All that remain are the ghosts of people long gone, myths about what once was, and fading memories of a different time. The school is again being assaulted by intense negative publicity in the press, on the electronic media, and among community and civic officials. What happened? Why didn't any of the reforms endure? Why have the reforms been replaced by alienation of students and teachers that is visible throughout the building? Both resort to flamboyant forms of street theater in order to get attention and make their points.

And what about the hundreds of parents who were involved in school-related activities each month? Where were the parent groups organized to support the jazz band, the gospel chorus, the football team, and the debating team? What about the forceful and effective Parent Teachers Association we had built up over the years? Parent involvement, staff informed me, had also faded. At first, monthly meetings continued to be held in the auditorium, as had been our habit when large numbers attended. As numbers dropped, the meetings were moved to a large classroom and then, finally, to the principal's office. Officially, the PTA still existed even though there were hardly any teachers who were still members.

By now, the reader might wonder whether I was looking for the dark side of the school—the warts and the shortcomings. After all, what head of any organization is pleased with the direction taken after he or she leaves? As the adage goes, the source of a river is never satisfied by its course.

Truthfully, I was hoping to find things otherwise. I wanted to see the reforms that I had worked so hard to achieve flourishing and alive. To see the school in such deplorable condition meant that I had to confront the question of my own responsibility for its present condition and for the fact that the improvements with which I had been associated—indeed, for which I had been the chief engineer—had not lasted. This is an uncomfortable question to ask, since I already knew the answer; unquestionably, a share of the responsibility was mine. It is a leader's job not only to provoke and support change, but to assure that it is long-lasting.

The simple fact is that although I attempted to build ownership for the reform efforts, I paid scant attention to increasing the capacity of the school's constituent groups to sustain those efforts. You might think I must have been pretty dense not to realize that institutionalization is the critical component of the change process; after all, without it, reforms are like a knife through water. But for me, the idea of institutionalization really was a curve ball. I, like many principals, deluded myself into thinking that acquiescence meant involvement and that cooperation meant collaboration. They do not. The question remains, what strategies might I have employed to provide the reform efforts with greater permanency?

So, this book came finally to focus on building the leader's ability to create and support reform. More importantly, it emphasizes the importance of sustaining reform—with the hope that one day, when readers make a return journey to their schools, it is more personally and professionally gratifying than mine was.

Kenneth J. Tewel
New York City

Acknowledgments

This book owes its origins to people who are gone. First and foremost is my best friend and partner, David Gross, who told me that it was time to write it and for helping me to follow through and get it organized. His enthusiasm and support were critically important in my starting out; memories of him helped me finish. This is his book as well as mine.

I would like to pay tribute to my friend and mentor, Helen Storen Reid, the most gifted and far and away the most influential teacher I have had. In the thirty years of our friendship, there has hardly been a day when I have not learned from her—lessons about teaching, schools, learning, children, and life. In a world where common sense about schooling is not at all common, Helen brought a refreshing sense of idealism and purpose.

A debt of gratitude also goes to Ed Meade, Jr. When Ed was Chief Program Officer at the Ford Foundation, he described his work as "interrupting people's lives." He interrupted mine fifteen years ago and since that time has had a profound influence on the direction of my career, my thinking, and my writing. Ed and I discussed the structure and content of this book during our early morning "power breakfasts" at Blimpies on lower Fifth Avenue in New York City. Each time I met with Ed, I came away with a little more perseverance and courage. He had the audacity to scorn the conventional wisdom and then the power to rewrite it.

Imagining that the status quo really can be different and that you can make at least a piece of the world anew is the most mysterious of human gifts, and one that can easily get you accused of being whimsical or insane. Although the thoughts contained in this book are exclusively mine, I am indebted to the Partnership Program of the Panasonic Foundation for much of the information contained in Chapters 6 through 11.

I have also had the good fortune to have had the help and encouragement of collaborators. Thanks are due to a number of people who shared their knowledge with me in person or through correspondence. Among them are my friends and colleagues at the Panasonic Foundation: Executive Director Sophie Sa and Program Associate Ann Kreidle, as well as Judith Renyi, former Director of CHART, and Marty Vowels, Vice President of the Center for Leadership in School Reform. There are also those who were good enough to read portions of the manuscript: Steve Fink, Assistant Superintendent of the Edmonds School District in Washington; Frank Till, Deputy Superintendent of the San Diego Unified School District; and Ron Ottinger,

School Board Member, San Diego Unified School District. Betteanne McDonough, formerly Assistant Principal at Lane High School, and Paul Stero, a good friend and a member of Lane's graduating class of 1982, also deserve acknowledgment. Thanks also go to others who shared their knowledge: John Bevilacqua of Lane's class of 1980; Anita Strauss, of the New York City Public Schools Division of School Libraries; Michael Holzman, of the American Council of Learned Societies; and my colleagues Jack Seiferth and Howard Margolis, Professors of Education at Queens College. A measure of thanks goes to my friend Nicholas Monte, who helped set things right when they weren't going well. He contributed more than he knows.

Some, moreover, to whom I owe the greatest debt are too numerous to mention. The teachers, administrators, parents, and students in the schools I have worked in or visited did not know that they contributed to this book. They have taught me that islands of decency, humanity, and creativity can be created and sustained in the least likely places.

Perhaps it would be most appropriate to end at the beginning, by acknowledging my profound indebtedness to my late aunt, Nina Zamotin. On my visits to her home in Fort Lauderdale during the final years of her life, I would regale her with my adventures and misadventures as a high school principal. She would listen to each word, nod, and say, "write it down, Ken, write it all down." So, I finally did—for her, for David, for Helen, for Ed, and especially for those who will play leadership roles in America's high schools at the millennium.

1

Introduction

In 1990 a report published by the Educational Testing Service (ETS, 1990) detailed general improvement efforts made by American schools in the 1980s. Entitled *The Education Reform Decade*, it described the variety of attempts made to improve the nation's schools and then listed the end-of-decade results. Generally there was no improvement in any area.

Responding to this study, two researchers at the Stanford University Center for Policy Research in Education (Smith and O'Day, 1990) had this to say:

> The past decade has seen a blizzard of reports, federal and state legislation, and local efforts designed to stem the "rising tide of mediocrity" in American education. Two U.S. Presidents have announced goals [that number is now three], tens of governors have anchored their campaigns on educational improvement, and hundreds of thousands of educators and citizens have spent countless hours in reform efforts across the nation. Yet for all this effort, evaluations of the reforms indicate only minor changes in the typical school, either in the nature of classroom practices or in achievement outcomes. For the most past, the processes and content of instruction in the public school classrooms of today are little different from what they were in 1980 or 1970.

For that matter, one might add 1960, or 1950, or 1940.

What started in the 1980s with a call to arms in the *Nation at Risk* report and its successors has, as yet, barely touched the nation's high schools. The march toward changing organizational structures, politics, interpersonal behaviors, and cultures is a long journey that has barely begun despite pressure from many quarters.

The largest nationwide study of accredited public schools to date reveals that while there is some disjointed reform activity reported in the nation's high schools, the rate of change is sluggish at best and very uneven (Cawelti, 1994). In this study, high school principals were asked to indicate the degree to which their schools were involved in some 36 reform activities grouped under five major components of high school reform: curriculum/teaching, school organization, community outreach, technology, and monetary incentives. Results were obtained from 3,380 of the over 10,000 accredited high schools surveyed. Among the findings are that only seven high schools in the entire country reported general use of all seven critical reform elements identified as being essential for a comprehensive whole school change effort. These elements include site-based management, setting clear performance standards for graduation, performance assessment, use of the block schedule, extensive involvement in business/industry collaboration, use of technology, and interdisciplinary teaching for a more integrated curriculum.

It's not that school people are unaware of what needs to be changed. The criticism of the American high school has been specific. The charges are quite clear:

- Low achievement, both on tests of basic skills and of general knowledge in core subjects

- The impersonality of large high schools, with many students feeling no sense of belonging

- The predominance of students as passive learners and lack of motivation to work hard at their education

- The failure to shift from teaching as delivery of information to development of enduring intellectual skills, such as critical thinking, and helping students construct their own meaning from classroom experiences

- The failure to meet the instructional needs of language minority students and culturally different students for a challenging curriculum

- A curriculum that is fragmented, thereby rendering students unable to make important connections to real-world phenomena

- The failure to provide learning experiences that better prepare students for transition to the work world after graduation

THE WAY THINGS ARE NOW

The American high school, designed for another age and another task, is in deep trouble. Symptoms of distress are building all around. They are high on the agenda of a public exasperated by the inability of educators to develop coherent remedies to schooling's most pressing problems: dropout rates, in some cases as high as 50–70%, and teachers and administrators who are demoralized and who have given up on truly educating their students. Given the disturbing facts that past reform efforts have not lived up to their promise, a pervasive sense of disappointment that is too diffuse and intangible to be easily confronted has overtaken the public conversation about high schools. The things that generations of Americans were taught and still want to believe about a high school diploma—that graduation will open the door to a better life—no longer seems to fit the high school they pass on the way to work each day.

Big city high schools are suffering the most from the gap between what is and what must be, particularly those that serve the most vulnerable students. The yawning chasm between fact and wish is so distressing that many understandably turn away from the implications, resisting the diagnosis that something very serious is wrong: so to speak, they are in a stage of denial. Those who think that this is simply the trough of a cycle that will see the return of confidence in high schools in the near future don't fully understand the situation.

Peter Senge of the Sloan School of Management at MIT talks about what he calls the Parable of the Boiled Frog (Senge, 1990). He says that if you drop a frog into boiling water, the frog will immediately hop out without suffering much damage. If, however, you take the same frog and put him into the same pot filled with cold water and gradually heat it, you get a completely different result. Initially, the frog will swim actively. As the water temperature increases, the frog becomes more lethargic and eventually just lies there. When the water reaches 212 degrees, you have a boiled frog!

Today's high schools are, in many respects, boiled frogs. The external environment has gradually changed and they have done little in response. Instead, many teachers and administrators have relied upon a belief that the customers—students and parents—will keep coming and that things will soon get better. They are wrong.

The charges against high schools listed above may be specific, but that does not mean they capture people's attention. Correcting the problems is hard work and it's easier to avoid the truth. Therefore, too many people dismiss the visible dysfunctions in the high school down the street or across from the shopping mall as someone's fault. It's easy to evade the truth. There are, after all, so many convenient culprits.

Some assert that the problem rests with those now in authority: school administrators, central office officials, and boards of education. City people claim that whatever obvious flaws now exist, urban high schools—those in deepest trouble—have always been afflicted with the responsibility of educating the bulk of the nation's poor and, consequently, were always filled with defects and contradictions. Still others say it's the teachers' fault: they no longer really care about the kids. The principals are accused of being in it only for the money and power.

Although one can build a case for any claim, these evade the present reality. The fundamentals of decay are deeper than personalities; with few exceptions, they cannot be cured by replacing the teachers or the principal or by developing some glitzy new program with a catchy acronym that will attract better kids. Where does one find better kids? Does anyone imagine that parents are hiding them at home? Furthermore, it has been proven that filling a school with unrelated programs, however promising, does not improve the school as a whole. Finally, the nature of the problem in schools, although inherited from another era, is to a certain extent, of our own making. At the very least, they reflect the failure of practice in too many places. Today's educational problems cannot be answered by citing the shortcomings of previous eras.

The blunt truth is that high schools are in much deeper trouble than most people wish to acknowledge. In many places, the substantive meaning of high school education has been hollowed out. What exists behind the formal shell is a systemic breakdown—particularly in large cities—of the high school as an institution. In many places the connective tissue that once tied communities to their schools no longer exists.

In place of a meaningful and purposeful educational program, many schools embrace a culture of sham—false appearances—as they respond to the public with an artful ballet of rituals and displays that are without serious content. New programs are planned, announced with great fanfare and ceremony, and never implemented, or, if implemented, never evaluated. Promises made and never kept have become the accepted way of doing business.

The shape and façade of an institution that knows what it is doing remains in place and appears to be functioning, however. The day-to-day mechanics of schooling operate as if everything were fine. Teachers and students report each day; classes are held, bells sound for successive periods, students change classes, grade cards are issued, graduations are held on warm sunny days in June. Students resplendent in caps and gowns with hopeful faces still smile into cameras to mark the occasion. The rituals and folkways associated with high school continue to be acted out. The more meager the student achievement, it seems, the more grandiose the ritual.

Meanwhile, each year new discussions are convened at the national, state, and local levels around the search for reforms that might restore the public's trust in high school education. A veritable fortune in foundation grants and tax levy development money has been spent trying to devise solutions. Unfortunately, most approaches are selected for ease of implementation rather than long-term efficacy. Each quick-fix or magic bullet leads to predictable disappointment as people begin to survey the terrain for the next panacea.

The results thus far are so dismal that teachers, parents, and students are seeking refuge in other types of educational settings. Teachers, for their part, are fleeing to other professions. Parents with the financial means place their children in private schools. Transitional programs to higher education are springing up on college campuses around the nation. All of this does nothing but avoid the real problem: the inadequacy of the local high school. Reform, more reform, and reforming yet again has become the perennial occupation for those associated with high schools. Nothing tried lasts more than a few years, rarely longer than its creator remains involved and active.

Yet redesigning high schools so that the reforms are long-lasting is, in fact, very much within the competency of current professional personnel and within the range of current financial resources. However, the question remains as to whether or not society has the desire, leadership, persistence, and creativity—the sheer passion—to really challenge the change process and develop a different kind of school, one that will serve *every* student.

For change to occur and for it to last, all constituent groups must have genuine ownership of and active involvement in the change process. In a school community, this means parents, teachers, administrators, students, and members of the business sector all have a voice and are welded into a partnership relationship in which shared decision making is the major method of operation. Each constituent group, via its representatives, must have the ownership and empowerment that goes with it.

Strangely enough, though, when parents, community, civic officials, and students—the school's customers—organize themselves to confront the deception, they find themselves too marginalized by educators and "the system" to make much difference. When a maverick principal or a group of teachers tries to challenge school culture and daily practice, they find themselves confronted by mountain-high obstacles inside and outside the school. The result in too many instances, for those who care enough to try, is a debilitating sense of stalemate and a climate of torpid doubt.

The relationship that divides school staff members and the communities they serve—one that approaches contempt in many cases—is both a symptom of the erosion and an active ingredient in furthering the deterioration. One problem is that the views each has of the other are not based on current reality. Many teachers, for their part, think of families and parents as they were when they themselves were growing up, even though the social fabric of our nation continues to undergo profound changes. Today only 7% of students come from the type of family that might have been considered typical a generation ago: two parents in the home and only one a wage-earner. Today nearly half the children under eighteen years old live in a single-parent home. Clearly, a family's ability to get involved in the education of its children is most greatly affected by the presence or absence of family resources, especially income or the number of parents in the household (Schneider and Coleman, 1993).

Thus, while parental involvement has steadily won new support among educators during the past ten years, parents have gotten harder to reach. A parent who works a night shift, cannot afford to miss a day's pay, and has no power to rearrange his or her schedule, for example, will obviously find it more difficult to attend school meetings scheduled during evening hours.

As educators face larger numbers of students with deep social, emotional, and learning problems, they become more reliant on the support of parents. As students grow older and begin asserting their independence from their parents, many actually discourage their parents from coming to school. Added to this, high schools tend to be larger and more complex, leaving parents unsure of whom to contact. As a result of these and other factors, parental involvement drops off sharply by the time students reach high school. Communication between school and parent ebbs, and suspicion rises. Teachers feel that they are left hanging. We are being held responsible, they say, for whether or not parents support the educational process. Feeling alone and isolated, some teachers develop a siege mentality. We'll draw the wagons into a tight circle, they vow. Outsiders are our enemies.

Despite such distrust, principals, teachers, and parents share many common feelings about the desperate situation. All of them, for example, complain constantly about their own powerlessness to alter circumstances. All blame the system, all talk nostalgically about the "old days" when things were better. All ponder, but seem unable to act upon, the structural reforms that might somehow restore sense to schooling.

Theoretically, democratic institutions are supposed to have the capacity to adapt to new realities. Sooner rather than later, they should be able to react to what parents and students and the community at large want and need. The most troubling circumstance about the current situation is that in most places these self-correcting mechanisms can no longer work for high schools because too many of the people who work in them have closed their minds to alternatives. If the social contract that ties community life together is to endure, change must come quickly. If anything was learned about educational reform during the 1980s, it has been that single initiatives cannot simply operate in isolation. They must be part of a comprehensive reform strategy. Therefore, change must be focused on the entire school and it must be fundamental and comprehensive, that is, it must be radical and complete.

Before proceeding further, the issue of pervasive blame-placing that typifies many high schools—a characteristic of dysfunctional institutions and relationships—should be addressed. Whatever fissures and infirmities inhabit the high schools, teachers, and administrators of today are not on the whole less capable than their forebears; neither are parents as a group less interested, even though the complexity of the challenge facing education today certainly makes it look that way. Over the years, teachers and parents, and even school administrators, have, to some degree, been cut out of a responsible place in the thinking and planning process. There are narrow roles allocated to citizens and teachers and also to principals. When each on occasion cries out that something fundamental is wrong, they are frequently dismissed as pursuing narrow self-interest. The contours of the power structure at the school, district, and state level make it difficult for them to unite as a community on behalf of better education.

A central irony is that while school administrators, teachers, parents, and community members are frustrated by their unmet expectations of each other, the dialogue between and among them has become so weakened. Putting processes into place to restore a healthy climate of responsive change requires that all people in the school community feel and actually *are* responsible for the future of the school, both theoretically and practically. This is a task that people at the school and community level feel is far beyond them in most places. Most school leaders—principals, other administrators, and teachers—are not trained to be change managers. They are often faced with pressures for reform, but have no real idea how such an effort should be organized and what roles they should play.

In sum, the public compact between the lay public and high school educators has been broken. The alliance that is necessary for the development of a genuine commitment to public schooling in the United States is now crippled and neglected. Although the decline of high school education has implications for everyone, certain sectors of the population suffer from the loss more personally and severely than everyone else: the students least advantaged academically and economically.

Thomas Kuhn, in his book *The Structure of Scientific Revolutions*, describes how old paradigms frequently blind one to new approaches that could greatly enhance progress. Kuhn explained that crisis is often the only thing that brings about major change (Kuhn, 1962). That is precisely the predicament in which high school educators and others associated with the institution find themselves today. The old way of doing things is so ingrained in people's minds and habits that change is blocked, leading to even greater problems.

PURPOSE OF THIS BOOK

This book is grounded in the belief that current high schools are a relic of a former age. They cannot be reformed, resurrected, or restored. No amount of tinkering with the upright typewriter is going to turn it into a dedicated word processor. It is time for a new system of high schools, a need that is both important and urgent. However, it cannot be solved until all who have a stake in their remaking—parents, teachers, students, school and district administrators, and others outside the school community—are alerted to what is wrong, what needs to be done, and how they can contribute to the effort. This book is intended to do precisely that.

It is being written to help school leaders comprehend the need for high school reform, to help them appreciate the barriers that stand in the way, and to assist them in getting the reform journey started off in the right direction. Perhaps the experiences recorded in this book of those who have taken the first hesitant steps toward genuine reform will generate the will among readers to redefine what high school education means and how it can be made effective.

Uncovering the patterns of these underlying realities and suggesting approaches to make comprehensive and fundamental reform long-lasting will be the primary tasks of this book. Frequently, these deeper meanings are difficult to uncover amid the bewildering daily facts that present themselves in institutions serving more than one thousand, and sometimes as many as three or four thousand, young people. However, these deeper themes represent the real source of the general discontent with our high schools. These are the unpleasant truths that educators, parents and community, and others must face if we are to have a new beginning, if new kinds of high schools are to be created. At the very least, it is important to first understand what is going on prior to suggesting remedies.

Schooling is not a game; neither do schools exist to decorate neighborhoods. They exist to "keep" and acculturate the young people to the agreed-upon terms by which we live together as a nation. At its best, schooling can help to create the kind of society its members would like to have. Thus, in order to examine the condition of high schools in America, it is necessary to explore the contours of a lengthy list of issues and themes such as interdisciplinary curriculum, scheduling, the lethal effect of school size on student engagement, and the fragmentation of the structure of knowledge. In each case the overriding purpose is to plot out patterns that can assist in alleviating the current sense of powerlessness.

The book will also generate some practical principles for the leadership and management of change in high schools. The objective is to provide administrative and teacher leaders with tools that make it easy for them to do their jobs, to create the conditions in which change can succeed and be long lasting.

The book's content is based on the day-to-day work of ordinary administrators and teachers. It focuses on the problems of designing and implementing major improvement programs at the high school level. The purpose is to use the experiences of real schools that are struggling to reform to illuminate the issues that confront any school that is working to improve itself. Therefore, most chapters include brief visits to real schools involved in real change.

Some argue that the only way to reform high schools is to tear them all down and start over. Others believe that reform may best be stimulated by creating new schools based on new ideas. These proposals include, for example, the legislation authorizing "charter" schools in such states as Minnesota and California and efforts in a number of urban districts to create "schools of choice"—schools started from scratch, such as the New Visions schools in New York City or the America 2000 proposal to create hundreds of innovative new schools. Still others argue that simply putting choice into the system will fix everything.

A variation of these approaches is found in efforts to create "schools within schools," which preserve the conventional school structure for most students but recruit teachers to fashion alternative programs for students who elect to enroll in them. Such efforts have, at their core, the belief that professional educators in general are unable to carry out more effective ways of organizing their work, primarily because they are constrained by the structure and culture of the public high school.

That approach is a fantasy. Few people are lucky enough to be able to start a school from scratch. Although new and radically different schools have an important place in changing people's thoughts about high school education, the notion that such schools will lead to systemic and comprehensive school change is simplistic. Creating new schools is not a cure-all for the schools already in existence. Only systemic change of the multiple variables that make high schools what they are will bring about the kind of dramatic improvement and student growth that is needed.

The major premise of this book is that high schools *can* reform and that the work *can* be undertaken by average people in any school. It is not that everything now being done is wrong, but simply that everything now being done needs to be questioned.

The issue nevertheless remains, as those who work in high schools are quick to point out, whether principals and teachers *can* create real change or whether school board policy, district practices, and state regulations constrain their inventing a new kind of school that works better for their students. To answer the question: yes, principals and teachers can create real change, and no, district or state policy does not constrain change as much as teachers and principals say and think it does. The many schools cited in the book are testing the proposition that it is possible to improve schools from within, as Roland Barth (1990) phrases it, and that wholesale and comprehensive change can be accomplished with a unified school community and effective leadership from the principal and others.

The reforms discussed in this book inhabit the vast concealed space that hierarchically organized districts and states do not control: that space in most high schools is currently empty, filled neither by district and state mandates nor by teacher and parent initiatives. Therefore, all the ideas and suggestions contained in these pages can be applied almost anywhere with little, if any, cost and with no additional permission from those in positions of authority at the district and state level.

Thought, rather than reaction, is the key to effective leadership. Thus, the book emphasizes the thinking that must undergird any reform effort and, no less important, the ways in which thinking can drive action. Many books on school reform purport to be "how to do it" books. Although appropriate techniques and strategies for accomplishing reform are crucial to the success of any change initiative, there is also a need for a "how to think about it" book. Right thinking results in right action. This book is intended to be both.

The book is also different in another way. Most publications directed toward principals and other school leaders are written by policy makers, college professors, and professional reformers who lack firsthand knowledge of their subject. They are, for the most part, researchers and observers about schools; they are not and have not been practitioners. My professional life, on the other hand, has been grounded in high schools. Over a span of 30 years, I have been a high school teacher, union leader, assistant principal, principal, and central office administrator. In addition to my current work as an associate professor teaching administration and supervision at Queens College in New York City, I have also been a consultant on reform and restructuring in Panasonic Foundation Partnership districts around the nation. As Mark Twain said, "The person holding the cat by the tail knows more than the people watching."

Despite the face that high school communities have not yet grasped at the need to change, the conversation among elected officials, ordinary citizens, and educational policy makers is about the need for reform—a new kind of reform without the centralizing improvement strategies that dominated the reform agenda in the 1980s. In their place have come approaches designed to empower teachers and parents and to transfer control of educational decision making to the school and to local communities.

This wave of reform has become known as the restructuring movement. Its advocates have focused on issues such as the professionalization of the teaching profession, the empowerment of school communities through site-based management, and changes in the governance, management, and organizational structure of schools, as well as changes in the teaching and learning process. It has paralleled, in many respects, educational, political, and private sector reforms that are unfolding in nations throughout the industrial world.

The radical nature of the change in the schools cited throughout the book is in their capacity building, not in the immediate programmatic changes, which are quite traditional. If the ways in which teachers work together are improved, as well as the ways in which they work with administrators, schools may ultimately have the capability to solve the learning problems that today's students possess. Furthermore, they may also become equipped to deal with the as yet unimagined learning problems of the students who will be in high school ten years from now. One of the most encouraging changes in the schools mentioned in this book is the development of a different ethos among teachers and a different relationship between the school and its customers.

The schools used as examplars of innovative practice have not changed their form and function so much as they have developed processes for reflection and ongoing improvement. Many have become their own internal *agents provocateurs*. They are relentless in questioning their own practices. At every opportunity, they ask themselves, "Why do we do things this way?" Sometimes, when they can imagine creative solutions, they ask, "Why not?" They then challenge themselves, their colleagues, and the district to make it happen.

High school teachers in Minneapolis receive school profile information on student achievement that is directly linked to curriculum initiatives, thereby giving teachers the ability to base school decisions on hard evidence. In one high school, teachers take "time out" to study the data and then plan modifications in the school's program and approach to learning. In Louisville, teachers use scores on student achievement tests or other assessment instruments as clues to tell them in which areas to design new student programs. In New York's New Visions schools, teachers have expanded their conception of their work, taking responsibility for school design, organization, and continual improvement.

In all three cities, and elsewhere as well, school and district administrations have acknowledged that when teachers and parents become the prime owners of reform, it is more likely that they will be implemented and, with support and leadership, will be long lasting. Individually and collectively, they provide valuable information about educational improvement. They reveal the difficulties as well as the possibilities of restructuring.

The formula for successful reform is no secret. Information garnered from reforming schools, such as those identified in the chapters that follow, as well as the findings from national research identifies the components that make for successful high schools: small size, school-based management, and a commitment to collaboration, thematic curriculum, strong personalized attention, and rigorous academic performance standards.

This book also chronicles my own personal journey as an educator. Some portions of that journey traversed the roughest terrain in the world of school reform. It includes my experiences as principal of three New York City high schools. The first, Franklin K. Lane High School in Brooklyn, was, prior to my arrival, a school more known for violence, vandalism, and social disruption than for teaching and learning. It was the most violent school in a city of many violent schools. The second, George Westinghouse High School, was a classic (and very traditional) vocational/technical high school. It served 2000 boys, most from the poorest sections of the city. In spite of this, the school became one of eight in the nation to win an award from the President of the United States for a partnership with the electronics industry. The school is currently being cited in publications by the National Alliance of Business as a model for the use of total quality management. The third, Stuyvesant High School, is clearly the best school in the nation using any standard measure of student achievement. I became principal of Stuyvesant at a time of extreme alienation among faculty, students, and parents and stagnation in the development of the educational program. Believing that even the nation's best school can be better, we launched an effort that revitalized the school and led to support from the Board of Education for a new $90 million facility that, after many delays, finally opened in 1992. My experiences with change at the three schools are included in this book in the hopes that they will resonate with significance for the reader.

The book will also draw upon my current work, that is, the knowledge I have acquired as a consultant to changing high schools in some of the nation's leading restructuring districts—those in partnership with the Panasonic Foundation. Since 1987, I have led workshops, conducted strategy sessions with teachers and administrators, facilitated thinking and planning sessions at the school and district level, organized support groups for teachers and principals, and, at all times, in all of these places, have been a quiet unobtrusive observer of the change process.

The book was designed to speak to diverse audiences who are interested in the improvement of high school education. Although addressed to principals and other school leaders, it should appeal equally well to those who study the restructuring of high schools and to those who are in any way engaged in restructuring projects at the school, district, and state levels. There is much here that will be of interest to middle or entry level school administrators and to those who educate them: perspectives on the evolving role of a new type of high school administrator; views on the connections among alternative ways of learning, teaching, and the organization and governance of schools; the highly complex nature of developing a new kind of school culture; and a variety of other topics. It is designed to be useful to practitioners, who are the ones that must move theory and conjecture into reality. The goal for those who are committed to high school reform is to go beyond the theoretical discussion of restructuring to describe specific, concrete, and workable approaches for transforming schools.

School principals will be drawn to the discussions on the new social dynamics involved in leading transformational change efforts. A high school that is truly changing needs a principal who can articulate a vision, provide direction, facilitate those who are working to accomplish the change, coordinate the different groups, and handle the various forces impacting schools today.

Some now believe that there is less need for leaders such as principals. They note the newly empowered teachers and the establishment of leadership councils, and they ask why principal leadership is needed. This book takes the view that restructuring schools need a principal's leadership more than those that are not changing. This book should, in fact, be particularly useful to school principals. It defines anew what it means for principals to be in charge. They are one of the primary audiences for whom the book is intended.

Policy makers will find clues for the development of facilitative structures and processes for school-based improvement efforts. This volume should appeal especially to members of the school reform community, particularly those seeking information about ways to help high schools develop the capacity for sustained growth.

For this group, the nation's school reform community, the book is also a call to remember. The beginning of the second wave of school reform in 1987 was one of bright promise. Now, seven years later, those hopes have been modified, and the promise appears reduced by the seeming intractability of the barriers and by the reluctance of high school principals and teachers to engage the deeper implications of the need for change. What started out then as an effort to create whole schools that would be successful at educating all students has now turned into a much more limited effort to set up small units, mini-schools in a way, that resemble the self-managing street academies created during the 1960s.

Although one can successfully argue that small high school units are the way to go, and this book supports that argument, the abandonment of the larger goal is troublesome. The task is now more important than it has ever been before, but the situation has never appeared less hopeful. Reformers, in too many cases, are packing their bags, giving up, and moving on to other things.

OVERVIEW OF THE CONTENTS

The book begins in Chapter 2 with an explanation of the core concepts of *restructuring,* to deepen the reader's understanding of this overworked and frequently misused word. More importantly, in an effort to build the capacity of leaders to provoke, support, and sustain change within the school, the chapter identifies and explains the significance of those disabling habits of mind and practice that dominate most traditionally organized high schools and inhibit the school reform process. Sustaining whole school change is the focus of this book, and leaders should not underestimate the amount of effort involved. Accordingly, Chapter 2 includes a description of schools' "learning disabilities," so to speak, that leaders must understand prior to planning strategies for building involvement in the change process. Much of the resistance to change among high school educators can be found in these mindsets and thinking patterns of policy makers and practitioners. Overcoming them and moving the school forward is what the book is about.

Chapters 3 and 4 consist of an in-depth look at the change process at one school, Franklin K. Lane High School in New York City. They provide a realistic and somber look at short-term successes and long-term failure of an early restructuring effort. Both chapters describe the sandtraps that exist in every school and how easy it is to fall into them. They feature sections on each of the stakeholder groups and explain how the shifting school dynamics affected them, how and why some supported the restructuring effort, and why some felt threatened and resisted. Finally, Chapter 4 studies the lessons learned during the five years of the Lane change effort. The chapters provide a firsthand look at a real-life situation where I and others struggled, and sometimes failed, to make change long lasting.

It is not possible to talk about reform without a clear notion of what new kinds of high schools can and should look like and how the people who work and learn in them will go about their daily task of educating young people. Chapter 5 begins with a picture of an average day in a school where today's reform efforts in structure, curriculum, instruction, governance, and community relations have become part of daily practice. The chapter then goes on to describe briefly the different reforms—schools within schools, school-based management, cooperative learning, shared governance, for example—that are part of today's restructuring terrain. The chapter provides names and addresses of people to call and schools to contact if readers want more information. The chapter should give readers an introduction to what is happening and where.

Chapter 6 focuses on leadership. It is not possible to create a new type of leadership without understanding its different elements and how it compares and contrasts with traditional leadership paradigms. The chapter begins with descriptions of the new roles that leaders play within a restructuring organization: leaders encourage and facilitate improvement.

As has happened all too often over the years, the restructuring flame is apt to sputter out unless it is correctly lit and adequately fueled. Chapter 7 explains how school leaders can ignite the fire so that it remains lit. Although restructuring concepts appear to make sense, implementing them in a real-life organizational setting is difficult, and getting the change process off to a successful start is a crucial first step. This chapter gives readers a theoretical framework for the different stages of the change process and then follows up with practical suggestions for getting the change process started. It presents the restructuring experiences of Beacon High School as seen through the eyes of teachers and administrators. The chapter concludes with a step-by-step process that leaders can use to guide a school through the process of developing a mission, vision, goals, and strategies to guide the restructuring effort.

In Chapter 8, the issue of professional development is explored. If teachers are to work together differently and to use new and more effective instructional strategies, then they must be provided with new models for their learning. Professional development is key to any restructuring effort.

Chapter 9 emphasizes the central role that the school's middle managers play in designing and implementing a restructuring initiative. Although some books on restructuring stress the importance of gaining commitment from the organization's managerial staff, they usually neglect to offer practical suggestions as to how this can be accomplished. Essentially, the manager's role is key. Managers need to become skilled at working with others to think through and implement improvement in the school's approach to providing education. Equally important, managers must work along with others to establish an organizational culture that nurtures and reinforces ongoing improvement through collaboration. All of this is easier said than done.

Chapter 9 also provides insights into the often chaotic world of the typical high school middle manager when a restructuring effort gets underway and why they are likely to feel like "losers," as if the sand has shifted beneath them. The chapter describes the process undertaken by three high schools to equip middle managers with new skills and to provide them with a safe and secure place in the new organization.

Chapter 10 focuses school leaders on the development of new skills to help facilitate the building of new relationships with the school's teachers. A restructuring effort rebuilds not only the school, but many of the interpersonal relationships with it. The chapter provides suggestions for creating new and more purposeful relationships between the school's leaders and staff members by examining different aspects of working in conflict situations and suggests ways in which focused listening can help resolve disputes. It then goes on to offer strategies for surveying and assessing staff opinions so that they can receive and provide important information from and to groups of teachers and the entire faculty.

Chapter 11 addresses how to do it. This chapter ties the book together by highlighting the major elements of a successful organizational transformation. The core of the restructuring approach is the conviction that leadership must rely on the people within the school community to do the work to analyze and come up with improved methods of providing students with a superior education. Chapter 11 offers suggestions, tactics, and overall strategies that can be employed in implementing a restructuring initiative at the high school level. These are the basic tools of restructuring and the keys to success.

Restructuring is not a one-time, one-year program; once new ways of working are introduced into an organization, they must be constantly supported and reinforced. Names and places of schools that are using them are also provided in Chapter 11. This last chapter summarizes and synthesizes the information contained in previous chapters. It is intended to prepare and inspire readers to lead a restructuring effort on their own.

This book does not rely upon a single model of what high school education should be, but advocates important values and processes, as well as characteristics and structures that, experience shows, are directly related to student success. It includes suggestions for some basic tenets of how people ought to work together and the processes they can employ.

By no means does this book assume that high school education in America once existed in some perfect form that now is lost. On the contrary, the United States as a society has never achieved the full reality of the democratic idea in the way high school education was constructed for young people. Ideally schools are supposed to be the learning places of a democratic society. One can easily make the case that what is currently learned in high school is not democratic, nor does it encourage or promote the democratic principles to which Americans say they subscribe.

Ideally, this book should be read "unconsciously"—as an experience. Readers ought not to restrict deeper insights by rejecting what they currently disagree with or do not fully understand. The book is meant not just to be read, but to be *used* and its ideas and suggestions freely discussed. The margins can be used to scribble thoughts, feelings, why something will or will not work—whatever comes to mind. It is most of all a work book, providing ideas that can be tested in readers' own schools as they embark on their own journeys of reform with students and fellow educators.

References

Barth, R. (1990). *Improving Schools from Within.* San Francisco: Jossey-Bass.

Cawelti, G. (1994). *High School Restructuring: A National Study.* Arlington, Virginia: Educational Research Service.

Educational Testing Service. (1990). *Education Reform Decade.* Princeton, New Jewsey: ETS.

Kuhn, T. (1962). *The Structure of Scientific Revolutions.* Chicago: University of Chicago Press.

Schneider, B. and Coleman, J.S. (Eds.). (1993). *Parents, Their Children and Schools.* Boulder, Colorado: Westview.

Senge, P. (1990). *The Fifth Discipline: The Art and Practice of the Learning Organization.* New York: Doubleday.

Smith, M.S. and O'Day, J. (1990). Position Paper on Education Reform Decade. Palo Alto, California: Stanford University Center for Policy Research in Education.

The Way It Is:
Thinking and Planning Barriers
to Reform in High Schools

The goal of this chapter is to set the context for the chapters that follow. The first section provides a clear but brief explanation of the need for what is meant by the term "restructuring." Further on in the chapter is an exploration of those embedded institutional patterns of thinking and behavior that render high schools resistant to fundamental and comprehensive change.

Some readers may recall the scene in the movie *Teachers,* starring Nick Nolte, in which one particularly odious faculty member with a propensity for monopolizing the school's sole duplicating machine is given the nickname "Ditto," for obvious reasons, by his colleagues. Ditto seems to exist in a world of his own. He ignores fellow teachers who must wait in line at the copier while he grinds out the "busy work" assignments that constitute his class lesson. Ditto's private and routinized world also extends to his undecorated classroom. He follows the same instructional procedures each day: he remains seated at his desk, shielded from students, virtually unseen behind the daily newspaper he is ostensibly reading. Students file into the room at the beginning of each period. At the sound of the late bell, the first student in each row stands and takes copies of the duplicated material placed each day at the left-hand corner of the teacher's desk. Students then spend the full class period completing the assigned work. Their heads are lowered and their eyes focused on the papers in front of them as they concentrate on completing the many short-answer questions that fill the worksheet.

Ditto remains behind his newspaper throughout the period. During the class session, not a word passes between teacher and students or among the students themselves. Each student works silently at his or her seat.

One day, however, Ditto silently suffers a massive heart attack, slumps down behind his still open newspaper, and drops dead right in the middle of a class period. The teacher's death behind the newspaper is not noticed by anyone, since it does not disrupt practiced classroom routines. Students collect papers, as is their practice at the end of each class period. They add these to the pile on the right-hand corner of the teacher's desk, and then, as is their habit, quietly file out of the room. All the while, Ditto remains behind the newspaper—dead.

The next class files in. Students take their assigned seats. At the bell, the first person in each row stands, takes a copy of the duplicated material from the left-hand corner of the teacher's desk, and so on. This routine continues until the last period, when someone finally notices that the teacher's newspaper hasn't moved for some time—the only clue students have that something is wrong.

Although, in the movie, Ditto's relationship with colleagues and his approach toward his instructional responsibilities to his students might be an extreme and amusing example, the basic outlines of the story are too common. Most students in high school today have at least one Ditto-like faculty member or class experience on their daily schedule. For some, unfortunately, the day is filled with ditto sheets and busy work.

Some high schools are saturated with teachers who have done things exactly the same way for twenty or more years. They rarely, if ever, think about whether or not their mode of operation makes sense any longer. Such teachers may brag about having twenty years' experience but, in essence, they haven't really taught for twenty years; they have taught for one year twenty times—and learned nothing on the journey. That one way of doing things—well learned, highly practiced, and thoroughly embedded in their psyche—is at the core of their thinking about the school, how it ought to function, what constitutes instruction, and the role they ought to play in providing it. They have no other pictures of schooling. That's it.

Principals too fall victim to habits and practices that restrict thinking about new and different ways of doing things. Most high school principals agree that something very serious is wrong with high school education, that is, when speaking about high schools in general and about schools with which they are not associated. However, when mentioning their own schools, principals claim that everything is fine. These schools are doing all they can under difficult circumstances. They provide special programs for high-risk students and have caring teachers who work closely with students and regularly contact parents. Principals are quick to rattle off the achievement of the few graduates who win awards and distinguish themselves. They sound, to a certain extent, like one principal who, when challenged by the district superintendent to lead a school change effort that would fundamentally rethink high school education, made the following comment:

> Other schools may be in need of reform. Ours, however, is essentially healthy. We do all the new and innovative things identified in the reform literature. The faculty regularly discusses schoolwide problems and strives to meet the educational needs of those students who want to learn. The school has an array of discrete and clearly identifiable programs to deal with such problems as class cutting, classroom discipline, and dropouts.

This principal was unable to recognize that anything was wrong and, therefore, was not in a position to alter the situation. Any effort to reform or to create something new presupposes that educators can recognize institutional deficiencies and can formulate a more desirable state of affairs for the students. Regrettably, many cannot.

One problem with conceptualizing reform might stem from the word itself. Reform is generally thought of as "amending the defective, vicious, corrupt, or depraved. It also aims to remove an abuse, a wrong, or errors" (Rich, 1991, p. 152).

"Well," principals and staff members might conclude, "if there's something so terribly wrong with the school, and I've been associated with the place for so many years, then there must be something wrong with me." This is not a conclusion that people generally care to confront.

THE CASE FOR CHANGE

Since the turn of the century, American social and economic systems have changed immensely, and information about teaching, learning, and human motivation has expanded enormously. However, high schools remain basically unchanged. Even the grandparents of the current student generation would feel fully at home in them. Grandma and grandpa would quickly see that subject matter is organized as it was when they went to school. An array of new units and topics have been added, such as nuclear energy or genetics, and a few have been deleted, but the basic structure of knowledge is unchanged. The class schedule would be familiar to them as well. There are still those 40–50-minute periods with classes meeting at the same time each day. They would recognize the marking and grading procedures, as well as the organizational and management structure of the school. Those vice principals and department heads are still around; teachers still spend most of their day in their self-contained classrooms doing what they did then—teaching developmental lesson plans. Chances are that the principal's office is still in the same place that it was when the grandparents went to school.

Some things are different. It would surprise them that boys and girls are now in the same physical education and career/business classes. There are an equal number of males and females in the home management classes. They would certainly remark at the relaxed, friendly nature of the conversation between teachers and students. Some of the social interactions have changed, but most other aspects of schooling remain the same. The world has changed; high school has not.

Despite the steadily growing criticism of the educational system in every quarter and the increasingly strident demands for change, progress on reform at the high school level, as noted in Chapter 1, has been painfully slow.

In 1970, at the height of the student disruptions that coincided with the protests against the Vietnam War, I vividly remember a conversation with colleagues at the Queens College School of Education where I was teaching while on a one-year leave from my high school job. There was general agreement among those present that the demise of the comprehensive high school, as it has always been known, was imminent. They were certain that, as a result of the widespread student outcry about lack of relevancy in the curriculum and insensitivity in management and policy, the high schools would never be able to continue in the same way they had been.

"The pieces of the educational revolution are just waiting to be picked up and put together," promised one professor.

The revolution was at hand. Those in the forefront of the school change movement at the time had every expectation that the high schools of the last three decades of the twentieth century would be very different from those of the past.

They were wrong, dead wrong. Today, one is struck by the divergence between what they thought would happen and what has actually occurred.

The pieces of the educational revolution are still waiting to be picked up and put together. Why has it seemed impossible to make past high school reform efforts stick? Many people have certainly tried, and spent careers and millions of dollars in the process. It's not as if the keys to what makes a school successful are not known— new knowledge makes it possible to create schools for the twenty-first century right now. Why can't schools that are not now successful be restructured into places that take better care of the students who attend them?

Without tracing the history of high school reform and how the current desperate situation was created, which is not the purpose of this publication, it is important to provide a clear definition of restructuring, in particular of how restructuring applies to high schools.

At statehouses, governors' mansions, and state agencies across the nation, politicians, bureaucrats, and educational reformers have put restructuring schools and school systems at the top of their agenda (Mitchell and Beach, 1991).

A WORKING DEFINITION OF
HIGH SCHOOL RESTRUCTURING

In order to clarify terms, restructuring means, first, and perhaps most important, the decentralizing of authority: that is, devolving authority from the state level to the district, from the district to the school building, and from building administrators to teachers, pushing decision making down to the lowest appropriate level in the system or the school. In some places, this is called *site-based management* or SBM. It provides authority consistent with responsibility. Timar (1989) defines it as "changing the ways that schools do business. Improving organizational competence..." Restructuring, however, means more than just delegating authority to lower levels of the system or school. It also involves a basic change in accountability.

The change in accountability relates to a set of changes in school governance. Murphy (1990) refers to these changes as voice and choice, involving two specifics. First, restructured schools empower teachers, parents, and students; second, they expand the school community. They unite parents, professional educators, businesses, universities, foundations, and the general populace into a collective force dedicated to the improvement of schooling for all children. In sum, a key aspect of restructuring is giving people at the school level authority that is both equal to their responsibility and, at the same time, tempered and checked by real accountability, defined in a variety of ways.

Obviously related, even requisite, are the concepts of teacher empowerment and of professionalism. This means more formal decision making influence on the part of the school community, but, more importantly, it means a larger role in defining the work of teaching as well as major changes in the design of teachers' work. This is nothing new. In an internal document prepared for the McDonnell-Douglas Corporation during 1946, Peter Drucker, one of the most respected management experts in this century, wrote that "any institution has to be organized so as to bring out the talent and capabilities within the organization; to encourage men (and women) to take initiative, give them a chance to show what they can do, and a scope within which to grow" (Belasco, 1990, p. 6).

There are other important aspects of restructuring; all involve still additional changes in roles, rules, and relationships. One is curriculum restructuring or alignment. New, more integrated, and cohesive curricula must replace the fragmented smorgasbord-like approach to curriculum that typifies the learning program in the traditional high school. The new curricula must fit or be in alignment both with the aims of schooling and with one another.

Tied to this are changes in instruction, especially a new emphasis on the student instead of the delivery system (Schlechty, 1990). Instruction becomes less teacher-centered and more student-focused, less generic and more personalized, less competitive and more cooperative (Sarason, 1990, 1993). Murphy (1990), examining the elements of restructuring, defines three aspects of this change in curriculum and instruction: (1) mastery or outcome-based learning, (2) developmentally based learning, and (3) the personalization of learning. He calls the new system "teaching for understanding."

The emphasis is now to be on a learner-centered pedagogy as opposed to the more traditional model of teacher-centered instruction. The image of teacher as the "sage on a stage" (Fisher, 1990, p. 83), in which teachers view themselves and are seen by students as curriculum area experts with information that they transmit by lecturing and telling, is now to be replaced by "teaching (that) is more like coaching, where the student is the primary performer" (p. 83). An interactive classroom, filled with dialogue as "the central medium for teaching and learning" (Means and Knapp, 1991, p. 12), will replace the didactic instruction (Newmann, 1991) that is at the core of the traditional developmental lesson plan used in most high school classrooms.

Schools, the theory goes, are to be viewed as "knowledge work organizations" (Schlechty, 1990, p. 42) where teaching is "facilitating the construction of meaning" (Petrie, 1990, p. 18). Students, then, are seen as "producers of knowledge" and their teachers as "managers of learning experiences" (Hawley, 1989, p. 32). This shift in roles and activity places the focus on learning and not on the delivery system.

Teachers are no longer to be in the business of transmitting information but are to become coaches (Sizer, 1984) who assist students to formulate their own understandings of their environment. Educating for insight and understanding will replace teaching as telling. In this new view, teaching becomes a more complex task that is more personalized. Concern about strategies will ebb as teachers focus on expanding their knowledge about a variety of approaches that will enable them to customize classroom experiences to the needs of individual students (Sizer, 1984).

Murphy and Hallinger (1993, p. 15) provide an excellent summary of the changes in teaching:

> The redefinition of teaching included within the restructuring movement means that teachers, historically organized to carry out instructional designs and to implement curricular materials developed from afar, begin to exercise considerably more control over their profession and the routines of the workplace.

This transformation plays out in a number of ways. Teaching becomes a more collegial activity (Murphy and Hallinger, 1993, p. 16).

> At the macro level, teachers are redefining their roles to include collaborative management of the profession, especially providing direction for professional standards. At a more micro level, new organizational structures are being created to allow teachers to plan and teach together and to make important decisions about the nature of their roles.

At the core of the restructuring movement, in other words, is the notion that the organization of schools should reflect the best theory and practice about teaching and learning (Barth, 1991). Some have compared the word "restructuring" to the new business buzzword "reengineering." Both aim to achieve improved performance by rethinking processes and coming up with novel solutions because they both start with the iconoclastic question, "Should we be doing this at all?" and then follow with, "OK, but then why are we doing it this way? Is this the best way to do it?"

Rather than trying to shoehorn new ideas about teaching and learning into existing school structures, which usually means that neither practice nor structure changes, the basic idea behind restructuring is that school organization should change, perhaps radically, to accommodate the new approaches to teaching and learning. Again, this is not a new idea. In fact, it has been around in precisely this form since at least the beginning of this century, in fact, since John Dewey. This is also true of the other elements of restructuring as well. Site-based decision making, teacher professionalism, and an enlarged parental voice in school affairs have a history of their own and extend back to the beginning of the century (Murphy, 1992).

Although restructuring involves a comprehensive transformation of the schooling process, it is important to note that the basic change begins at the individual school (Goodlad, 1985). Since each school and district has its own unique traits, characteristics, and needs, the restructuring process is, by definition, highly personalized and unique.

Although there appears to be no shortage of high schools that have embraced restructuring rhetorically at least, or, more precisely perhaps, tentatively and timidly, there is still a good deal of confusion about exactly what the word and, more importantly, the underlying concept means.

A number of researchers have reflected on the vagueness of the concept (Newmann, 1991; Tyack, 1990). That vagueness may be intentional and, perhaps, an advantage. Murphy (1993, p. 2) makes the point that "definition of terms at high levels of abstractions is a long acknowledged method of building initial support and momentum for an idea." As Goldman et al. (1991) suggest, "The definition of restructuring is being created daily as educators translate it into myriad programs and behaviors" (p. 2). By its very definition, restructuring emphasizes its local nature, making it reasonable to mount a defense for Mitchell and Beach's (1991) assumption that "the term restructuring means just what it means to those who are wrestling with assessing it and implementing it in the schools" (p. 2).

A fairly concise working definition that is appropriate to this publication can be found in *High School Restructuring: A National Study* (Cawelti, 1994):

> The central goal of high school restructuring is improving student performance on important outcomes contained in the curriculum of the future. Thus, restructuring involves designing fundamental changes in the expectations, content, and learning experiences for a curriculum appropriate to tomorrow's world. To achieve this goal, restructuring utilizes creative incentives, different organizational structures, new and improved instructional technologies, and broader collaboration with community agencies and parents.

The definition offered by Cawelti suggests that the major components of high school restructuring must interact, with a focus on improving student performance on the knowledge and skills included in the school's curriculum.

Too often, as experience has demonstrated, a change in governance alone, such as site-based management or shared decision making, is frequently and erroneously called restructuring. Disappointing results by schools pioneering such decentralization plans suggest that the centerpiece of change might better have been the curriculum and organizational structure of the school. Changes in organizational structure can facilitate improvement, but it is essential that from the outset these changes be focused on the real goal of restructuring, which is improved student achievement.

The likelihood of significant improvement in student performance is highest when several elements of the system are simultaneously redesigned. It is important that the central components of the school's restructuring—students, curriculum, and learning—be kept in the forefront of the reform effort. A significant danger, however, is that the restructuring approach to high school reform requires that attention be given to most, if not all, of the major aspects of the school enterprise simultaneously. In these circumstances, with so much to consider (and with most of a high school's personnel resources expended on maintenance activities just to keep the place running), high school administrators tend to focus on only one piece of the large picture. It would be challenging enough if all that had to be done was to implement one innovation at a time. Those involved in restructuring high schools, however, must cope with multiple innovations simultaneously. Overload can result, often caused by a combination of too many pressing needs when a school generates far more innovations than can be efficiently managed by its political system and its ingrained mindsets.

A second danger, as Barth (1991) suggests, is that restructuring becomes a "catch-all, or garbage can, into which many loosely defined ideas about school reform can be tossed." In such circumstances, it is easy to see how people can become fixated on discrete and isolated pieces of reform and, in the process, lose the larger picture and the primary goal, which is fundamentally improving high school education for all the children served by the school.

DOES RESTRUCTURING MAKE A DIFFERENCE?

Seven years into the restructuring movement, its effects on student achievement remain, for the most part, unknown. For one, there is a dearth of research reported on high school restructuring in the professional literature. Most of the studies of planned educational change have emphasized the elementary and middle school. There is clear consensus in the literature that approaches that work at those levels may fail when transferred to the more complicated and turbulent environment of high schools (Neufeld et al., 1983). Moreover, serious difficulties exist in attempting to assess the interaction of the many variables that are believed to contribute to school improvement. Murphy (1993, p. 20) puts it as follows:

> . . . attempts to turn the educational enterprise upside down in the absence of data about the best way to undertake its reconstruction seem premature. Second, the likelihood that certain components of the restructuring agenda (e.g., choice, teacher empowerment, school-based management) will lead to enhanced out-comes for students is open to serious question.

Others are asking the same question (Cohen, 1989; Malen et al., 1989). There is also the issue, asked more frequently these days, of whether or not school-based management and shared decision making are the appropriate vehicles to use in trying to improve student achievement. On the other hand, many are optimistic about the potential for restructuring to improve education at the high school level. It is important to remember that building the capacity of any organization to chart its own future takes time and patience.

There is, at last, one recent study that deserves a close look because the school district involved has had a sustained commitment to school restructuring for over a decade. An independent research report prepared by Regina Kyle for the Jefferson County Public Schools in Kentucky and the Gheens Professional Development Academy identified three categories of high schools according to their sustained commitment to school restructuring. About 35% of the county's schools were in

Group I: these schools had a record of three to five years of commitment to systemic restructuring. About 45% of the schools were in Group II, a more initial stage of restructuring: these schools had been involved in some change, but on a less comprehensive basis. The remaining 20% of the schools were in Group III, which consisted of schools that had not yet made a commitment to school restructuring.

The Gheens Academy (established to provide leadership and support to Jefferson County public school personnel through training) examined whether or not there were differences in improvement in these three groups of schools. Schools in Groups II and III served as comparison schools and were selected to match Group I on the basis of socioeconomic and ethnic characteristics of students and student mobility rates. Three kinds of indicators were used: (1) growth in student achievement on the Comprehensive Tests of Basic Skills (CTBS), (2) the annual rate of change in achievement on these standardized achievement tests, and (3) change in such factors as attendance, parent and student satisfaction, retentions, and dropouts (termed positive involvement).

The data show that in the Group I high schools with a three- to five-year commitment to restructuring, students increased the percentages of those scoring at or above the 50th percentile on the CTBS 100 percent of the time, compared to 75% of the time in Group II and 83% in Group III. Students in Group I schools improved achievement on the CTBS at an annual average rate of 7.2%, compared to 3.6% for Group II and 5.5% for Group III. Increases in attendance, parent and student satisfaction, and graduation rates, and decreases in suspensions and dropouts, were reported 69% of the time in Group I schools, compared to 56% and 44% respectively, for the Group II and III schools.

Because of the sustained commitment to restructuring needed to be included in Group I, it seems reasonable to attribute these differences in improvement to the school's extensive involvement in restructuring. No doubt more sophisticated and complex measures of student performance will emerge in future evaluative work to reflect the authentic assessment activities now being undertaken in many high schools.

In light of these results, why are high school administrators and staff members having such a hard time responding to the demands for reform? Why does it seem to be more difficult to restructure high schools than those at any other level? James Keefe, in *The High School Magazine* (1994), identifies four reasons why most attempts at major school restructuring have failed: (1) lack of vision, (2) lack of plan, (3) lack of resources, and (4) lack of support. Louis and Miles (1990, p. 7) attribute failures to

> problems that were directly related to the complexity of their organizations and settings. These include adult–student tensions, conflict with special interest groups, political pressures or tensions, conflicts with the district office, and problems in reaching agreement among the staff over the desirability of the reform effort's goals.

The problems, unfortunately, go further and much deeper. Although all of the reasons listed above are plausible, they omit the powerful thinking habits and mindsets that inhibit change, which are discussed in the next section of this chapter.

THE INSTITUTIONAL BARRIERS TO RESTRUCTURING

Schooling is typically thought of as a local or state responsibility, since it is locally financed, locally controlled, and locally administered. It was designed that way, the explanation goes, to make it responsive to local needs and aspirations and to give it a flexibility or adaptability not enjoyed by schools in most other technologically advanced nations, where, for the most part, policy and practice are controlled at the national level. The truth, however, is that in terms of practices and operating regularities, American high schools may be as centralized and regularized as those in other nations, perhaps even more so.

The well-defined traditional way that high schools are organized has developed over the years a set of customs, traditions, and rituals that gives classrooms in Seattle, classrooms in Little Rock, and classrooms in San Diego an unsettling similarity. Students moving from one city to the other find comfort in the sameness that exists throughout the thousands of high schools across the country. The sameness is not simply in the curriculum, the course offerings, or instructional strategies but also in the character and organization of the school systems of which they are a part. Each is managed and controlled by a bureaucracy with granite-engraved definitions of role, status, and established practices and procedures.

Growing up and flourishing around the bureaucratic network at the school and system level are mindsets and thinking patterns that have become incorporated into the expectations of the parents and students served by the institution as well as the teachers and administrators who staff them. In fact, in some places, these mindsets and expectations function so well that the people in an institution can virtually carry on without direction. They know exactly what they are supposed to do.

Through a complex set of circumstances too lengthy to explore in this book, at one high school in New York State all five school administrators were unable to report to their jobs at the close of summer vacation. Coincidentally, the district superintendent took a sudden leave of absence and was unable to assign temporary administrators to the building to oversee the opening of school. Consequently, the school had to open without any administrative direction. Teachers and parents feared chaos.

Their concerns, however, were groundless. The school opened without incident or mishap. Everyone did what he or she had done during previous years. Each person had a role to perform; each person knew what it was. At this school, as at most conventionally organized high schools, each role is severely circumscribed; each staff member has his or her "acre of ground." People respect the boundaries of their responsibility and authority; not infringing on others' turf was an important cultural norm.

These mindsets, along with the traditional school structure and organization that they have created and which in turn fuel and maintain them, have created an institutional learning disability, so to speak, one that is no less crippling than the one experienced by a dyslexic child trying to make sense of the words on a page. The next portion of this chapter, drawn in part from ideas about the importance of systemic thinking presented by Peter Senge in *The Fifth Discipline* (1990), is designed to help readers recognize attitudes and actions in their own schools that are inhibiting staff capacity for growth and to clarify and deepen understandings about high school restructuring.

BARRIERS TO REFORM

Narrow Job and Role Definition

Most high school staff members describe their jobs as the series of tasks they perform each day ("I teach science," or "I take attendance"), making no mention of the greater purpose of teaching. Most see themselves as a small, insignificant part of the school organization ("I'm only a teacher, with little influence on decisions that affect the whole school," or "No one listens to school aides around here"). They do their job as specified in the staff handbook. They take care of the daily tasks, put in their time, and cope as best they can, for the most part isolated within their own offices and classrooms. Consequently, they tend to view their responsibilities as proscribed by the boundaries of their immediate tasks. For example, teachers teach the content in their subject areas. Other related responsibilities, such as advising students about school adjustment or personal problems, are tasks for the school guidance counselor. Teachers feel that is not their job.

The impact of narrow job definitions can be illustrated by a situation recently observed at one high school in Minnesota. A social studies teacher using costly video equipment to record a simulation activity about labor–management relations was unaware that later that same day, barely 150 feet down the hallway, a science teacher was using a second piece of identical video equipment to record a biology experiment. Still later that day, further down the same hallway, a foreign language teacher was using yet a third piece of the same equipment to record a one-act play written by a student.

Each department in this school purchased and maintained ("squirreled away" would be a less professional, but more appropriate, term) its own video equipment. Each department restricted equipment use solely to department staff members. None of the three teachers, when questioned, was aware that other departments possessed the same expensive video equipment. None saw the duplication as wasteful; none saw anything wrong with having multiple video units when one could have been shared.

Sadly, the isolation in the use of video equipment at this school matched, and, in fact, was likely a consequence of, isolation on all issues affecting teaching and learning. Each teacher was proud of his or her accomplishments with students; each characterized himself or herself as innovative. All three cared deeply about their students, but all were completely focused on the learning activities in their own rooms. None felt responsible for the interactions in the school as a whole.

The effects of such a situation are clear: isolated classrooms with successful teachers in otherwise failing high schools—teachers with little sense of obligation to the improvement of learning in the school as a whole.

Is it possible to build a good school when teachers confine their involvement to their own classrooms? Obviously, the answer is no.

Evading Responsibility

Typically, there comes a point in the school change process when staff members must identify their priorities for improvement. Unfortunately, however, the tendency is to begin by evading responsibility. Many point fingers at students ("They are not serious about learning") or parents ("They don't care about their children's education") or the central office ("they tie our hands"). The reasons for the school's failure to meet instructional goals, staff members maintain, rest with forces over which they have no influence.

Some school staff members have elevated evading responsibility into a fine art, finding someone or something other than themselves to blame for everything that goes wrong. The enemy is everything "out there" that prevents the staff from doing a good job. Administrators blame teachers, teachers blame parents, parents blame teachers and administrators, and everybody blames the superintendent and central office.

Is placing blame on others an unreasonable response from teachers and other staff members who feel powerless to alter the conditions under which they work? As long as a situation prevails in which staff members feel powerless, the school community—all the stakeholder groups—will continue to invest intellectual energy into finding outside villains. Is there any purpose in accepting responsibility if one is denied the concomitant authority to implement one's best ideas?

Some educators suggest that site-based management (SBM)—basically the devolution of authority over educational matters from central offices to schools—will automatically cure schools of the insidious practice of evading authority. SBM is discussed in greater detail in Chapter 5. The problem with SBM in the short run is that it feeds the notion that something significant is happening, that teachers are beginning to grapple with important educational issues. Frequently, however, all that is occurring is that the day of reckoning is being postponed, as shown further on in the chapter.

SBM can give teachers the mistaken impression that they are finally in charge of the school's future direction. They begin to believe that it is now possible to cease waiting for solutions to come from outside; at long last they can face and solve the school's most pressing problems. Words like "proactive" and "assertiveness" begin to appear in the minutes of staff meetings and in the faculty lexicon.

One illustration of the dangers of this false impression comes from a high school in California that held full staff planning workshops for the first time. This school agreed on a mission statement, set up action teams, and created the framework for an elaborate planning process. What did all this action focus on?

Regrettably, at the top of the staff agenda were efforts to get parents to be more responsible and make students behave better. In other words, the school took a more aggressive stance in fighting the same outside enemies; evading responsibility had a new disguise. Staff members at this school were still unwilling to recognize the ways in which the school structure and their own teaching practices were among the major causes of the school's problems.

Focusing on Events Instead of Long-Term Patterns

Typically, staff members view school life as a series of events, such as imminent budget cuts for instructional supplies. The issue for the staff becomes how to respond to the event, rather than to search for the real underlying cause. A preoccupation with events distracts school people from seeing the more significant, longer-term patterns that lie behind the events. More importantly, it keeps them from understanding the causes of those patterns and realizing that the most significant problems facing the school are often those slowly intensifying ones that prevent the school from achieving its educational mission.

The inability of many high school staff members to recognize and respond to slowly developing problems that threaten the success of the organization can be illustrated by a high school in New Mexico. For 50 years, and throughout the 1960s, the district's only high school had a national reputation for high academic achievement. Nearly all the students went to college. Many received prestigious scholarships and national awards.

The situation began to change very gradually as the dropout rate started to climb; however, the changes escaped the attention of the school faculty. In 1975, dropouts accounted for less than 3% of the student population. In 1980, they were less than 8%; in 1983, they were still under 13%. By 1987, when the dropout rate was 21.3%, and clearly a crisis, the school finally took a close look at the problem. This school's internal apparatus for sensing threats was geared to sudden disruptions, such as a racial incident, and not to subtle, gradual changes.

It is still not clear if, even now, this school has faced the implications of the gradually rising dropout rate. When I last visited the school in 1993, teachers were still focused on responding to such symptoms as erratic student attendance rather than the fundamental problem: lack of student engagement in the school's learning program.

Equipping the high school community to see slow, but important, underlying changes requires taking the time to pay attention to subtle shifts. The old adage that you can't redesign an aircraft while it is in flight and the minds and bodies of the crew are devoted to keeping it airborne also applies to schools. It is impossible to rethink a school's structure and instructional program while staff energy is fully engaged in keeping it operating.

Intellectual Isolation and the Quick Fix

Most teachers learn by reading about the practices of others and by reflecting on and discussing their own experiences. In most high schools, however, teachers have little if any time in their workdays to read and discuss the implications of educational research or to talk together about their classroom experiences. Even in those cases where teachers are encouraged to meet together to reflect upon classroom practice, they are, because of school structure and staffing patterns, unlikely to learn from each other's experience or, in other words, to perceive the consequences of their actions.

Even if high school educators were better able to thoughtfully discuss research, share their experiences, and consider the implications for their schools, a related problem would be likely to occur: the quick fix. The following example illustrates this dilemma.

Research indicates that in both minority and legally desegregated schools, practices such as homogeneous grouping, tracking, and retaining students tend to systematically constrict, rather than expand, the life experiences of African-American males (Oakes, 1985). When a school retains African-American males in the ninth grade or tracks them in homogeneous groups, it restricts their future options. However, it is years before the consequences are seen. By that point, many of the teachers may have left (Merton, 1968).

Is anyone there to see the direct relationships between tracking and the student dropout rate? In most cases, no. Schools work on short timelines. This motivates policy makers, school administrators, and program personnel to search for ways to produce immediate results. Their thinking falls along these lines: we must lower the dropout rate quickly. It would look good if the statistics could show improvement within a year, preferably by the next district budget referendum. Therefore, let us encourage the principal to devote time to those easy-to-take steps that might deliver dramatic results in a short time period.

The long-term interests of students would be better served if the principal devoted time and energy to facilitating ongoing staff reflection about the statistics on student performance trends as they relate to school practices. The quick fix simply postpones a genuine solution.

Principals have grown accustomed to the multiple demands for quick results. Their daily job tasks reward quick responses to contain any and every unanticipated emergency. Therefore, many preservice training programs for administrators focus on the development of responding skills. The ability to lead a school community in examining cause-and-effect relationships that last longer than a year or two, however, is different from the ability to apply an immediate fix to demands for improvement.

Moreover, most principals would argue that skills of thinking and reflection are not valued by their districts; in some cases, such skills can be inherently threatening. Principals are trained never to admit that they do not know the answer, and most organizations reinforce that lesson by rewarding the people who excel in advocating their views, not inquiring into complex issues (Drucker, 1989).

As one Minnesota principal stated, "Even if we feel uncertain or ignorant, we learn to protect ourselves from the pain of appearing uncertain or ignorant."

The Minnesota principal may have a point. When was the last time a principal was rewarded for raising difficult questions about current school practices rather than solving urgent problems? The reward system impedes progress toward new understanding that might threaten the status quo.

Structural Fragmentation

Traditionally, organizations attempt to overcome the difficulty of examining the systemwide impact of decisions by dividing the system into manageable pieces that are easier to see and comprehend (Sarason, 1990). These pieces (for example, functional divisions such as curriculum departments) can, however, create a type of thinking that cuts off interaction, as discussed in Chapter 3.

Although administrators give lip service to the need for fundamental overhaul, that concept is difficult to grasp, and the answers to questions about how to achieve it are hard to come by. It is easier to deal with the immediate steps that can be taken in the social studies department or the science department. The result is that an analysis of the most important problems in a school, the complex issues that cross functional or department lines, becomes an exercise that threatens the way the school is organized and the job functions by which staff members define themselves.

In summary, these thinking and planning disabilities are only a part of a larger number that shape the understanding of how schools are and can be. It is essential that those in leadership positions make provision for incorporating opportunities for exposure of these mindsets to staff members. People must understand how they think and act before the institution can build the capacity for change. As long as such disabling mindsets are a part of the very fabric of high schools in action, they act as barriers to the successful implementation of any school-based reform effort. They cripple creative thought and, unless revealed and dealt with, have the potential for undermining any effective and long-term change.

In conclusion, the movement toward school-based reform is a journey filled with many potential pitfalls for high school principals and other school leaders who begin the trip without even studying its complexity. After all, some people say, what could be so difficult about giving schools the authority and responsibility to make important decisions affecting the education of their students? Isn't that what school people have been asking for? Isn't that the way it should have been all along? Aren't we only righting the wrongs? Just as there are no simple, straightforward answers to these questions, neither is there an easy way to restructure high schools. Why? Simply put, restructuring at the high school level strikes at the foundation of the way most people think about schooling, the roles that people ought to play, and how the institution ought to go about the business of educating children.

Too often initiators of change underestimate how complex serious change really is. Restructuring is complex in the sense that those undertaking it literally do not know what the solution will or should look like at the early stages. In other words, it is complex by virtue of the fact that the solution has not yet been developed. It is complex in that the exact nature of the reform is not known. The pursuit of complex change requires a risk-taking, problem-solving, inquiry–feedback mindset and corresponding mechanisms for action. Any high school that begins looking seriously at initiating a school-based reform effort must deal with the school's thinking and planning disabilities. They must eventually change if the venture is to be successful.

The restructuring movement currently occupies center stage in the effort to improve high school education. This second chapter has defined and described restructuring at the high school level, what it means, and how roles and relationships within the school community will be changed. The chapter also serves to familiarize readers with some of the thinking and planning barriers to change in order to equip school leaders with the understanding they will need as they plan change strategies. The next chapter provides examples of ways in which these and other barriers to reform mediated the change process at Franklin K. Lane High School in Brooklyn, New York, and how short-term success turned into long-term disappointment.

References

Barth, R.S. (1991). School: A community of leaders. In A. Lieberman (Ed.), *Building a Professional Culture in Schools.* New York: Teachers College Press. pp. 129–147.

Belasco, J. (1990). *Teaching the Elephant to Dance.* New York: Crown Publishers.

Cawelti, G. (1994). *High School Restructuring: A National Study.* Arlington, Virginia: Educational Research Service.

Cohen, D.K. (1989, September). Teaching Practice: Plus Ça Change... (Issue Paper 88-3). East Lansing: Michigan State University, National Center for Research on Teacher Education.

Drucker, P. (1989). *The New Realities.* New York: Harper and Row.

Fisher, C.W. (1990, January). The Research Agenda Project as prologue. *Journal of Research in Mathematics Education,* 21(1), 81–89.

Goldman, P., Dunlap, D.M., and Conley, D.T. (1991, April). Administrative Facilitation and Site-Based School Reform Projects. Paper presented at annual meeting of the American Educational Research Association, Chicago.

Goodlad, J. (1985). *A Place Called School.* New York: McGraw-Hill.

Hawley, W.D. (1989). Looking backward at educational reform. *Education Week,* 9(9), 35–36.

Keefe, J.W. (1994). Redesigning your school. *The High School Magazine,* 1(2), 4–9.

Kyle, R.M.J. (1993). *Transforming Our Schools: Lessons from the Jefferson County Public Schools/Gheens Professional Development Academy, 1983–1991.* Louisville, Kentucky: Jefferson County Public Schools. p. 27.

Louis, K.S and Miles, M.B. (1990). *Improving the Urban High School: What Works and Why.* New York: Teachers College Press.

Malen, B., Ogawa, R.T., and Kranz, J. (1989). What Do We Know about School Based Management? A Case Study of the Literature—A Call for Research. Paper presented at the Conference on Choice and Control in American Education, University of Wisconsin, Madison.

Means, B. and Knapp, M.S. (1991). Models for teaching advanced skills to educationally disadvantaged children. In *Teaching Advanced Skills to Educationally Disadvantaged Students.* Washington, D.C.: U.S. Department of Education. pp 1–20.

Merton, R. (1968). *Social Theory and Social Structure.* New York: Free Press.

Mitchell, D.E. and Beach, R.A. (1991, March). School Restructuring: The Superintendent's View. Paper presented at the annual meeting of the American Educational Research Association, Chicago.

Murphy, J. (1990). The educational reform movement of the 1980s: A comprehensive analysis. In J. Murphy (Ed.), *The Reform of American Public Education in the 1980's: Perspectives and Cases.* Berkeley, California: McCutchan. pp. 3–55.

Murphy, J. (1992). School effectiveness and school restructuring: Contributions to educational improvement. *School Effectiveness and School Improvement,* 3(2), 1–20.

Murphy, J. (1993). Restructuring: In search of a movement. In J. Murphy and P. Hallinger (Eds.), *Restructuring Schooling: Learning from Ongoing Efforts.* Newbury Park, California: Corwin Press.

Neufeld, B., Farrar, E., and Miles, M.B. (1983). *Review of Effective School Programs: Implications for Policy, Practice and Research.* Cambridge, Massachusetts: The Huron Institute.

Newmann, F.M. (1991, February). Linking restructuring to authentic student achievement. *Phi Delta Kappan,* 72(6), 458–463.

Oakes, J. (1985). *Keeping Track: How Schools Structure Inequality.* New Haven, Connecticut: Yale University Press.

Petrie, H.G. (1990). Reflecting on the second wave of reform: Restructuring the teaching profession. In S.L. Jacobson and J.A. Conway (Eds.), *Educational Leadership in an Age of Reform.* New York: Longman. pp. 14–29.

Rich, J.M. (1991). Rationales of educational reform. *Urban Education,* 26, 149–159.

Sarason, S. (1990). *The Predictable Failure of Educational Reform.* San Francisco: Jossey-Bass.

Sarason, S. (1993). *The Case for Change.* San Francisco: Jossey-Bass.

Schlechty, P. (1990). *Schools for the 21st Century.* San Francisco: Jossey Bass.

Senge, P. (1990). *The Fifth Discipline: The Art and Practice of the Learning Organization.* New York: Doubleday.

Sizer, T. (1984). *Horace's Compromise: The Dilemma of the American High School.* Boston: Houghton Mifflin.

Timar, T. (1989). The politics of school restructuring. *Phi Delta Kappan,* 71(4), 265–275.

Tyack, D. (1990, Winter). "Restructuring" in historical perspective: Tinkering toward utopia. *Teachers College Record,* 92(2), 170–191.

Lane High School Restructuring: The Plan and the Process

School restructuring is rapidly becoming the new buzzword among policy makers and practitioners, worshipped by some as the new magic bullet that will save education, criticized by others as "pie in the sky."

While the literature is becoming rich with case studies about comprehensive, planned educational change, the emphasis is on elementary schools (Louis and Miles, 1990). There are, as yet, few studies about high schools and even fewer about large high schools, particularly those in deep trouble. The main point here, as already stated in the first chapter, is that no category of school is in greater need of fundamental reform than large high schools, especially those serving economically disadvantaged students (Louis and Miles, 1990).

High schools are not being totally ignored. There has been, after all, a spate of recent movies and television productions about charismatic principals who have improved school climate. Some have depicted leaders who have taken violent schools and transformed them into safe ones. Others feature heroic teachers who, all on their own, usually against overwhelming odds, achieve remarkable results with students. These images put forth about high schools may inspire, but do not provide clarity about the improvement process (Neufeld et al., 1983). However, this is a critical time for high schools. There is a window of opportunity open for reform; if it is not taken advantage of, there may not be the chance again for many years.

This chapter and the one that follows are about Franklin K. Lane High School in Brooklyn, New York. They tell a story about the most troubled school in a city of many troubled schools. A former New York City Schools Chancellor once called Lane "the leper colony of the system…a Byzantine place…a rat's nest of conflict." The first section of this chapter traces the school's journey into crisis and its attempt to restructure. It provides a brief, but useful, discussion of the change process.

For seven years before my arrival as principal, the school was wracked by violence and disruption. Students were beaten, raped, and stabbed. On one occasion a science teacher was doused with kerosene and set ablaze while he was walking to his car on school premises. Ultimately, the presiding judge of the Federal District Court for the Eastern District of New York ordered the school phased out and then reopened with a new principal, a new attendance zone, a new organizational structure, and a new instructional program. Since my assignment as principal coincided with Lane's period of reorganization, I came face to face with the issues that are the subject of this book. Thus, this is my story; it is a story about short-term dramatic success and long-term failure.

Since I am writing a generation after the story began, I have the benefit of being able to look back at the events at Lane with new insights and, perhaps, a more objective lens shaped by time and fate, two subsequent assignments as principal at other New York City high schools, and, more recently, experiences with many other reforming high schools around the nation in Panasonic Foundation Partnership Districts.

The accelerating interest in school-based, whole school reform (David, 1989; Sarason, 1990) raises several important issues for persons involved with change in high schools. Among the issues to be addressed in this chapter are the processes involved in planning and carrying out the structural redesign of a large high school and what steps educational policy makers and practitioners can take to nurture these change efforts. The strategies we used and the mistakes I made at Lane will inform the remaining chapters of this book, as well as, I hope, the way principals and other school leaders approach high school restructuring.

BACKGROUND AND SOCIAL CONTEXT

Straddling the border between Brooklyn and Queens, Franklin K. Lane High School sits between two very different communities. To the north and east, a blue-collar, working-class, white neighborhood that is predominantly German, Italian, and Irish in origin borders the school. The homes in this area are small and close together, well-kept with meticulously maintained flower and vegetable gardens and carefully manicured lawns. People in New York call this type of community "Archie Bunker territory." Local residents bristle at the term and resent the characterization.

One of New York's largest black and Hispanic ghettos with overcrowded tenements lies to the south and west of Lane. Before World War II, middle-class Jewish families lived in this area, but in the 1950s increasing numbers of blacks and then Hispanics moved in as the Jewish families left. From the late 1960s on, this community was a center of black militancy, particularly with regard to community control of education. It is also an area characterized by poverty-level subsistence for the largely unskilled labor and welfare recipients who live there and by levels of crime and violence that today are among the highest in New York City.

Lane has been the high school for this entire area since the mid-1920s, when it was housed in a converted elementary school. In the mid-1930s, as the population in the area surged, the city constructed a new building. It occupies a huge site encompassing four city blocks. The most striking feature about Lane is its sheer size. In a city with many very large high school buildings, Lane stands out as the largest. Its architecture is modeled after a midwestern university campus.

From the outset, the student body was predominantly white. Until the early 1960s, Lane was a traditional academic high school. Members of the staff placed the ratio at 80% white to 20% minority students. During the mid 1960s that ratio began to change; racial tension built as fights between different racial groups erupted on school grounds and in the immediate neighborhood. The student body started to shift from a white majority.

Over a period of three years beginning in 1966, the central Board of Education changed the attendance district so that only a small portion of the white middle-class areas to the north and east remained, while it added more and more areas to the south and west. Queens parents in the small area of Woodhaven and in the immediate neighborhood of Cypress Hills, which remained in the Lane attendance zone, balked at sending their children to the then changing and hostile environment at Lane. They attempted to dodge the system with false addresses and opted instead for specialized, vocational, or parochial school placement. Students zoned for Lane filled the local Catholic high schools as the community virtually gave up on a school that it now considered an intrusion in the neighborhood. It was now serving the children of other people who lived far away, children that people in the community were suspicious of and did not want in the neighborhood.

After 1970, the student population soared to over 4000. Racial strife in the school continued to grow as the number of black and Hispanic students increased. By 1974, whites were only 10% of the school population, just eight years after having been 70%. The increase in the number of black students can be attributed to the enlargement of the ghetto areas to the south of Lane. It also seems also to have been the result of a conscious decision by the central Board of Education. Lane would become the school for minority students in Brooklyn; the neighboring high schools to the south would remain preponderantly white.

By the early 1970s, the students attending Lane were extremely disadvantaged economically, unaccustomed to urban life, and poorly prepared for the traditional academic education provided at Lane. Attendance became a major problem. Property owners on the periphery of the school grounds complained vehemently about loitering, drinking, and drug use in the area of the school. They directed their appeals to the school administration, to the police, to elected officials, and to the central Board of Education.

Various political and religious groups began to take an interest in the events at Lane, with the Black Muslims, The Five Percenters, and the Rastafarians becoming active among students. Elsewhere in the community, the Brooklyn Conservative Club and the Knights of Columbus also focused on the events at the school. It was not a good mix, and it helped to bring events at the school to the boiling point.

Faculty members reported that these groups held unofficial meetings in hallways, classrooms, and playing fields. Community meetings drew larger numbers of people from political fringe groups. Pressure built from citywide teacher and parent groups to end those in-school sessions, but the building administration appeared both unwilling and powerless to do so. Power inside the building gradually shifted from the school officials to the students. In the surrounding community, the initiative passed to right-wing political groups. Staff members who were there at the time describe Lane as a permissive school with an unrealistic tolerance for wrongdoing. The problems of the school were compounded because it was in the midst of a frightened neighborhood bent on correcting the chaotic situation at Lane by taking matters into its own hands.

Some members of Lane's faculty who were on the staff at the time describe the period as a "seven-year siege of guerilla warfare." Official incident reports filed at the time describe bands of students and intruders roaming the corridors of the building, attacking anyone who was in their path, burning bulletin boards, and looting classrooms. Students had their hair set on fire in hallways and on stairwells. Gambling and drug dealing was rampant throughout the building.

According to a former dean, knives were more frequently seen than pencils. Stabbings of students and bystanders were frequent occurrences. Teachers claim that there were few, if any, attempts by the administration to involve the staff in developing solutions to the chaos. The immediate community fell victim to the same vandalism, as marauding gangs of students committed property crimes daily. Lane became notorious throughout the city as a "jungle," after an incident in which a student intentionally set fire to a chemistry teacher made national headlines. The central administration, embarrassed by the incident, brought additional security guards into the school to patrol the halls and the cafeteria.

None of these measures were successful. How could they be? Lane's problems were structural, organizational, and educational. An endless stream of security guards using every means at their disposal proved unable to curb the violence, vandalism, and mayhem. The turmoil continued. Instructional issues faded into the background as staff and students struggled to get through each day. Divisions widened among staff members as teachers on different sides of issues openly accused each other of racism in widely distributed letters that circulated almost daily in the school.

In the mid-1970s, members of Lane's staff joined with parents in filing a suit in federal court. They maintained that the central Board of Education had deliberately zoned the school to produce a predominantly black and Hispanic school. The court case concluded when Federal Judge John Dooling ruled for the plaintiffs; Lane's parents and staff had won. Lane became the first school north of the Mason–Dixon line to be placed under a federal court order to achieve integration and quality education.

The court order had three main provisos. First, there was a mandated rezoning to redress the racial imbalance. The New York City Board of Education was required to develop a plan that would result in a student population that was 50% white and 50% black and Hispanic. Sections of the ghetto to the south were dropped and white areas to the north were added to the school's attendance area. Second, in order to reduce the student population and correct the racial imbalance, the school was not to admit a freshman class for the 1975–76 academic year—a move that resulted in the transfer of almost half the teachers to other high schools. Third, the school's approach to education was to be rethought by school staff, parents, and community officials. School staff was given the authority, indeed, the responsibility, to redesign the school, its instructional program, the allocation of personnel time, the format of the school schedule, and virtually all school rules and roles. There were only two constraints: State Education Department regulations and negotiated labor agreements had to be observed.

The reopening of the school and the implementation of the court order was to be overseen by a blue ribbon advisory commission of distinguished educators and civic leaders. The divisions among the different groups within the school and the community had been so great that a nationally noted labor mediator had to be brought in by the mayor of New York to get the various participant groups to work together on the advisory commission. It took all his considerable talent and extraordinary patience to get the different parties talking to one another. Keeping them working together, however, took more time than he was willing to devote. He became fed up with the interminable squabbling and removed himself from the picture as soon as he could, in fact, as soon as the school reopened.

The federal court order unleashed a wave of controversy in the community. Parents attracted wide media coverage by staging demonstrations against the forced bussing of white students from distant neighborhoods. There were sit-ins at neighboring feeder schools and community-wide protest meetings sponsored by local block associations. One woman managed to get into the newspaper and on the evening news by chaining herself and her child to the flagpole of the high school from which they were being transferred. (Actually, the plan never stipulated that anyone be transferred; however, the woman made her point and received a great deal of attention, which was her primary goal.) The leaders of the white community, who were needed to make the plan viable, were instead hostile, suspicious, and determined to scuttle the effort.

Essentially, the court order stipulated that the "old" Lane, as it was to become known, was to be phased out. Since the old Lane had a dropout rate of nearly *80%,* it took only one year for the student body to shrink to 1200. The old Lane faculty was to be reassigned to other high schools as the student population decreased. Within a year, only 70 teachers remained. A "new" Lane was to open in September 1976, with entering ninth and tenth grades admitted only from the new attendance zone. The new feeder pattern was to contain a student population evenly divided between white and minority children.

One community leader characterized the plan as an Alice in Wonderland adventure. It had, he said, "not a chance in hell of succeeding." Moreover, he vowed that he would organize others into opposing the plan. Unfortunately, he was typical of community sentiment at the time.

A NEW ADMINISTRATION

The search for a new principal to head the new Lane was divisive, filled with invective, controversy, and interference by the citywide teachers union, The United Federation of Teachers (UFT). I was appointed principal in May of 1976, scarcely four months before the new Lane's scheduled opening.

First Day on the Job

A description of my first hours on the job unveils many of the school's deeper problems. I arrived for my first day of work at 11 A.M. after having met at Board of Education headquarters with then Schools Chancellor Irving Anker. The scene that greeted me at Lane bore testimony to the work that lay ahead.

There were hundreds of students lined up on the broad esplanade immediately in front of the building. They seemed to be in no rush to get anywhere. They appeared content as they lounged about sitting on cars, dancing around garbage cans, enjoying the bright sunny day, that is until a bell sounded. They then proceeded into the building. There was no one checking student programs at the front door, no one checking to see whether or not they were all students. When I inquired about the curious situation, an assistant principal responded "Oh, they're late."

"At 11 A.M.?" I shot back.

"Oh, they come in that time everyday. It's when lunch begins, you know. They generally miss morning classes and come for lunch."

"Do they go to afternoon classes and does anyone check?" I continued, doing a poor job of hiding my dismay.

"Well, some of them do go to classes after they eat lunch, and it's impossible to really check since it would overwhelm the staff in the cutting office. Besides, teachers don't file the cutting forms since there would be too many and we don't have the resources to keep track of it. It's just out of control."

So it was—all of it.

After this distressing first impression on the street in front of the school, I entered the building. I was immediately struck by its beauty. Broad marble halls were lined with imposing Corinthian columns. It was a setting that took me back to the movies of the 1940s in which students spent their final, idyllic days of innocence before going off to war. There were clusters of students collected in every hallway. They appeared to be having a fine time. Groups of boys and girls deep in conversation with their contemporaries. Some were listening to "boom boxes" that could be heard in nearby classrooms. Weren't there supposed to be lessons going on in these rooms? Strange that no one was complaining about the noise. A few students near a science lab were dancing to the beat of the music; a few more were arguing the merits of disco versus rock. It was an altogether pleasant scene, except that classes were in session and no one seemed to care.

I asked the security coordinator if this was passing time for the change of period. "No," he stated, "it's always like this. A lot of kids don't go to class."

After being warmly welcomed by a group of staff members who happened to be in the vicinity of the general office, I indicated to the security coordinator that I wished to take a walk around the building prior to the faculty meeting scheduled for later that day.

"Don't go alone," he said, "it's dangerous up there. Something could happen to you."

"Like what?" I asked.

"Well, you could run into a group of students who aren't friendly, or you could wander into a fight between some students, or there might be something you can't handle. After all, the kids don't know who you are. However, on second thought, that might be a good thing, given the climate in this place."

I assured him that I could handle anything I encountered and set off on my own. The assistant principal, however, still concerned about my safety, gave me a walkie-talkie so that I could signal for the help he was certain I would need. What I saw in the classrooms and the hallways made me hopeful and depressed at the same time. Most of the occupied classrooms contained, at most, seven or eight students; the remainder were presumably cutting. Perhaps they were among the throngs in the cafeteria or out in the school yard. Cutting was so rampant at Lane that few teachers bothered taking attendance. Halls were filled at all times with students—and who knows who else—who roamed freely without being challenged for passes by staff members.

A few teachers were making a noble effort at making it sound and look like a real school. They were teaching lessons; in some cases, students were actively involved in the classroom activity. They were outnumbered, however, by the number of staff members who assigned busy work and then spent the remainder of the period at their desks doing crossword puzzles, knitting, or preparing shopping lists. Only a few were grading homework papers. Like Ditto, they could have died, and it is doubtful anyone would have noticed. Even so, faculty members seemed to care about each other. They welcomed me to the "Lane family."

The signature piece of this first tour of the school occurred when I reached a series of old-fashioned, enclosed, sit-down phone booths in an alcove on the first floor. Within a single booth were a male and female student. The head and upper body of the boy were clearly visible through the glass, the second student's head much lower, with only her hair showing. I would soon learn why they were in this awkward position. I opened the phone booth door and saw them committing an unspeakable act that did not require use of the telephone.

"What are you doing?" I blurted out, an inane statement I regretted later on as word of this encounter spread around the school.

"What do you think we're doing, stupid? And what business is it of yours? We ain't makin' no noise. After all, the bell ain't rung yet and we ain't late."

The first change I enacted at the school was to remove the enclosed phone booths.

Beginning Work

Within a week of my arrival, I arranged to meet with various groups at the school: the Lane Advisory Commission, building administrators and supervisors, representatives of the Lane UFT Chapter, members of the hastily convened faculty planning teams, representatives of the parents, leaders of the various community block associations, and student groups to organize a process for rethinking schooling at Lane and to develop and win support for a series of mutually agreed upon goals. Essentially, what was needed was a partnership with all the stakeholder groups and a major effort to expand their collective vision of what was possible.

It seems now that there was a crisis mentality and, at the same time, a naivete as to the way I approached the initial phases of the change process. I hoped that the synergism of an involved and enthusiastic staff and parent community would carry us through and tried to establish an atmosphere where practical negotiations could occur and disagreements be aired. I should have known that such an approach was futile at Lane. The best predictor of how a school will engage the change process in the future is the way it has done so in the past. Had I known that at the time, I would have handled things differently. Lane did not have the capacity to tackle the change mandate given to it by the court order on any but the most superficial level.

Early on, we (the staff and I) foolishly decided to attack every problem at once. Within six months we ran into the same trouble as many government administrations: lack of focus and the inability to make the system respond. It seemed to us that we had no time to turn things around. We felt that we had to show immediate improvement in every area. Of course, we were wrong. We could have educated each constituency, involved them in developing a timetable for change, and then provided them with periodic updates.

We held a series of planning meetings with representatives of the various groups to identify what would be changed and how. At the outset, there was no overall planning framework, nor was there an explicit theory of change guiding the reform effort. It was the only experience I have ever had with the school change process where no participant said, "Let's keep what works." *Nothing* at the school worked for students or teachers. There was a need for ongoing team building and decision-making skills before any of the planned reforms could be implemented. Neither I nor anyone else at the building was versed in the literature or the process of change. In retrospect, I would characterize all of us as having more guts than brains. We saw the job to be done and plunged ahead.

It soon became obvious that each group was anxious to participate in creating a new and more successful Lane, but was deeply suspicious of the role to be played by the others. The rhetoric of collaboration was surely there, but collaborative behavior was not. Teachers individually and collectively vowed that they welcomed genuine parental and community participation in all important policy decisions. Conversely, without recognizing an inconsistency, they also voiced concern that "outsiders," defined loosely as anyone who was not a teacher, not play a role, even a severely circumscribed one, in decision making on school policy or program development. Teachers were even reluctant to include parents on the planning teams charged with security and safety problems.

One teacher summarized a prevailing view: "Parents are transients. They can't be trusted with the future of the school. They've let us down before when we counted on them. Why should we count on them again?" The scars of the troubled years remained. Faculty anxiety about inviting others to share in the change process, frequently displayed as a preoccupation with process and requests for clarity of roles, infected thinking and planning throughout the five years I remained at the school, although to a diminishing degree.

I arrived at Lane equipped with powers that can be considered extraordinary for a principal. The stipulations of the federal court order and its timetable for change anchored my authority and reduced my dependence on the Board of Education for permissions and approvals. I approached work with one focus: change must happen and it must happen quickly. The skills for making change happen, I frequently said, must be distributed throughout the school and in the community. This meant building capacity among staff and parents to initiate and sustain change efforts. Who was there, though, to help us build these skills? We had none of the resources and expertise available today in schools and districts to help with change. Therefore, ill-equipped faculty volunteers and parents worked with members of the school's administrative team throughout that first summer as they designed the new school's governance framework, organizational structure, and educational program.

It was only much later that I realized that the teachers who worked that summer were not representative of Lane's faculty as a whole. They were younger, more innovative, and more flexible than the rest of the staff, and they were not active participants in teachers' union affairs. Most were relative newcomers to the school, in a word, outsiders—not considered to be members of the club by the old guard. Relying on teacher volunteers was a haphazard way to build staff ownership for the new Lane. Although the goal, building involvement and ownership among staff, was right, the strategy employed was wrong. It was a mistake that resulted, over time, in a growing feeling of disenfranchisement among some veteran faculty members. It polarized the staff, accentuated the "us and them" mentality, and weakened the faculty's ultimate acceptance of the redesign plans when they were presented. Although buy-in and volunteerism are important in any reform effort, it is even more important to be more inclusive and encouraging than we were at the time. The timetable was everything to us. If broad-based support had to be sacrificed, it was a price we were willing to pay in favor of meeting the court-ordered deadlines. Restructuring cannot take place "under the gun" of external mandates. It can be helped along by outside pressure, but internal needs and comfort with change are also important. If I had a second chance, I would probably put the issue of representation and broad buy-in before the faculty as an issue for discussion and resolution.

The planning teams visited other high schools undergoing change. They consumed the educational literature and developed preliminary plans. These devoted groups of teacher and parent volunteers not only developed the framework for a new and, even by today's restructuring standards, innovative instructional program, but they also put together and executed a remarkably effective public information campaign that won over suspicious communities and transformed public perceptions about Lane's being a viable educational option for their children.

School representatives fanned across Queens and Brooklyn. They spoke at civic and community meetings, church breakfasts, and private gatherings, all on their own time, in their attempt to stimulate vocal and visible community support. On each occasion, the message was the same: Lane would become a safe school. It would have innovative and exciting programs; it would become a model of an integrated urban high school. Trust us with your children.

Most people, including officials at the Board of Education, were convinced the plan would fail; in fact, there were some on Lane's staff who believed that central officials hoped it would fail. Central board officials said that they knew Lane's faculty. It was lackluster, fractious, and not primarily interested in educating all students. The only interest they had, according to one high school borough superintendent, was to get "white kids back into the building."

School system officials were not alone in their pessimism. There were very few in either the minority or local white community who gave the Lane Redesign Plan, as it came to be known, more than an even chance for success. Everyone hedged their bets; their skepticism was understandable. This was, after all, the first attempt to reintegrate the student population of an urban high school north of the Mason–Dixon line. It was also the city's first attempt to use a planned comprehensive school-based approach to transform a failing high school through a partial closing and then a reopening.

The job ahead was awesome. There had to be dramatic and immediate improvements in the school climate: violence had to be eliminated, the support of a hostile and fearful parent community won, and an educational restructuring that included a new school organization implemented, all at the same time. There was still more. A central office, dubbed the "Livingston Hilton" in many quarters (the street address of the administration building), known for staggering inefficiency and rigidity, had to be won over. The school still depended on the High School Division of the New York City School System for all management and support services. How could we win the system's support for a school program that reconfigured the structure of knowledge (forcing central office departments to work together collaboratively for the first time) and challenged central office data systems, citywide bus schedules, and student assignment zones?

Lane reopened on schedule in early September. A banner headline atop the front page of the *Long Island Press* proclaimed "Lane Holds Breath." There was more than arrested breathing going on. Had reporters looked closer, they would have heard sighs of relief and seen more than a few tears among those who had devoted years of effort for that day. Clara Jones and Gus Dennis, outgoing and incoming presidents of the parents' organization, one black and a community activist for many years, the other white and an official of the local conservative party, stood side by side and held onto each other as 3300 students streamed into the newly scrubbed building past massed television cameras and newspaper reporters. Lane's staff had won its first battle. The summer's work had been successful. There were no pickets and no incidents. Remarkably, the school's integration goals were achieved on Day 1 and not, as planned, during Year 4.

There were 130 teachers on staff: 70 remained from the "old" Lane and 60 were newcomers. The school was exempt from the union-negotiated automatic transfer policy based on seniority. An elected committee of teachers interviewed and selected candidates for vacant positions. Theoretically, this might sound ideal. What more could one want than to hand-pick a new staff for what would be a new school? In actuality, it was something quite different. There weren't enough applicants to fill the vacant positions. The old Lane's reputation for violence, vandalism, and lawlessness limited applicants to the brave and the desperate.

In attendance were 1200 students from the old Lane and 2100 from the new, reconfigured, court-ordered zone. Ninety percent of the eleventh and twelfth graders were black and Hispanic. Seventy percent of the ninth and tenth graders were white. For that first academic year, there were, in effect, virtually two different schools with two separate instructional programs in operation within the one facility. Naturally, this bizarre arrangement complicated the transition. We were phasing out the racially segregated old Lane, with its traditionally organized educational program based on subject departments, while beginning a new integrated Lane with a new approach to education. It was like having one plane land and another take off on the same runway.

THE NEW SCHOOL PLAN

The plan for the new school provided for a major change in the organization, in the content and structure of the curriculum, and in the relationships among the different stakeholder groups within the school community. The new Lane was to be a radical departure from the organizational and programmatic patterns at the other 110 New York City high schools and was to contain new roles for students, teachers, administrators, supervisors, and parents. It was hoped that the new school would attract a more diverse student population, that it would provide for better management of

Lane's huge organization, and that it would build a broadly based constituency among community members for a school viewed as an orphan: no one wanted to be associated with it, and no one in it wanted to be responsible for its educational performance.

The problem was that the redesign plan did not fit well with the school's or the district's culture. Although we knew vaguely about the importance of school culture on a theoretical level, we did not realize how essential it is to have a fit between culture, process, and organization if efforts are to last. Initially, the planning teams approached the redesign process as if it would include only curricular innovations. However, the groups of teachers and parents soon realized, after visits to other schools, that innovation frequently either is not carried out successfully or has little or no impact on student learning, due to a host of organizational problems that arise to impede practical application. For example, one proposed innovation, career-focused interdisciplinary institutes, required new kinds of instructional material. The planning committees wondered if teachers would choose to use the new materials or, if so, if they would use them properly. Thus, the planners advanced the notion that curriculum innovations had to be buttressed by a new type of organizational structure and a revised schedule that could build curriculum planning time into the teacher workday. This would then provide opportunities for groups of teachers to solve day-to-day implementation problems such as, for example, how to use new types of instructional material.

Before too long, committee members realized that implementation of a series of fundamental curriculum innovations required changes in a variety of interrelated institutional arrangements. In addition to the already mentioned changes in the scheduling of staff and student time, there was also the selection and utilization of instructional strategies and the school's departmental organization, which was seen as a barrier to interdisciplinary instruction. The curriculum and instructional changes also affected the mechanisms for making decisions and, naturally, created, in the process, new roles and relationships among all school stakeholders.

Even more important than the structural and programmatic changes, there had to be a change in school culture and ethos. The old Lane's working style was based on a laissez-faire attitude: "I'll leave you alone if you leave me alone." That became translated into "No one will pay attention if you neglect your teaching responsibilities." The new Lane, however, was under the gun and highly visible with little margin for error. A suspicious community and an ever vigilant Advisory Commission kept the school moving forward. There was no slack; everyone felt the pressure. The new school had to be built on a system of strict staff accountability with responsibility for clearly delineated outcomes. Although, at the outset, accountability largely focused on climate, management, and organizational issues, later on teaching and learning goals came to the fore. That is when the trouble started.

As previously mentioned, I felt driven to accelerate the change agenda. I saw a small window of opportunity and wanted to take advantage of it before it closed. It was expected that Federal Judge John Dooling would retire before long, members of the advisory commission—many with citywide interests and responsibilities—would move on to other projects, and the broad latitude in hiring granted by the teachers' union would expire after a year. Staff, responding to my pressure, struggled over time to ensure that each identified problem had a solution in progress or on the drawing board. Some were coping efforts, of necessity, cosmetic; others were morale boosters. Still others actually changed the conditions of teaching and learning at the school. Thus, piecemeal change became comprehensive whole school change. As I acknowledged earlier, at the time we were novices with the change process. None of us realized that extensive change required a commensurate support system, such as a far-reaching staff development program for teachers and administrators to cope with those embedded stabilizing factors that can impede successful implementation. We also were unaware that curriculum innovations would be easier to carry out and sustain than the changes in organization and roles. On top of all this, there was stress, a factor we were totally unequipped to handle.

The redesign plan, as it came to be known, was an amalgam of the ideas presented by the various planning teams to a self-selected faculty, parent, and student coordinating committee (not, unfortunately, a representative one, as discussed below). The curriculum initiatives were aimed at making the school more responsive to student needs and interests. Interdisciplinary mini-courses were introduced to make the curriculum more appealing and to eliminate barriers between subject departments. The academic year was divided into four modules of ten weeks' duration each to allow for shorter working periods and more immediate awards for students. Guidance services were reorganized to eliminate fragmentation of responsibility among different individuals in the pupil personnel department.

The components of the redesign plan were (1) ten-week cycles, (2) Career Institutes, (3) a family structure for homeroom classes, (4) omnibus counseling, (5) a new grading system, (6) new roles for teachers, students, administrators, department heads, and parents, and (7) a new public image for the school.

Ten-Week Cycles

The school year was divided into four cycles, each of ten weeks' duration. Each cycle would consist of two marking periods, the first at the end of five weeks, and the second at the conclusion of the cycle. Students would be awarded half-term credit for the successful completion of each cycle's work.

The four-cycle school year had many advantages. It accelerated the pace of instruction throughout the school. No longer were there the slack periods that occur during the middle of the term in schools on a semi-annual or annual schedule. Gone too was the sense of hopelessness that envelops students in traditionally organized classes when they become aware early on that cutting, erratic attendance, or failure on tests have made trying to pass a futile effort.

In time, unfortunately, the staff also discovered that the four-cycle year had severe disadvantages that mediated their effectiveness. A major goal of the redesign plan was to eliminate the fragmentation of the traditionally organized high school curriculum. Regrettably, cycles had the opposite effect. They created a new type of structural fragmentation by eliminating continuity from one instructional unit to another or from the teacher for cycle 1 and the teacher for cycle 2. In other words, a cycle schedule required greater coordination among teachers than was possible using the traditional whole school master schedule and the traditional 45-minute period blocks.

Compounding the problem, and confounding school schedulers, was the added burden imposed on an already overworked administrative, guidance, and program staff who now had to do twice the work in the same amount of time. The two major challenges posed by cycles became how to establish curriculum continuity and how to reprogram the school four times a year with no loss of instructional time.

The Career Institutes

Interdisciplinary Career Institutes grouped courses from different curriculum departments into three-year career-oriented programs that usually included a nonpaid internship at a field site. These career-focused clusters of courses connected school and workplace. For example, the Performing Arts Institute included courses in dance, choral and instrumental music, drama, theater, and stage technology. An Institute Certificate of Completion was awarded to students who successfully performed on an employer-developed battery of career-related skills. There were four other clusters as well: public service, business, arts and sciences, and industrial technology.

The changes in the way the school organized knowledge—the interdisciplinary nature of the Career Institutes—made an anachronism of the school's traditional organization based on subject area departments. The old Lane had twelve department heads who had operated virtually independent baronies, little subject area fiefdoms, who defined their jobs as managerial and worked exclusively with teachers in their own curriculum area. Each department was located in a different wing of the building. As in most traditionally organized high schools, teachers from different subject area departments rarely interacted with each other beyond the social level or on union activity, and almost never planned or taught together.

The curriculum thrust for the new Lane, however, necessitated cross-discipline planning and the coordination of implementation strategies, at least for scheduling purposes, among teachers in different subject areas. In order for the Institutes to function effectively, department heads and teachers had to begin working on instructional initiatives across subject boundaries. This required rethinking the school's administrative and supervisory organization to come up with a design that made it easy for the needed interactions to take place. It did not make sense for people to struggle against an outmoded structure in their effort to achieve institutional goals. It made more sense to change structures to accommodate program goals.

The problem, however, was that the department heads saw the changes as being imposed on them, as sort of a leveraged buyout of their independence. For most people, having a job is the minimum requirement. Having a job means playing a role that one is comfortable with and from which one receives professional fulfillment. How could we expect people to participate in the elimination of the roles by which they defined themselves professionally? However, as far as the planners were concerned, the change in the functions of department chairpeople, in turn, drove a rethinking of the roles of other personnel categories.

A Family Structure for Homeroom Classes

The new interdisciplinary curriculum design opened new possibilities for a reorganization of homeroom classes to achieve the school's integration goals. During the first two years, 90% of the juniors and seniors were from minority groups, and 70% of the freshmen and sophomores were white. Ungraded, career-focused family units for purposes of homeroom organization and school management would promote greater interaction among older and younger students. The new arrangement had an added advantage. It eased the establishment of cross age tutoring, student mentoring, and peer-led group guidance sessions.

Omnibus Counseling

As in many high schools, particularly those that are large, guidance and other support staff operated in a detached way from the school's educational program. As with other school functions, the guidance department, too, had exclusive possession of a building wing for their offices. Similarly, they wished to maintain exclusivity and control over their area of expertise, in this case student adjustment and career- and college-related issues.

At Lane, as at many schools, specialized guidance functions were carried out by separate individuals, an arrangement that forced students to relate to a number of different individuals. Typically, a student would see one counselor for course scheduling, a second for career advice, a third for dealing with a family crisis, a fourth for health concerns, and so on. The planning committees felt that such an arrangement exacerbated problems of anonymity and created additional confusion for students as they shuffled from one staff member to another. As at many large high schools, most members of Lane's teaching staff had little information about what guidance staff did with their time and consequently felt that their contribution to the school was negligible, at best, and perhaps even a waste of resources. Many simply felt that the traditional way of organizing guidance services aggravated the serious communication problems between and among members of the guidance staff and between guidance staff members and teachers. The general sense was that students were being cheated and that they needed more.

Lane's redesign plan addressed these concerns by the integration of guidance services with the new nongraded homeroom classes and the new curriculum framework. There would be one individual responsible for all aspects of the guidance process—programming and scheduling, career and college counseling, class cutting and attendance, and intervention during crises—as it is at small schools. Guidance and instructional services would be coordinated at regularly scheduled team meetings that could include subject area teachers, guidance counselors, and the home base teacher.

A New Grading System

Something had to be done about the lack of student success at the old Lane. In some courses, such as algebra and geometry, fully 85% of the students were required to repeat because of failure or excessive absence. Most of those repeating failed the second time as well. There was deep suspicion among teachers that the traditional high school grading and promotion policy, in addition to the curriculum, was a primary cause of the dropout rate.

The faculty devised a new marking system that was and is quite unusual. Unlike the number grades used at the other 110 New York City high schools, Lane students received letter grades. No notation was entered on permanent records for failure, nor was a student's grade point index adversely affected by failed courses. At other New York City high schools, failing marks were recorded on permanent records, and policy was bound by a complex systemwide coding system governing failing grades, e.g., 41 = nonattendance.

Parents, students, and teachers adapted quickly enough to the new marking system, but officials at central headquarters did not. There was relentless pressure from the central office to make Lane conform to the grading procedures at other New York City high schools. After all, they argued, colleges would have trouble interpreting Lane's new grading system, and it would place students at a disadvantage. When this proved to be false (in fact, most college admissions offices understood and favored Lane's detailed student transcript), we then were told that we were causing confusion and "unnecessary" work at other schools. They had to devote additional staff time to interpreting our student records. That was true enough, but they also had to interpret transcripts of students transferring from outside of New York City as well. Neither were good arguments, but central officials persisted in their opposition to anything that was different about the way we did things.

As Lane returned to Board of Education jurisdiction, the pressure to conform intensified. There was no longer a vocal and assertive advisory commission to advocate for the school. One year after my departure, the data processing unit within the high school division at central headquarters prevailed, and the school reverted to the traditional number grading system typically used at all other New York City high schools.

New Roles for Teachers

Faculty roles underwent dramatic change as teachers for the first time assumed major responsibilities for policy decisions, program development, and school governance. During any month, there were ten to fifteen faculty task forces planning innovations and grappling with school administrative and policy issues. In addition, staff members designed a new managerial body representing all school stakeholders: an Instructional Cabinet intended to coordinate, monitor, and initiate additional change efforts. The new group was charged with setting measurable instructional objectives for all courses, developing strategies to attain those results, and assessing attainment at the close of the school year. In other words, the Instructional Cabinet provided Lane with a new structure for the institutionalization of change, as well as a formal mechanism for focusing on educational issues.

It didn't work. Department heads felt that it intruded on the conventional tasks entrusted to them, tasks that they felt defined their professional status and place in the school. They threw one bottleneck after another in the way and effectively prevented the group from organizing itself and getting on with its work.

A second illustration of the changed faculty role was a new type of collaboration between the school administration and the teachers' union. This joint venture was organized around weekly meetings with the union's executive board to discuss schoolwide managerial issues not specifically within the purview of the negotiated citywide contract. We believed that a new type of school required a new type of relationship with the union that addressed issues beyond those of wages, hours, and working conditions, which are typical of the traditional teachers' union. It was hoped that the new relationship would lend the support of the union, the official teachers' bargaining organization, to the planned changes and encourage greater teacher involvement, as well as identify areas of potential friction early on. Quick action might avoid festering problems that could erode morale.

New Roles for Students

Student roles changed from passive recipients of predetermined services to decision makers about conditions affecting learning. This was done to generate student support and to invest students more deeply in their own education. The planning teams saw student empowerment as a strategy for reducing student–faculty alienation and, given the suspicions remaining from the days of the old Lane, for increasing teacher commitment to the school. An active and involved student body would generate many more extracurricular activities that would in turn create pressure for a wider decision-making role for students. Such a student role might stimulate deeper involvement of yet more teachers concerned about having their traditional rights and prerogatives encroached upon.

Students assumed a decision-making role on issues ranging from building regulations, security, and class cutting to the allocation of student-generated funds.

Student groups, such as the Big Siblings, Peer Counselors, Adoptive Parents, and the Council of Homerooms, were organized and assigned the job of monitoring in- and out-of-school behavior. We arranged schedules to permit guidance counselors to run group problem-solving sessions on school issues, with official classes once every six days. These were not the traditional group guidance sessions. They focused student attention on Lane as an institution and provided students with an opportunity to explore their role in making it a better place. Topics at these sessions ranged from orientation to school programs to strategies for resolving intergroup conflict to improvement of school tone.

New Roles for Administrators and Department Heads

Lane had two assistant principals for school administration and twelve department heads when I arrived as principal. One assistant principal was responsible for school operations, and the other handled pupil personnel services. Each department chair headed a subject area department and was responsible for staff supervision and program development. Unlike the practice in most school districts, a department head in New York City has line authority over staff and earns the same salary as an assistant principal for administration. (In New York City, department chairs are called Assistant Principals—Supervision; however, for purposes of convenience and clarity for readers who might think this strange, they are referred to in this book as department heads). The fact that department heads have line authority over personnel makes them a formidable power block in the school. Organizational development specialists or change theorists would perceive this as resistance at the middle management level. It was a perception that we did not fully appreciate at the time.

Although difficult to imagine by anyone who has not worked at a school in crisis, most of the department heads, like the old Lane faculty, had spent little time on instruction. Moreover, most had never mastered the essentials of classroom management, curriculum development, or personnel evaluation. In blunter terms, most knew hardly anything about teaching and learning. During the school's troubled years, most of them had held assignments dealing with student discipline and building security. Becoming a department head was offered as a reward. Even those brought in from the outside were hired for their familiarity with security and discipline issues.

One department head had spent only one term in the classroom before being relieved of her teaching responsibilities to serve as a dean of discipline. She was the terror of the dean's office, feared by teachers and students alike. Unfortunately, she never altered her approach when she became a department chairperson. Her teachers, in fact, enjoyed calling her "Attila the nun" (her former profession). A second department head had spent two years teaching out of license. These were hardly qualifications for a leadership position in curriculum and instruction.

The seven-year-long climate of crisis at Lane provided the department heads few opportunities for sustained work on instructional issues. Thus, their relationships with teachers were more frequently based on power derived from line authority than from instructional expertise, making them ill equipped to play a leadership role in the change process and, moreover, psychologically unable to cope with the substantial organizational shifts and altered role responsibilities that were part of the redesign plan.

The redesign plan required that department heads work in teams, sharing jurisdiction over instructional matters such as interdisciplinary courses and the Career Institutes. Their ability to work within a collaborative framework was critical to the success of the redesign plan. They had to be on board. The old adage about educational change—that changing a school by changing administrators and supervisors is like changing the course of the Mississippi by spitting into the Ohio—does not hold water in this case. Collaboration among heads was a key ingredient in the redesign plan. Their outright sabotage of their new, less independent roles proved to be a major stumbling block from the start.

New Roles for Parents

An important component of Lane's redesign was an expanded role for parents and community members. I had never had bitter experiences with these parents and community members during the troubled years, and I viewed community and neighborhood residents' direct involvement in all phases of policy and governance decisions as a way to ensure that problems would be dealt with in a timely manner. The community would bring a special urgency and understanding to decision making because it was their children whom the school served.

Clearly, the old Lane's undistinguished record provided evidence that an entrenched school bureaucracy (administration, department heads, the union) had become calcified, unable to respond to the expressed needs and aspirations of parents and others in the local community. They had shown themselves to be either unwilling or unable to comprehend or address the desperate problems of a rapidly changing community and had excluded them from a real voice in school affairs. To be fair, working conditions at the old Lane had created a siege mentality among all staff, an environment in which it is difficult to think and plan collaboratively.

Strengthening bonds between school staff and members of the local community could be one strategy that might reduce the entrenched suspicions that had accumulated over the years. A firm connection between the community and the schools' professional staff would serve as a source of vitality and as a focus of ongoing problem solving, a connection that had not existed previously. It was important to me that community participation at Lane not be "symbolic" and that such participation not be manipulated by the school's educational establishment in order to co-opt reformist elements within the community. The involvement of Lane's community represented an insurance policy, one that would not allow the school to slide back into chaos.

Developing a significant community role on the high school level is not simple, however, and long-established patterns of parental noninvolvement, hostility, and alienation had to be altered. Some parents optimistically suggested that one way to reduce isolation among different school groups would be to establish a parent–teachers' association, which would include staff members, instead of a parents' association, where teachers could only participate as guests. This was a departure from traditional practice in New York City high schools, although it followed a pattern prevalent in most elementary schools.

At first, parents and teachers were reluctant to get involved with one another in any type of organizational relationship. Watching them interact during the early days, I was reminded of two wrestlers circling the ring, seeking out weaknesses in the opponent prior to launching an attack. While, in theory, most teachers supported efforts to build a parental presence in the school, in practice they opposed parental involvement in major decisions. Teachers readily welcomed more contact with the parents of youngsters doing poorly in school, but vehemently opposed parents sharing portions of their own traditional role in school affairs.

A New Public Image for the School

Improved public relations was a key factor in trying to revitalize the school and its image. Teachers directed the initial effort at feeder public, parochial, and private schools in the community. Members of the Fine Arts Department designed colorful and informative brochures with the help of media consultants who donated their time. A team of teachers and parents set up a speakers' bureau. They sent advance scouts to public meetings to discuss Lane's new program. These individuals then became the liaison between that feeder school and Lane. Whenever a teacher or parent from that school contacted Lane, they were automatically referred to their own permanent representative. It made the school's effort to improve its public image both personal and efficient.

One faculty/parent task force encouraged representatives of citywide and local newspapers to visit the school to see what was going on. They had practically camped out at Lane during the period of the disruptions and had seen the school at its worst. Now, staff and parents wanted them to know that things had changed. We staged special media events to attract public attention and, after a time, established a press relations office. Groups of interested teachers were trained in writing press releases. Corporations paid for advertisements in citywide and local newspapers. Headlines like "Miracle on Jamaica Avenue—Comeback at Lane" and "High School Renaissance in Queens" helped fuel the transformation of Lane's public image and get the message of change into the community. The enormous attention devoted to public relations and an elaborate campaign to educate parents and others may have been the reason that a traditional community suspicious of change supported an educational design that was, at the time, a radical departure from practice in other New York City high schools.

IMPLEMENTATION OF THE REDESIGN PLAN

Unfortunately, since Lane's redesign and rezoning coincided with New York City's near bankruptcy in 1976, promised supplementary funds for the school never materialized. Unlike other New York City high schools, however, the court order provided Lane with the authority to make its own budget decisions, similar to the authority held by most school-based management schools today. A revised rules structure, an altered departmental organization, a four-cycle school year, interdisciplinary minicourses, guidance families, Career Institutes, a no-fault marking system, and new, altered roles for faculty, students, and parents were implemented by redistributing the school's meager operating funds as the staff stretched an inadequate budget to the limit.

The new and more collaborative relationship with the union also brought benefits. Some new programs requiring special teacher resources were made possible by increasing class size beyond contractual limits, a step tacitly approved by a faculty willing to make sacrifices in order to give the redesign plan its one shot at success. The shift in budgetary authority from central office to school at a time of draconian budget cuts was a critical element in the ability to implement the plans for change. For Lane, the authority to plan and act was more important than dollars.

The city's desperate financial condition had at least one benefit. For starters, it prompted one faculty group to turn to the private sector for help. At one terribly exasperating moment, when everything seemed to be falling apart and it appeared as if the planning teams were about to give up, one teacher casually suggested that we gather together representatives of local block associations, parents' groups, and civic officials to tell them that we had failed, that the job was too big to accomplish during a time of fiscal crisis. As one social studies teacher quipped at the time, "Instead of a shovel to help us build a new school, all we've gotten is a teaspoon with which to dig our own graves." To which a second teacher added, "And you may as well invite the corporate sector—they at least have the money to pay for coffins."

An initial meeting of community officials and business leaders turned out to be just what we needed. One banking official set the tone with a promise to work with parents to develop a funding base for a new football program; another made a similar commitment to the school's nascent gospel chorus, and a third pledged corporate support for the development of a mineralogy program.

Thus, the city's precarious financial situation turned out to be an asset in building community support and involvement. The Society of Friends of Lane, comprised of representatives from community agencies, churches, corporations, and volunteer groups, was established to coordinate the support received from external groups and to become advocates for the school in its dealing with the central Board of Education. I viewed it as a replacement for the rapidly disintegrating Advisory Commission.

This group quickly expanded its function beyond fund-raising. Over time it came to symbolize the tapestry of intermingling responsibilities among the school, community, business, and civic/social organizations. Ultimately the Society grew so large that it had to be reorganized into an executive board and seven subcommittees, each of which solicited support for the dozens of new projects and programs that emerged as the new school grew.

The school's alumni were also mobilized to help. A number of Lane's early graduates had become prominent: the late Sam Levenson, the humorist; Warren Phillips, president of Dow Jones; Red Holzman, former manager of the New York Knicks; Franklin Thomas, president of the Ford Foundation; Anne Jackson, the actress; Jose Greco, the guitarist; Alfred Kazin, the writer; and Earle Hyman, the actor. They were glad to lend their names and devote time to building the new school.

Portions of the building were named in honor of distinguished graduates. This had the effect of drawing positive attention to the school and also served to inspire current students. Sam Levenson, for one, agreed to raise funds to buy equipment for new high interest courses such as photography, hematology, and genetics. In one talk to the faculty, he remarked "Folks, if you need a helping hand, you'll find it at the end of your arm." No one could have expressed it better. The new Lane was to be built by the energy, creativity, and forbearance of its faculty and parent community, since support for the redesign plan—for that matter, for the school—was practically nonexistent at the system's central office.

References

David, J. (1989). Synthesis of research on school-based management. *Educational Leadership,* 46(8), 45–53.

Louis, K.S. and Miles, M.B. (1990). *Improving the Urban High School: What Works and Why?* New York: Teachers College Press.

Neufeld, B., Farrar, E., and Miles, M.B. (1983). *Review of Effective Schools Programs: Implications for Policy, Practice and Research.* Cambridge, Massachusetts: The Huron Institute.

Sarason, S. (1990). *The Predictable Failure of Educational Reform.* San Francisco: Jossey-Bass.

The Restructuring of Lane High School: Ruminations and Reflections

How well did Lane's restructuring efforts pay off? Where did Lane stand five years after the implementation of the redesign plan? Very simply put, the school prospered and flourished. It received local, statewide, and national recognition for its accomplishments. The U.S. Congress cited Lane as one of ten national models of "school turnaround" (U.S. Government, 1978). Local and state education and political officials were now happy to associate themselves with the school and made periodic pilgrimages to Lane to bask in the reflected glow of one of the few urban high school success stories of those days. Lane was no longer the pariah of the system, although it continued to be an administrative nuisance to central officials. It became a place that teachers wanted to transfer into when they left other schools. It was able to attract newer, younger, and more progressive teachers, who in turn further enriched the educational program with their ideas and their enthusiasm. Early success, however, came with a heavy price.

Student enrollment soared as Lane became the school of choice in South Queens. Student population rose to 4000 within a year, and then to 6000 by the beginning of the third year. The school was operating at 150% of capacity, requiring the institution of multiple sessions running from 7 A.M. until 5:00 P.M. Students and staff were coming and going all day. It became difficult to tell who belonged where.

The four-year dropout rate plummeted from 80% to slightly more than 20%—still unconscionably high but, by any measurement, a dramatic improvement. The percentage of students performing on or above grade in reading rose from 26% to 63%, and those performing on or above grade in math rose from 23% to 61%. The percentage of students going on to higher education climbed from 31% to 73%. Teacher absenteeism dropped from 9.7% to 4.7%.

Although Lane prospered, the redesign plan itself did not fare well over the long term. Certainly, it produced a school that students and parents loved. Little was known, however, about the meaning of the success indicators. There were no longitudinal studies to ascertain whether or not the Lane experiment actually improved the schooling experience for teachers and students. Many questions remain:

- Does the improved student performance reflect the changed student population? It most likely does, although the new student population would not have come to Lane without the changes at the school.

- Had the achievement level of the least capable student improved? It most likely had: many more of them remained in school through to graduation.

- Were marginal students attending the new Lane more successful than they would have been at the old Lane? There are no definitive answers to this question since scores were never isolated by student cohort. The school had no resources to track indicators of progress, the system had no interest in it, and at the time, there were no data systems in place with the capacity for providing the school with any meaningful statistics of student progress. The sad fact is, it is still true in most places that restructuring schools neglect to follow the progress of students over the long term. They still lack proof that it is their reform efforts and not other factors that are producing changes in student achievement.

How does one go about planning and carrying out radical change in an institution still traumatized after seven years of chaos? Is it more difficult when the changes must be started all at once or are crisis conditions a needed stimulus to change? This book will provide some suggestions to the first and second questions; the third, however, remains largely unanswered.

I learned from the Lane experience that major changes require significant time and resources; we didn't have either. We also lacked sufficient knowledge about the change process itself. We did it by the seat of our pants. We rarely thought about the strategic issues that must be engaged if one wishes to overcome the obstacles that are likely to arise during changeabout. The result was that, over time, innovations were "swallowed up" by forces that tend to maintain organizational stasis. Schools can tolerate only so much change and still tend to the business of keeping school (Hall and Hord, 1987).

THE LESSONS LEARNED

Lane's rebirth as a viable school was accomplished by a court-mandated redesign that involved a multi-pronged effort to restructure the organizational, curricular, and instructional program. The Lane experience with structural change can be filtered down to a number of interesting questions:

- What was the effect of "specialness" on the change process?

- What was the effect of school size on the implementation and institutional-ization of change?

- What are the implications for change when one tries to improve a school in crisis without changing the faculty?

- What effect did increased demand on teachers have on their performance?

- What effect does the system's central office have on the change process?

The Importance of Being Special

The court mandate provided a sense of urgency and the aura of power. That power provided a rationale for circumventing Board of Education procedures and strengthened our hands with central board officials. It also made faculty members more hesitant than would otherwise be the case in opposing change; it muted opposition by placing opponents of change in a psychologically disadvantaged position. It also drove resistance underground, and there were guerilla attacks at unexpected moments.

Designation by a district as part of a reform effort confers a special status on a school, one that serves as a catalyst or incentive for change, as it did at Lane. Separate from the actual activities or support received, this symbolic and socializing role is harder to describe but seems a fact in the success of many schools. Today, identification as part of an "elite" group of restructuring schools by high-level district officials who support and value change sometimes provides encouragement in the face of inevitable setbacks and discouragement. It also encourages risk-taking in some schools and prompts requests for waivers or assistance that might otherwise be out of the question.

The effect of "specialness" on the change process helps to underscore the complexity of school reform. Similar to a "Hawthorne" effect but perhaps more powerful, special status gives school people confidence that they can find help and solve difficult problems. For example, I have observed that schools informally designated as "school-based management/shared decision making" or "restructuring" schools (the term depends on the district) often see themselves as able to tackle fundamental changes in their structures and instructional programs *without* clear authorization from district administrators. They take it upon themselves to deal with process issues, develop a vision, set up new schedules, or teach with an interdisciplinary approach. One school staff described it to me as "emerging from the closet."

Specialness also helps in the development of new types of relationships with high-level district officials. Those formerly dreaded visits by the superintendent and his or her immediate staff take on new meaning. They become visible evidence of special status, important validation for the principal and the teaching staff, and an important factor in maintaining the connection and identification with the district's new value system. For most schools, special status is desirable. It encourages teachers, lessens the sense of isolation, rewards administrators through greater visibility for the school, and, for the most part, provides credible validation in the community for the change effort.

Early on, Lane became the darling of the media, appearing in professional journals, in newspapers, and even on national television as a model of innovation. Reporters knew the school from the time of turmoil. The change at the school gave their reporting a "then and now" handle. Numerous groups invited teachers and administrators to present at local and national conferences. For the teachers, such professional opportunities were further evidence of their changing role in the school.

Specialness has its negative side as well. Presentation to an endless stream of visitors and media attention consumed the staff's time and energy. Staff members were having a hard enough time figuring out what they were doing. Living in a fishbowl divided their attention and added stress.

One particular incident stands out. When CBS filmed a documentary on the school's Encounter Program (Tewel and Chalfin, 1980), only selected students and teachers were invited to participate. The remainder of the school felt excluded, and many questioned the presence of the TV crew in the school. Although it is exciting for a school to have attention from visitors, researchers, and the news media, and the attention does help raise enthusiasm for the school in the community, the long-term outcomes of such publicity are not positive. Such media attention diverts needed energies and creates a fishbowl environment that is not helpful to continued growth. Public visibility, moreover, raises resentment among some teachers and certainly reduces support among administrators at the central office.

Structural Change and Size

The redesign plan called for a school of 3000 youngsters on single session, not 6000. The doubling of the student population was unanticipated. The smart money at the central board was betting on failure, so why waste time planning for the implications of success?

The redesign plan focused on personalizing the school for students, but the explosion in population made implementation a management nightmare. For example, ten-week cycles meant that the entire school had to be scheduled four times each year. If correctly done, this process entailed individual counseling with students, matching grading and marking data with student course requests, and producing 6000 individualized schedules, all within a three- to four-week period. The cycle turnaround process became even more difficult since the district scheduling software had no capacity to accommodate students participating in work/study, community service, and in-school activity programs at specially designated times. Scheduling software to handle nontraditional student schedules is still a problem in many school districts. "It doesn't fit into the schedule" is something I hear frequently as I wander the country to work with restructuring schools.

At one point, it took the program office staff four twelve-hour days to resolve the schoolwide conflict matrix. When the number of classes meeting each period exceeded the number of classrooms, the school had to go on three overlapping sessions, which added new problems.

I now know that there were other ways to handle scheduling issues. We could have carried the concept of Career Institutes to its next logical step by creating genuine self-managing, self-scheduling mini-schools. Such an arrangement would have personalized the school for each student, streamlined school management, and given teachers greater control over their working life. Neither I nor other members of the staff knew about this option at the time. Our lack of knowledge about scheduling alternatives doomed the cycle format to failure.

In time, the administrative burden created by scheduling proved to be too much for a school administration reeling under repeated financial and personnel reductions. Lane's huge size made it almost impossible to operate the school, sustain the instructional changes, and maintain forward momentum in the change area. As the management problems grew, school staff spent geometrically increasing amounts of time trying to keep one step ahead of the next approaching deadline. They narrowed their scope of interests as they focused almost exclusively on their own areas of responsibility and became less concerned with the school as a whole.

The school's administrative, guidance, and managerial staff became almost totally consumed by the mounting burdens caused by educational ideas that carried with them procedures that were no longer practical, even though they might be creative and exciting. Procedures that could be handled efficiently with 3000 students did not work when that number doubled. Eventually, the staff's perspective on innovation became governed not by the intrinsic educational merit in an idea but by how much managerial effort it would take to accomplish. For many at Lane, weariness caused by an increasing student population and decreasing resources strained the abilities and patience of the school staff to the point of exhaustion. Reason waned as anger and frustration grew. Staff members at every level pointed with anger and resentment at the culprit: the redesign plan.

Structural Change and Faculty Culture

Is it a good idea to attempt to rescue a high school in crisis with the faculty that participated in its deterioration? The Lane experience suggests that the answer is an emphatic no. For many years the staff had divided along racial, political, and social lines. Most of those who survived the troubled years were drawn together or irreparably split apart by the experience. They shared a common approach to handling things. As an illustration, some supported and others opposed the redesign plan. They fought for it or against it with the same vigor and callous disregard for its effect on the schools that they had brought to their disputes during the years of turmoil. In the days of the old Lane, they brutalized staff relations and continued to do so during the five years I was at the school.

The earlier seven years of chaos dominated the imagination of staff members who had lived through them. They viewed school affairs through a lens ground to fit a school in crisis and, as a result, focused almost exclusively on safety and security. These teachers remained haunted, almost paralyzed, by memories of violence and vandalism and the potential for physical harm to themselves and their personal property. They envisioned potential catastrophe behind each new initiative. They treated staff members willing to take risks as if they were wounded swimmers in shark-infested waters. An illustration is the problems that occurred when the school instituted overlapping sessions to accommodate the burgeoning student population. As with most schools, the primary purpose in assigning rooms is to give teachers a home base. This policy was continued at Lane, even after there were not enough rooms to go around and they had to be shared. One hopes to provide teachers with a place to keep materials and to make the classroom a learning home for the kids where they can keep projects and completed work on display. This meant, however, that teachers might be teaching in isolated portions of the building during the last part of the day when there were only twenty or thirty classrooms in use out of a total of ninety-five.

It was not long before a delegation of staff members scheduled an appointment to discuss the manner in which "school administrators were placing teachers in physical danger." It was a somber group. They were scared. They saw potential problems that did not seem real to me. During the meeting I could hear the anguish in their voices. They could not get beyond their fear of teaching in a half-empty building.

Further, and of greater concern, the old Lane faculty possessed almost no communal experience focusing on instructional matters. Of course, there were individual teachers who taught exemplary lessons and who thought deeply about teaching and learning. There were teachers who remained current in their knowledge of teaching strategies and their interest in children's education. Theirs, however, was not a shared experience, and it did not improve the school as a whole. Their knowledge as well as their teaching remained isolated in what Phil Schlechty, president of the Center for Leadership in School Reform in Louisville, Kentucky, calls "self-contaminated classrooms."

My perusal of the minutes of faculty meetings prior to the redesign of the school revealed that items related to curriculum and instruction had not been discussed by the faculty as a whole for three years. Given the traditional isolation of the classroom and the chaos in the school, teachers rarely discussed anything but issues involving the maintenance of safety and security. At the outset of the reform period, most teachers were indifferent to the implications of the instructional or organizational innovations as long as they felt safe in their classrooms. If educational redesign was the price for getting a secure environment, they would agree to almost anything.

When one considers the traumatic history of the school and the lack of a stable organizational structure, the old Lane teachers required more sustained emotional support—tender loving care, perhaps—than the administration could provide. It was almost as if they searched for opportunities to feel alienated from the administration, the parent community, and the new staff members. They drew themselves into a tight circle for protection. They shut their ears and their minds to new ideas and new staff members, whom they repeatedly characterized in local union publications as "recent arrivals, who were not as seasoned as those veterans who had toiled at Lane for years."

Most new staff members (those assigned to the school after 1976) viewed circumstances differently. These teachers, for the most part, came to Lane because they wished to work in a different type of school. Most supported instructional change efforts and volunteered to serve on the planning task forces. This group grew in numbers as the student body increased and within two years outnumbered the holdovers. Their energy fueled the change process as the pace of reform quickened. Over time, the increasing strength and influence of the new teachers created a backlash and unleashed a struggle among faculty for control of the union chapter.

In time I came to believe that the redesign plan would have fared better had the old Lane been shut down and all staff members reassigned to other high schools. Although one can argue that high school reform in America will succeed only after the discovery of the clues to changing the teaching corps ("You have to plow with the mules you got," as farmers are fond of saying), there are those extreme cases in which failing institutions traumatize staff members to the point at which they develop a negative synergy that is injurious to them as individuals and to the institution as a whole.

During the early 1980s, I was placed in charge of framing and implementing a strategic plan for the redevelopment of the New York City High School Division and had an opportunity to apply some of the lessons learned at Lane. In planning for the reconfiguration of other schools in crisis, I insisted on three things: (1) the old school must close, (2) staff members must be reassigned, and (3) the student population must be capped at the number specified in the school's redesign plan.

The Problem of Demands on Teachers

At Lane, the newly developed high expectations for teachers that were part of the redesign plan were not matched by new and higher expectations for students. Most of the changes had more immediate impact on teachers than on students because, understandably, the initial focus was on structure and instruction. After all, the Lane effort was, in essence, a recognition that changes in instructional practices in school would not be fully implemented and would be extremely difficult to sustain without teacher involvement and appropriate organizational changes. For example, we saw how changes in classroom practices (the Career Institutes) had to be supported by changes in how teachers worked, communicated, and planned together; how students would be grouped; how resources and time were allocated; how teachers and students were evaluated; and how much support for change there was from parents. The conventional wisdom was that capacity for change could be built through equipping teachers with the necessary skills.

Unfortunately, of course, it had costs. The traditional or hierarchical organization of high schools makes no demand on teacher time for decision making. We never knew whether the time costs of a shared decision-making structure had the desired effects on student outcomes. The emphasis was on program planning and implementation and making the new organization work efficiently. Less time went into rethinking classroom practices and program evaluation.

Clearly, recent indicators from many studies (Dade County Public Schools, Report on SBM/SDM, Phase I, 1991) already show the visible benefit of shared decision making in higher levels of teacher satisfaction about their work and strengthened professionalism. However, educational historians (Ravitch, 1983) have argued that the educational reforms of the first half of this century spawned reactions such as back-to-basics movements and demands for accountability precisely because they did not communicate high expectations for *student* performance and, therefore, were perceived by the public as lacking content and condoning lazy instruction. In fact, the educational reforms of the late 1960s fell prey to yet another back-to-basics movement that still haunts schools.

Teachers in schools today, however, believe that the changes in instruction and school organization will ultimately increase opportunities for students. Rather than being seen as simply more "challenging," they see the changes as providing support for students to achieve current academic goals. For example, teachers at one high school I work with in Minnesota regularly point out the parallel between the similar demands on teachers and on students for higher-order thinking.

While initially the emphasis in most schools and districts is on empowerment and local school determination of needed changes, it is important that in the future high schools focus more on high expectations for students in addition to the increased demands on teachers.

The Link Between Change and Student Achievement

Many changes at Lane were proposed and adopted because the planning teams thought they seemed like the right thing to do. Although teachers and parents were conscious of the effects they would like to achieve, few discussed, let alone ever attempted to reach consensus about, the desired student outcomes. Moreover, there was no real evidence that the efforts would be likely to produce the desired effect on students.

Even in those efforts where desired outcomes were explicit and teachers were clear about what they wished to achieve, there were still problems with the kinds of measures to be used as indicators of success, as in restructuring schools today. At Lane almost no effort went into the development of comprehensive procedures for assessing change efforts. Teachers then, as today, agreed that there was a mismatch between forms of assessment and school goals. They agreed then, as today, that the public demand for accountability through standardized achievement tests was misguided and inappropriate. However, then as now, they felt powerless to change public perception about assessment. More troublesome, many teachers today do not see changing the public perception as their responsibility. Even those teachers in the vanguard on assessment issues today still complain, perhaps correctly, that the solution rests beyond the local school.

At Lane, as at most restructuring schools today, very little teacher energy was directed toward demonstrating the effects of innovation on student achievement. By and large, most teachers viewed measurement in traditional and narrowly defined terms as a technical enterprise synonymous with traditional testing (i.e., standardized achievement tests such as the California Achievement Test) used by many high schools. While it is true of many high schools in general (a characteristic of the field, so to speak) that changes in instruction and organization are seen as desirable goals in themselves and are not viewed as requiring evidence about their ultimate effects on students, more data are required from restructuring schools, much more. How will teachers know whether or not new programs are successful in raising student achievement levels if they do not look for and cannot explain which particular program (or within programs, which component) or process contributes to success or to ineffectiveness?

Structural Change and the Role of the Central Office

The Lane Redesign Plan produced a model that was hardly compatible with existing practice at other New York City high schools. It challenged thinking about how high schools should be organized and education delivered. It also created bureaucratic problems at the central office because its instructional programs crossed the jurisdictional lines of the traditional curriculum departments. Career Institutes, as already explained, included a correlated curriculum in academic and vocation/career/business subjects. How would these programs be listed in Board of Education catalogs? Who at central headquarters could take credit for them? Who would want to pay for modifications to facilities if they could not then claim credit for the program? Such were the disputes that rocked central headquarters as the Lane plan was implemented.

Moreover, there was great suspicion at central headquarters that the Lane staff was determined to make city school system bureaucrats look bad, a notion fueled by the board's past history with the school and by the high visibility of the Lane experiment in the news media. The suspicions at central headquarters were fanned by the fact that Lane's mandate for planning and implementation bypassed central board officials. Frankly, in a major mistake on my part, I never let them forget it. I should have done the opposite and tried to draw central officials into the process. Once the Lane plan became operational, it depended on central office support or, at least, understanding. Within the board, there was a lack of sensitivity to the components of the Lane plan among officials charged with budget allocations, personnel, curriculum support, and pupil personnel services.

The instances of interference are legion as central office officials made life difficult on a daily basis. The interference was not intentionally disruptive; rather, it disrupted because it did not take the school context or needs into consideration. The central bureaucracy in New York City is so unstable, and people change jobs so often, that most central office officials knew very little about the school and its history. They viewed requests for waivers from district policy as attempts to evade centrally imposed restraints. They were unwilling to alter the standard districtwide system for allocating categorical financial and personnel resources to the school. Although budget authority resided at the school, that in some ways becomes meaningless if the authority does not include the ability to move funds from one category to another. Since Lane's new instructional program required different staffing arrangements, the school administration was faced with a difficult choice: violate either Board of Education regulations or the court order. We decided to ignore board policy and, if challenged, to appeal to the court. We juggled resources and submitted "creatively" prepared figures to the High School Division. This was most certainly not an effective way to build a purposeful and supportive relationship with the central office.

Additionally, the Lane plan posed an even greater threat to board policy since it ran counter to districtwide trends. Central authorities were rushing toward tighter control and greater standardization among the city's high schools with uniformity of curriculum and increased regulation. While the district was distributing a citywide curriculum that prescribed standardized assessment instruments, teachers at Lane were developing a student-centered instructional program.

"What would happen if we had 110 different school schedules and 110 marking and grading systems? How would we keep track?" one high-level central office bureaucrat asked.

"Keep track of what? Why do you need to keep track? The state department of education comes in every five years to reregister the school. Let them keep track," I responded.

"That is my job and I'm going to do it," he stated, clearly thinking I had lost my mind. How could a school system work if people didn't spend their time keeping track?

Orchestrating a complex, multi-part improvement effort, developing the planning skills among staff, and fitting the program components into existing state regulations all required adroitness in buffering the work from central office interference.

Central office problems were not unique to Lane. Louis and Miles (1990) report that in their study of urban high school reform, four out of five schools experienced conflicts with the district offices as a "pervasive element" during the planning stage.

CONCLUDING REMARKS

The special circumstances surrounding the Lane experience with structural change have, in some ways, a limiting effect on the transferability of the lessons learned to other schools. Among the special circumstances discussed in this chapter are the federal court mandate that helped drive the change process and the fact that Lane was concurrently redesigned and rezoned for a new attendance district. Lane was virtually a new school, with one exception: the old faculty remained.

Beyond Lane's unique situation, applicability is further limited by the issue of whether or not "turnaround schools" undergoing dramatic improvement after a period of severe decline have internal dynamics that differ from those in more stable schools, i.e., those undergoing fewer changes. The answer to this question is unknown, but is raised for the benefit of readers.

Some threads emerged at Lane that do have significance for others currently involved with structural change. Foremost among these is the critical importance of strategic thinking. There is probably a tendency among school practitioners who spend their days performing to take for granted the deeper meanings in the events that occur around them as they manage the change process. In coping with a demanding schedule and the management of an institution in which 6000 children and 300 adults interacted for nine hours each day, I rarely had time to think about what I was doing or to focus on those aspects of the change process that were necessary to ensure success. It is precisely such foresight and deep reflection, however, that might have eased the stress that accompanied change at Lane and perhaps altered the outcome. My observations of principals around the nation reveals that lack of strategic thinking among all school stakeholders is a general problem that must be addressed by school systems before any type of real school-based structural change can take place.

There are other themes as well. Among them are the advisability of including in the planning process teachers representing all shades of faculty opinion on change issues; the importance of altering a school's administrative structure, such as subject department organization, to maintain compatibility with new curriculum and instructional innovations; the importance of ongoing communication about the innovations with all school groups—teachers, students, parents, business sector representatives, and civic and community leaders; and the importance of building a purposeful relationship with the central office. It is necessary to take into account all of these themes, as well as the importance of monitoring faculty mood, to preclude the development of stress.

References

Dade County Public Schools. (1991). Report on SBM/SDM: Phase I.

Hall, G.E. and Hord, S.M. (1987). *Change in Schools: Facilitating the Process.* Albany: SUNY Press.

Louis, K.S. and Miles, M.B. (1990). *Improving the Urban High School: What Works and Why.* New York: Teachers College Press.

Ravitch, D. (1983). *The Troubled Crusade: American Education 1945–1980.* New York: Basic Books.

Tewel, K. and Chalfin, F. (1980). Close encounters in the classroom: A technique for combating irresponsibility among today's high school youngsters. *Kappan,* 62, 56–58.

U.S. Government. (1978). Violent Schools, Safe Schools. Washington, D.C.: U.S. Government Printing Office.

5

The Reforms

Before providing readers with strategies for maneuvering through the turbulent waters of the change process, it is essential to refocus on the goal: developing the capacity of school leaders to work with other members of the school community to create a new kind of high school able to produce substantially higher levels of learning for larger numbers of students. It is important, then, to have a description of what such a school might look like and how it might work, with an emphasis on those features of the traditionally organized high school that must be changed. This chapter provides a brief glimpse of such a school as seen through the eyes of one student. It then goes on to provide brief descriptions of the reforms themselves, together with the names of schools and networks that readers can contact if they wish additional information.

Futurists and experts on organizational change emphasize the importance of mental imagery and visualization in achieving desired outcomes. The first step in accomplishing something significant is to create a vivid mental scenario of what it would be like if the dream came true. What follows is a vision of a twenty-first century school that has addressed many of the restructuring issues in high schools of today. The school has integrated its activities in improving curriculum, instruction, professional development, organizational change, assessment, and accountability while developing a deeper collaboration with parents and other community members. The description is not meant to portray what every school should be doing or to advocate for a particular model of schooling, but rather to convey an idea of the ways in which the concepts being addressed by restructuring schools might be implemented in one school.

WESTBROOK HIGH SCHOOL

John is eagerly looking forward to his three-hour social studies session this morning with Sally and Bob, his project team members. They have spent the last two weeks working together to organize a Lincoln–Douglas debate on issues surrounding the population explosion in Third World countries. They have prepared briefing papers, including a bibliography of printed and software resource materials, for distribution to other class members.

John is in his second year at the lower school at Westbrook. At any traditional high school he would be classified as a tenth grader. At Westbrook, however, all ninth and tenth graders work in ungraded groups until they are able to pass a battery of competency exams that permit them to move on to the upper school, which comprises the traditional grades 11 and 12.

The students in the lower school at Westbrook High are divided into six clusters of approximately 150 students each. Each cluster has a team of math, science, English, social studies, and humanities teachers. Two full-time guidance counselors divide their time among the six clusters. A bilingual teacher and two special educators spend varying amounts of time with each of the clusters, depending upon student need. In addition, each teacher functions as an advisor to a small group of students who meet daily for 30 minutes.

John is thinking about making some changes in the individual learning plan that he, his parents, and the teachers in his cluster have developed. He is increasingly unsure about his original decision made more than a year ago about what career path to take.

John had a choice of a number of different high schools; in fact, he could have chosen any school in the entire city. There were no longer attendance zones or student assignment restrictions other than available space. John originally chose Westbrook because the upper school had an excellent Legal Careers Academy. Ever since he was in elementary school he was fascinated by the legal profession. He remembered reading courtroom novels instead of joining his friends on the ballfield. He loved the action and verbal jousting that were part of the working life of a trial attorney. For many years he had had a picture of himself becoming a trial lawyer. Now he wasn't too sure. Lately he'd been thinking that he really wanted to write courtroom dramas about lawyers instead of being one. Didn't that mean he should think about becoming a journalist? He knows that a school across town has an Academy of Written Communications and Technology. Perhaps he ought to transfer there for the eleventh and twelfth grades.

It wasn't as if he would be leaving all his friends if he transferred to another school. Most of them were going through a similar process of decision making. Everyone had to decide about a career focus for upper school and that meant people would be heading in different directions. His friend Mike would be going to the International Studies Academy at another school across town and his friend Greg would be studying electronics and technology at a satellite program operating at the headquarters of a local corporation where he would have his academic classes and career experiences as well as an on-the-job internship. His friend Sara would be attending the Space Academy at Westbrook, the school's specialization in addition to law. A major portion of Sara's classes would be taught at a nearby aeronautics and space facility. Although Sara was not sure that she wanted to work in the aerospace field, she welcomed the opportunity to apply science, math, communication, and technology concepts and skills in a meaningful, adult-world context and to learn many skills applicable to other careers.

All of the lower school clusters and upper school academies combine academic instruction and career preparation. They are designed so that students can either go on to college, get advanced or specialized training, or move directly into a career. Partnerships among the high schools, colleges, and local businesses provide resources. All of the partners are involved in program design and provide opportunities for internships.

John's thoughts shift from planning for the future and return to the present. He should be spending his mental energy on the need to execute a computer search for additional source material for the debates that he and his team are working on. Thursday is the deadline, the day of the debate. Everything has to be finished by then.

Mr. Rodin, his social studies teacher, enters the room. He is returning from a cluster planning period where he and his colleagues are planning for ways of integrating the unit on world population into other curricular areas. They had originally planned it as a four-week unit; however, students had gotten so deeply involved in researching their projects that the teachers agreed to extend the unit to seven weeks. John is anxious to talk with Mr. Rodin, who is also his advisor. They had originally planned his individual education plan together, and now he wants to tell him about his thoughts on switching schools and areas of study for upper school.

Lower school had been an excellent experience for John. Like the other students, he had enrolled in the structured sequence of courses in which all students are prepared to think conceptually, solve complex problems, and communicate their ideas. The school had no remedial courses. John thrived on the lower school's approach to education. He had participated in courses that developed a strong academic foundation in language arts, mathematics, history, and science. This academic core also provided students with courses in the arts, health and physical education, vocational education, and foreign languages. The curriculum that comprises the core was rigorous and appropriately differentiated to ensure that all students operated at a challenging level. Students had to work harder, but the work was interesting and engaging. Those students who met high performance standards more quickly move on. Some moved on to upper school before the two years were up.

The new lower school core courses had replaced the fragmented department-based curriculum that his father had taken when he was a high school student during the 1960s in the same town. John's curriculum was not just new courses with new names. These courses and course sequences transcended the borders of the traditional academic curriculum. The integration of curriculum took a variety of shapes: for instance, a combination of math and science; history and English; or history, math, and the arts; or a combination of academic and vocational disciplines, such as sports and science or social studies and business.

One recent evening, John's father had compared his son's high school program with the one he had taken when he was a student. His father thought that the new core curriculum challenged and supported students to work harder and on more demanding assignments. It was rigorous and concept-driven, as opposed to solely fact- or skill-based, and it was accessible to a broad range of learners. For example, the traditional sequence of math, algebra, geometry, advanced algebra, and trigonometry had been replaced by a new course sequence, Math 1,2,3,4. Concentrating on important and complex mathematical ideas, the math curriculum was composed of eight strands: numbers, measurement, geometry, patterns and functions, statistics and probability, logic and language, algebra, and discrete mathematics.

Students' work in the new curriculum was often focused on projects they "constructed," using experiences related to the world outside of school and primary source materials they selected because of their appropriateness and personal connection to their lives. Learning activities put together complex concepts by asking students to apply skills across subject matter boundaries and to confront personal and group values related to their learning. It engaged students in the learning process so that they became active participants who could apply their knowledge to other areas of learning. This type of learning program was nothing new for John. It continued the approach used in the middle school he had attended. That school, too, was organized into clusters in which students worked with their peers and an interdisciplinary team of teachers.

Westbrook High School was different from the school John's father attended in other ways as well. At Westbrook, there was flexible use of instructional time under the exclusive control of an interdisciplinary team of teachers. The schedule made it possible for teachers working with a group of students to have the time needed to accomplish various objectives. The schedule was flexible, driven by the competing demands of the curriculum, and decided by the teacher team. One day they might spend the entire morning on a science project, just as they were spending today on social studies. The school also had longer blocks of time for student work. Blocks of time differed based on the nature of the instructional tasks. The traditional 50-minute class was deemed not long enough for students to solve complex problems, compose effective writing, or design projects that measured real progress. In addition, students had alternative ways to demonstrate attainment of high performance standards, and those who met these standards quickly were encouraged to move on.

Westbrook also had a longer school day, week, and year. Scheduling a longer school day (for example, from 7 A.M. to 6 P.M.) or a longer week (Saturday classes) made the school a learning center for the entire community, including working students and parents. Students in grades 11 and 12 could take the high school's program in the morning or afternoon, while they also took advanced courses at colleges and universities or participated in internships or other field work experiences with business, industry, schools, and private and public community organizations. The school year at Westbrook was extended by creating intersessions that allowed additional time for student support or faculty planning.

As great as lower school had been, John was looking forward to moving on. In upper school, he will be able to choose an organized program around a special focus that combines academic, applied academic, and field experiences. These program thrusts might be organized according to themes built around career fields, such as law or transportation technology. Once a student selects a theme, he has an opportunity to integrate academic and vocational curricula with a strong core curriculum. Many of the programs have been designed to meet college entrance requirements, while also providing students with career-related technical and practical skills.

Students at Westbrook are not tracked in either lower school or upper school; instead, they select a program based on their own interests and learning styles. The hope is that many more students than ever before, particularly students from backgrounds historically underrepresented in higher education, will take courses that prepare them for college. John's advisor, in his discussions with him, had stressed that John would not be locked into any program that he chose, but could move from one program to another if his goals changed. Students, in collaboration with parents and advisors, develop and revise personal learning plans that provide road maps to postsecondary and career goals. The plans are reviewed frequently by advisors and cluster teachers.

A special feature of the learning experience for John is the ability to work together with other students. His advisor stresses that it is essential for him to develop interaction skills in lower school because that is how he might have to work during his career.

Collaborating with others is enjoyable for John. It is much more desirable to work and struggle with others than to struggle alone. Working with other students helps him feel that he is part of a community of learners where everyone shares from each other's success. At the same time, John also has to do individual work and has personal responsibility for specific projects or parts of projects. Teachers still have an opportunity to judge his individual performance; these projects are important. Each student at Westbrook has a graduation portfolio that contains various assessment measures, including work samples in all core disciplines, awards, the standard high school transcript, a performance-based diploma, and statements about what the student has learned.

Actually, John's teachers are also modeling collaboration when they function as their own learning community. They share their own discoveries with students each day during their team meetings. They read about and discuss new ideas in teaching; they experiment with new approaches, and they plan evaluation and assessment together.

Working as a team is only one way in which teachers' lives are different. The concept of staff development at Westbrook has been broadened to mean more than simply training: it has become a vehicle for professional growth and ongoing renewal. For instance, participating in collegial support teams, classroom research projects, and curriculum development contributes to a teacher's effectiveness. Organizing study groups around issues or professional readings can bring new ideas into practice. Observing other teachers and having time to talk about classroom practices helps teachers feel more comfortable with new methods or curriculum.

Westbrook High School staff members have greater control over resources to support the new curriculum and student goals than teachers did when John's father went to school. Budget authority and decision making are decentralized so that most budget decisions are made at the school, primarily by teachers, but with the input of parents and others. The budgeting process allows staff to shift financial resources to implement their philosophy for improving teaching and learning. The budget development process provides meaningful choices, flexibility, and the maximum opportunity for success within state law, court orders, and district policies. The school staff is accountable for the resources used to improve program effectiveness as evidenced by increased student success.

Westbrook's principal sees to it that communication channels between teachers and administrators and between the school and the parent community are efficient, effective, and direct. The school suffers from none of the pervasive problems of isolation that characterized high schools in John's father's day. Ms. Arons, Westbrook's principal, checks for messages through electronic mail (e-mail) three or four times each day. Because Arons recognizes that school teachers have tight schedules but still need to connect and communicate with each other, the principal makes sure that everyone has an e-mail number and access to a networked computer. Arons sees this technology link as essential in a school with diverse faculty whose various schedules often keep them separate. Arons once explained it to Mr. Rodin as follows:

> Everyone knows I read my e-mail at least three times each day, so they can always get in touch with me, no matter how big or small the issue. Think of the time that saves teachers: what if people had to look for me, or interrupt my meetings with teacher teams, or write me notes that had to be delivered? Think of the time it saves for my secretary. It also makes me feel closer to the faculty, too—and there is less room for misinterpretation because I am dealing directly with everyone.

Not all students are as successful as John. Some encounter formidable obstacles in trying to master the demanding curriculum. Consequently, higher expectations for students are accompanied by more support in the form of individual attention, strong teacher involvement, and small group and individual learning opportunities before and after school. The school subscribes to early intervention through the continuous monitoring of student progress. An ongoing plan provides additional support for students needing more time, encouragement, or instruction. The school day may be extended, summer or Saturday enrichment programs offered, and specialized daily instruction provided. This support is not remedial, but is offered within a context of enriched opportunities for learning that builds on individual students' strengths. It is based on the concept that, whereas all students can learn, some students may need more assistance in one area than another.

Support such as tutoring and counseling, training in time management, note taking, writing reports, analysis, written expression, and critical thinking; adaption of the physical environment; and learning techniques, such as cooperative study groups and the inquiry method, are considered a normal part of the help that Westbrook offers to all students. Prevention is at the heart of this assistance. All students receive help in their personal, social, educational, and career development. Student support is proactive and positive, not remedial or indicative of failure, and it is integrated into the regular coursework. No stigma is attached to receiving or asking for support.

Westbrook High School is constantly evolving. The school is always in an ongoing process of planning, implementation, reflection, and rethinking the instructional program. Although all teachers do not embrace change, with its accompanying stress and sense of displacement, everyone knows that constant change is a feature of working and learning at Westbrook.

This concludes a brief visit to a typical morning at Westbrook High School, illustrating how it is dealing with some of the restructuring elements high schools are confronting today. The next portion of the chapter briefly describes and further explains some of these elements. It also provides readers with names and places to contact if they wish more extensive information. The section is divided into three subsections: (1) restructuring the school organization, (2) transforming the classroom, and (3) changing the school climate.

RESTRUCTURING THE SCHOOL ORGANIZATION

A major goal of restructuring the school organization is to enlist broader participation in school decision making and operation. The decentralization of authority within the school permits expanded roles for teachers in the processes of handling governance issues and planning school improvement activities. At the core of innovations such as shared school governance is the basic belief that professionalizing teaching by involving teachers in instructional teams and various governance councils will enhance teachers' professional lives and, more importantly, will result in enhanced student learning. Although there is much support for this trend, one must be cautious. Having teachers assume additional responsibilities without altering the traditional format of the teacher workday can quickly become overwhelming, as demonstrated in Chapters 3 and 4, and may distract from their energy for teaching itself.

A second organizational change focuses on the efficient use of instructional time. Innovations such as the block schedule and school subdivisions, or functional units, are meant to increase flexibility so that teachers can vary instructional activities. The extended school year has been proposed as a means of providing more time for student learning. However, budgetary constraints limit implementation in many places.

Still other elements of organizational restructuring aim to make the school a more humane and welcoming place that encourages and facilitates student learning. School-within-a-school and teacher advisee structures attempt to reduce students' feelings of alienation and disconnectedness by giving them more personal contacts with caring adults.

All of these approaches to restructuring the school organization are efforts to involve people—educators, students, parents, and others—in schooling in more meaningful ways. The hope, of course, is that such meaningful involvement will create the conditions that will ultimately increase student achievement.

Shared School Governance

Varieties of advisory councils, management councils, shared leadership teams, or restructuring coordinating committees represent a trend away from centralized school administration. Including those who are affected by decisions in the decision-making process is believed to enlist greater understanding and support for the introduction of changes in the school (Dade County Public Schools, 1991). High schools vary greatly in the degree to which they include parents in formal school governance structures, but teachers, students, and other employees are almost always included.

An example of shared school governance is the plan for a 13-member Site Committee in the Chiloquin Junior–Senior High School in Chiloquin, Oregon. The committee includes the principal, one classified employee, one external patron, three parents, and seven teachers. The committee mission statement specifies that the committee will focus on instructional improvement and staff development issues, basing decisions on 80% consensus.

A second example is South Mountain High School in Phoenix, Arizona, which employs a collaborative decision-making model in its School Improvement Team to facilitate changes needed for its diverse student body. A third example is Mission Bay High School in San Diego, California. Mission Bay has a provision in its governance framework that permits any staff member to attend and participate in governance team meetings.

School-Based Management

There are many names and definitions for school-based management (SBM), including school-site management, school-based budgeting, school-site autonomy, and shared governance (Clune and White, 1988). School-based management is a key component of almost all restructuring efforts (David et al., 1989; Fullan, 1993). As Bailey (1991) points out, SBM is about "who is the boss," which affects other key reform issues in education, such as what is taught and how it is taught. Although SBM is defined in a variety of ways, it is typically described as a change in governance structure that increases authority at the school site.

School-based–managed schools operate under plans affording varying degrees of latitude in delivering an instructional program appropriate for students, which may vary from one high school to another. The basic assumption of SBM is the same as that of decentralization efforts in general, namely, that personnel at the point of service delivery, e.g., individual schools, are better able to identify the specific problems and needs of their own students and schools. Thus, they should be given the authority, responsibility, and opportunity to alter procedures and practices to meet those needs. This added leeway and flexibility, it is further theorized, should better stimulate school personnel to improve their ability to educate and motivate students and enable them to introduce new ideas more rapidly to better match the needs of their own students. It is further assumed that SBM will encourage the development and implementation of new ways of educating students—ways that might meet resistance if imposed from the outside.

SBM, in other words, is a formalized way of enlisting broader participation and accountability among the constituents in a particular school. This is achieved by replacing central district requirements and decisions with more school-based power to allocate resources, set directions, and tailor a local instructional program to meet the needs of the student body. In practice, this can mean that schools are obliged to follow a district curriculum but are encouraged to seek improved student performance through interventions initiated by a local advisory group. Phrased another way, the district defines *what* is to be learned, and the school figures out *how* to achieve the results. Although school-site budgeting is a key indicator of the total commitment of a district to SBM, most schools have not gotten this far yet.

SBM has become a major educational reform movement in elementary and secondary education. Support has come from every type of forum. The Rutgers-based Center for Policy Research in Education has said that SBM has a "strategic position at the crossroads of major trends in state and local policy" (Clune and White, 1988). The National Governors' Association (NGA) has produced no less than three policy papers on SBM since 1988. These papers followed the NGA task force report "Time for Results: The Governors' 1991 Report on Education," which called for promotion of school autonomy and site management. The Carnegie Forum on Education and the Economy has called for restructuring schools to provide a more professional environment for teachers by increasing teacher participation in decision making (Carnegie Forum on Education and the Economy, 1986). Kentucky has mandated statewide adoption of school-based decision making in its Education Reform Act of 1990, which is to be fully implemented by 1996–97.

Although site-based management may be more applicable to larger districts, where central office roles have been perceived to be inhibitors of change, it is also being adopted in smaller districts across the country.

There is surprisingly little empirical research on SBM, considering all the hype devoted to it. In a literature review, Malen (1990) identifies only eight systematic investigations of SBM based on case studies, but stresses that these were not comparable because different versions of SBM were examined and different dimensions were the focus. Additional empirical research on SBM is under way, although the number of schools or districts studied remains fairly small (Hallinger et al., 1991; Taylor and Teddlie, 1992; Weiss, 1992).

Despite generally positive descriptions of the rationale for decentralization, or SBM, some of the literature raises concerns about the ability of SBM to impact student learning. Elmore (1991) notes that SBM lacks an explicit explanation or theory for translating organizational changes into changes in instructional practice and learning. In addition, new systems such as SBM must be implemented within the constraints of existing knowledge and relationships, which may neutralize their effect on the overall performance of schools. Finally, he points out that educational innovations in general are often poorly designed and/or implemented, often without a clear understanding of the processes and institutions they are trying to affect. Fullan (1993) makes a similar point about implementation, noting that rapid implementation of new structures, such as SBM, creates confusion, ambiguity, and conflict, which ultimately may lead to retrenchment. He suggests that an organizational culture conducive to change is needed if restructuring efforts, such as decentralization, are to succeed.

Some of the more recent literature raises additional concerns about the potential of SBM to have positive impacts on teaching practices or student learning. A recent study of a small group of teachers and principals indicates that neither group made much of a connection between new governance structures and the teaching–learning process (Hallinger et al., 1991). Taylor and Teddlie (1992) note that early literature on restructuring efforts predicts that changes in teaching practice could be expected, although this area has been largely neglected in actual research on restructuring. Their study in one district known for its SBM efforts suggests that teaching practices are not affected by teachers' greater participation in decision making associated with the SBM effort by the district.

In a similar vein, a recent study of twelve high schools across the country, six with and six without formal structures for teacher participation in decision making, found no evidence that such teacher participation increased the schools' focus on curriculum or teaching practice (Weiss, 1992). Although the schools with decentralized decision making are adopting more of the current educational reform initiatives (interdisciplinary teaching, block scheduling, etc.), these changes appear to be associated with the arrival of a new principal or superintendent with a reform agenda, rather than with the participatory role of teachers. However, shared decision making may be promoting greater support for or "ownership" of such innovations (Weiss, 1992).

School-Based Budgeting

Budget and expenditure flexibility are the responsibilities most commonly delegated to the school level in restructuring districts. Some school districts extend budget authority to schools in several phases (i.e., a small cadre of schools are initially given more budget authority on a pilot basis, with more schools added in later years). In some districts, schools have the option of applying for additional budgetary authority after a pilot phase. Generally, schools are not allowed to remove teachers and transfer personnel funds into other uses. However, in several districts, schools can make such transfers when a vacancy occurs.

A commonly used budget process is illustrated by an example from The San Diego Unified School District in California. Schools develop their own budgets by modifying a projected budgetary allocation prepared by the school district. The district budget office provides each school with estimated amounts for various budget categories based on projected enrollment, required pupil/teacher ratios, and so on. Schools may use these estimates and instructions provided by the district budget office to develop proposed budgets. As part of this process, they are able to transfer funds among line items defined by the district as discretionary accounts, such as substitute teachers, supplies, equipment, and per-session employment. They may also make modifications in staffing patterns, that is, a switch from one category of personnel to another. Schools can exchange a library aide for a counseling assistant. Resulting school budgets are subject to approval by the district.

No district currently allows individual schools to deviate from districtwide salary scales. However, schools are usually allowed to provide extra payments to faculty for added activities that the faculty often recommends, such as special tutoring services. In most places, individual school flexibility over personnel costs is highly constrained by school district policies (and often union agreements) such as maximum student/teacher ratios. The Boston Teachers Union and the United Teachers of Dade County (Florida) have contract provisions permitting the establishment of schools with different pay scales and staffing patterns, but these are not yet in operation.

At the high school level, most schools allocate budgets to individual departments and sometimes to teaching teams. These budgets are typically for discretionary accounts, such as supplies and other instructional expenses, but, unfortunately, rarely for staff. Teaching teams in some schools generally receive small budgets for supplies or student-related expenses, such as field trips and incentive awards. In too many cases, teachers are unaware of the amount of money to be spent or of the real latitude they have in making decisions.

In a number of school districts, schools are able to make ongoing transfers among budget accounts, although restrictions are sometimes placed on which accounts can be used or the amounts involved. The ability to transfer funds is especially popular with teachers. They enjoy the flexibility of modifying spending decisions as needs change throughout the year, rather than being locked into the initial budget developed before the beginning of the fall term.

In Prince George's County, Maryland, a high school site council that includes department heads can agree to transfer funds among departments as long as personnel allocations are not involved. For example, at one school, two of the departments needed additional funds to replace lost texts. The site council reallocated funds from a third department for this purpose. Transfers were made with the general understanding that those who gave up funds one year would benefit from transfers in the future.

The Santa Fe Public School District in New Mexico decentralized budgetary authority by allowing schools to transfer funds among a selected group of line items: supplies, staff development, and texts. These accounts were chosen because they were fairly easy to monitor by the school district, any errors were relatively easy to correct, and staff sizes and salaries would not be affected.

Many teachers indicate that they feel that under decentralized budgeting it is easier to obtain the equipment or supplies that they want. In addition to added departmental responsibility and flexibility in allocating procurement dollars, forms of decentralization typically simplify procedures for obtaining equipment and supplies. Social studies teachers at a school in Miami remarked that the ability to make local purchases allows them to do minor things that improve morale, such as repairing classroom facilities. In another school, English teachers note that departments have more flexibility in deciding how funds are spent and that some departments pool resources to purchase supplies or equipment. This is quite a contrast to the school in Minnesota cited in Chapter 1, where each department purchased and had exclusive use of its own expensive video units. The principal of one high school in Santa Fe suggests that it is not only faster but more efficient to have teachers deal directly with suppliers, rather than funneling paperwork through the school district's central office. As Hatry et al. (1993, p. 19) point out in their study of SBM:

> A high school in one district initiated joint department purchasing under decentralization to reduce duplication of equipment purchases. For example, the mathematics and science departments collaborate to purchase software that can be used by both departments. In another high school, the science and mathematics departments structure their budgets to increase purchases of mathematics and science-related equipment and supplies, such as calculators, microscopes, and laboratory supplies. They use discretionary and instructional funds to purchase computers for their departments.

In some districts, schools are allowed to carry over funds. In these cases, school spending patterns frequently depend on the "personality of the principal" (Hatry et al., 1993, p. 21). Some principals spend almost everything within a year; others accumulate funds and do long-range planning. In Poway, California, schools are allowed to carry over 100% of their unspent instructional funds and a percentage of staff units. The district superintendent reports that principals feel this authority is one of the most empowering features of the district's SBM model. On the other hand, in Edmonton, Canada, schools are required to spend all of their funds within a year. The Edmonton superintendent believes that schools are given funds to educate the children that are in the schools now, not those who will be there next year.

Ninth Grade Transition Schools

Ninth grade transition schools are a largely separate entity provided for students in the lowest grade in the school (almost always the ninth grade) to ease their transition into the upper grades.

In large high schools, parents and faculty members have become concerned that the institution overwhelms younger students as they enter high school. Many schools are responding to this problem by establishing student advisory programs, providing smaller classes and more interdisciplinary work with smaller units, and separating the entering class from the rest of the school as much as possible. Naturally, it is important that good planning precede implementation of such transition programs and that parents and students be involved.

An example of a transition program can be found at the Huntington Area High School in Huntington, Pennsylvania, which operates a ninth grade school-within-a-school to provide a more nurturing environment for the first-year high school student. Students' core academic courses and lockers are located in a special ninth grade wing of the building. Ninth grade students are also provided with group activities and small-group and individual counseling as needed.

Student Advisories

Many high school have traditionally grouped students by home room. Student advisories carry this idea further by expanding the responsibility of the teacher to counseling students and getting to know them. In the often impersonal world of the high school, such one-to-one contact with a specific, caring adult can increase students' sense of belonging and self-esteem.

Each teacher is assigned a group of students who are provided with a "home base" for academic, vocational, or personal assistance/counseling. Groups meet 20–30 minutes a day in some schools; in others, they meet for longer periods, but on fewer days per week.

Such a program exists at New Trier High School in Winnetka, Illinois, where selected faculty members serve as teacher-advisers for 30 students, are given a reduced teaching load for this purpose, and meet for 27 minutes each day. An Advisor Program is also being used in Wilde Lake High School in Columbia, Maryland, in order to ensure that there is an in-depth knowledge of each student by at least one adult.

Fairdale High School in Louisville, Kentucky, schedules a daily half-hour Teacher-Guided Assistance period for all students: an advisory group in which 17 students of mixed grades work individually and together on both personal and academic matters. A surprising 90% of students polled called it the best thing about their school.

At Pasadena High School, all 650 ninth graders participate in an hour-long advisory period three days a week. In groups of 20 to 30, students meet with their teacher-adviser for activities designed to foster leadership, build self-esteem, and resolve conflicts. By the end of the first year that this was implemented, this school, 75% of whose student body is made up of minorities, had a ninth grade attendance rate of 96%, twice that of any other grade in the school.

Bellefonte Area High School, a small rural school in Pennsylvania, has a daily 15-minute Active Communication Time period scheduled into the lunch hour. To help teachers who are uneasy about what to do with the time, the school provides a handbook of guidelines and suggested activities for the 15 student groups. Advisors do no work in isolation. They are backed by a team of professionals that is called in for counseling, guidance, or intervention when a serious problem arises.

Thayer High School in Winchester, New Hampshire, has an effective advisory program. As part of the school's effort to link restructuring schools through interactive television, they have prepared a video on advisories that is available from the school.

School-Within-a-School

The idea of organizing high schools into smaller units has gained wide support in the last decade. The school-within-a-school concept is used in many places to create smaller student bodies that encourage feelings of student involvement and belonging. The organization of schools into smaller units is not a new concept in school reform, as many veteran teachers can attest. House systems enjoyed a heyday in the 1960s and early 1970s as rapid growth in the size of schools engendered interest in humanizing them. Schools were organized into clusters of a few hundred students with a formula-driven allocation of faculty members. Students received most, if not all, instruction from their house teachers and participated in house activities that were created over and above the schoolwide extracurricular program. Small units have been found to dispel the alienating effect of large schools, support a more coordinated and concentrated approach to instruction, and allow teachers greater input in decision making.

Today, in almost any large city one can find at least one school that was built during the 1960s or 1970s to accommodate a house plan. However, few of these house systems survived to the present, in large part because a national trend toward broadening the high school curriculum necessitated increasing, not decreasing, the scale of schools during the later 1970s. Now, when the shortcomings of a specialized high school curriculum are being widely noted, especially the shallow and unequal instruction of students, small unit organization has resurfaced with even greater recognized potential for strengthening secondary schooling.

The most persuasive argument made for small units is that they allow teachers and students in large high schools to form bonds of familiarity, identification, and support. Small units do this both by limiting the number of teachers and students who interact with one another and by increasing the number of activities they share. Students respect and cooperate with teachers who know them and have repeated contact with them. Shared learning experiences promote a sense of community.

Small units are also more effective than larger ones in supporting a more coordinated and concentrated approach to instruction. The comparatively small group of cross-disciplinary teachers within a small unit finds it easier to share experience and act consistently across students' entire academic programs than would a larger group of teachers, who are organized not around students but around academic disciplines and special needs programs. Small units support a student-centered approach to instruction, as opposed to a curriculum-centered approach. Moreover, small unit organization lends itself to a deeper rather than broader curriculum, since the small scale of units cannot support a highly diversified curriculum. Unit instructors concentrate their efforts on core subject areas, emphasize understanding and application of concepts, and add variety by creating different curricular themes and special projects that cut across subjects.

Small units allow for greater teacher input into decision making. The small unit plan is generally accompanied by a decentralized system of governance that gives unit leaders (frequently called "lead teachers") authority over unit activities. Unit leaders are better positioned for two-way communication with teachers, students, and their parents than are centralized administrators.

Large high schools have their own special set of problems that can be remedied by an effort to break them down into smaller units. Some large schools establish vertical house plans. These are more appropriate for large high schools and have been used off and on for several years. The most common format is three or four smaller schools within a larger institution, each of which includes a cross-section of ninth through twelfth graders with largely its own faculty and student activities. These houses may or may not have a particular instructional focus. This idea remains one of the most viable plans for breaking up "bigness" in the American high school.

Today, house systems and similar strategies for creating schools within a single school building are being supported by policy in school districts across the country: New York City, and Rochester, New York, and Columbus, Ohio, have adopted house systems at the high school level. Boston was one of the earliest districts to experiment with the plan in its high schools; Philadelphia has embraced a charter school plan for all 22 of its comprehensive high schools.

Several schools provide examples of school-within-a-school structures. Reynolds High School in Troutsdale, Oregon, is organized into three houses of 320 students each and one house of 80 students, in order to personalize each student's learning experience while attaining his or her Oregon Certificate of Mastery.

Polytechnic High School in Long Beach, California, has a diverse student population of 3900 students who attend smaller "academies" of 150 to 200 students that focus on one of two areas: Advanced Placement courses or careers in international commerce. Plans are underway to establish five or six more academies that will focus on such areas as technology, the arts, English language development, and marketing.

TRANSFORMING THE CLASSROOM

Two popular instructional strategies are being considered by many restructuring high schools as likely to improve student learning in the classroom: cooperative learning and outcomes-based instruction. Additional strategies also described below are school-to-work transition, interdisciplinary teaching, alternative assessment techniques, and student grouping.

Cooperative Learning

In cooperative learning, students work together in learning teams. To succeed in cooperative learning, four conditions are essential:

- Specific positive interdependence between teammates
- Face-to-face interaction
- Individual and group accountability
- Utilization of specified and taught social process skills

The teacher is more of a facilitator of team productivity and a "guide from the side rather than a sage from the stage." When the cooperative learning format is used consistently, students show higher achievement, better social skills, better self-discipline, fewer discipline problems in school, higher self-esteem, and more acceptance of ethnic, racial, and other differences.

Cooperative learning is the most widely used restructuring element under the broad category of curriculum/teaching assessed by the ERS report on high school restructuring (Cawelti, 1994). Almost half of the respondents (47.6%) report that cooperative learning is in general use in their schools; an additional 40.4% report that this instructional practice is partially implemented.

Outcomes-Based Instruction

A second instructional strategy that may be used to help a school meet the learning needs of its students is outcomes-based instruction or outcomes-based education (OBE). This approach assumes that the school has a clear set of general learning outcomes on which students are or will be expected to demonstrate proficiency prior to graduation. The primary goal of the OBE approach is to ensure that all students successfully demonstrate the exit outcomes around which the educational program is ultimately defined. The strategy also shifts the focus away from the process of instruction and onto the results of instruction, from covering the curriculum to elevating learning success by providing the time needed for each learner to learn at his or her highest level.

Traditionally organized schools march students through the curriculum whether they are ready or not. After the teaching time allotted for each part of the curriculum is over, students generally take a test, which measures student proficiency. Then a gate is shut and students are marched into the next unit of instruction. A student with a 65% level of proficiency will go into the next unit with a 35% deficit, which probably continues—and likely will increase—throughout the year.

With the OBE approach, however, the entire instructional process focuses on providing students with the time they need to master the material. This is done through various types of "correctives": by using tests as diagnostic gauges of what is and is not learned and by spending more time on the latter. Students may take more tests on a particular topic and are thus stimulated to invest the amount of time they each need to master that material. When students have these opportunities, not only do their learning levels increase, their learning rates accelerate as well.

Outcomes-based education has encountered opposition in some communities and states because of concerns about the more nontraditional or hard-to-measure outcomes that are defined in some of the plans (for example, character development). This opposition may have slowed or influenced the movement toward OBE in many places.

An early innovator with OBE was Johnson City High School in Johnson City, New York, which has combined OBE with many research-based strategies. High schools in District 214 in Arlington Heights, Illinois, are also using OBE. Ralston High School in Ralston, Nebraska, has established a program for performance-based exit outcomes for graduation that also features an Individualized Learning Plan.

School-to-Work Transition

Many believe that there is currently a disproportionate amount of attention devoted to academic preparation of college-bound students, at the expense of preparing the half of each year's graduates who do not go on to college. In an effective school-to-work transition, the school collaborates with local community colleges and/or businesses to provide training in the skills needed for the positions likely to be available for students upon graduation; such efforts include apprenticeships and "tech prep" programs.

Examples of school-to-work transition programs include the Charles F. Kettering High School in Detroit, Michigan, which offers programs for technical preparation in such fields as business, media, health, transportation, and food management; Escondido High School in Escondido, California, which offers a Career Path program in similar fields as well as agriculture and social services; Westinghouse Technical/Vocational High School in Brooklyn, New York, with its Partners for the Advancement of Electronics Program; and Okeechobee High School in Okeechobee, Florida, which provides a Tech Prep program in cooperation with Indian River Community College.

Worklink is a computerized system, developed by the National Association of Secondary School Principals (NASSP) and the Educational Testing Service, that makes it easy for employers and work-bound students to find each other. Worklink organizes a variety of information about students that is of interest to potential employers, including (1) confidential teacher ratings of work habits, (2) workplace skills, (3) job-related courses and grades, (4) work experiences and references, and (5) honors, awards, and commendations. Using a menu, businesses can select job candidates by selecting work-related skills or work experience such as "data processing," and the computer will respond by generating a list of potential candidates who have those qualifications. Educators are enthusiastic about the system's capacity to not only quickly connect students with job opportunities, but convince students that schoolwork is connected to life work. For more information contact NASSP, 1904 Association Drive, Reston, Virginia 22091.

Interdisciplinary Teaching

The move toward a more integrated curriculum has been growing in recent years because of the recognition that students need deeper understandings of complex ideas and connections across subjects. This approach affords an opportunity to integrate important topics or themes throughout the curriculum, in order to help students see the connections between the knowledge and skills of different disciplines.

Although most people tend to associate the interdisciplinary approach with the humanities or the arts, it is no less appropriate in math and science. Uri Treisman, a mathematician at the University of California at Berkeley, researched learning among minority groups and found that the formation of collaborative study groups enabled minority students to succeed in their college calculus courses. He then went on to rethink the teaching of high school mathematics, maintaining that math needed to be more connected to the physical world. For example, a full day's curriculum could be devoted to the principle of motion. Students could study Newton's laws in the physics lab and, in their literature class, explore how the concept of motion applies to their lives through selected readings and writing assignments. A teacher at International High School in Queens, New York, working on such a curriculum, said (Center for Collaborative Education, 1994),

> Our goal as a team has been to provide students with an integrated experience across an entire day. The most difficult part is to rethink how we approach our own discipline. We [are] no longer teaching in isolation but trying to connect the separate disciplines.

An example of a school that has implemented interdisciplinary teaching is York High School in Yorktown, Virginia. The school's S.A.G.E. program is an interdisciplinary teaching program for 80 ninth graders involving four teachers of science, algebra, geography, and English. The teaching team has a common planning time within their block schedule. The program has been expanded to include sophomores during the current school year.

Rham High School in Hebron, Connecticut, has reorganized ninth grade schedules to enable teachers to integrate instruction and work across disciplines. Core subjects—math, science, English, and social studies—are grouped into the first part of the school day, along with a course in computer skills called Information Management. Students work on long-term projects that incorporate a number of disciplines. Capital High School in Santa Fe has developed the Gateways Program, which integrates social studies, philosophy, and the arts into a nongraded thematic series of courses that replace the traditional required courses.

International High School, one of New York's new small-focus schools, has 467 students from more than 60 countries who speak 40 different languages. The teachers abandoned a teaching program with 50 individual courses in favor of one with six interdisciplinary blocks. The school is now broken into six smaller schools, each one responsible for a block of students for an entire instructional day. The staff is organized into six interdisciplinary teams, each one responsible for two curricula based on such themes as invisibility and visibility, structures, conflict resolution, and beginnings.

Alternative Assessment Techniques

Many educators have become critical of standardized tests because of their lack of applicability to the local curriculum and their inadequacy as instruments to authentically measure student achievement. A standardized test of grammar bears little relationship to a student's ability to write well, and a multiple-choice science test does not measure a student's ability to apply modes of scientific reasoning to a laboratory experiment. In response to the need for better assessment, high schools are developing assessment plans that call for portfolios, projects, and other demonstrations of what teachers believe is important for students to know about a specific subject or skills area.

An example of an alternative assessment plan is Littleton High School in Littleton, Colorado. The school has established 19 standards for graduating classes from 1995 on, which will require 36 demonstrations of mastery using authentic assessment techniques. For example, students are required to demonstrate composition skills on three different kinds of writing at an established level of proficiency. Unfortunately, a recent change in membership of the Littleton Board of Education has resulted in the temporary suspension of the use of these assessments.

West Warwick High School in West Warwick, Rhode Island, implemented its "Performance Portfolio" during the 1991–92 school year. Each student's portfolio contains examples of experiences that the student gains in each course he or she takes during the three years of high school, demonstrating that the student has met the goals of the course and providing an anecdotal record of student achievement across the curriculum.

Student Grouping

Grouping students on the basis of measured or perceived ability is a very common educational practice. In fact, it has been estimated that more than 85% of the school districts in the United States use some form of ability grouping at the secondary level.

In theory, the fundamental purpose of grouping should be to place students in settings that best meet their learning needs. During the past two decades, homogeneous groupings by ability and track have become more popular in schools. In practice, however, the results of homogeneous grouping of students by ability do not warrant its continued use. A bedrock of this society is the belief that citizens be allowed to function in the least constraining environments possible. More heterogeneous grouping provides opportunities for students to learn in widening developmental ranges. Such arrangements allow movement toward greater heterogeneity. This is more natural and realistic than limiting learning opportunities within homogeneous, ability-grouped frames. Such a grouping is easier said than done. Teachers find it very difficult to teach mixed-ability classes under current teaching conditions. Nonetheless, the research is clear.

In the January 1989 *ASCD Curriculum Update,* Robert Slavin provided the following response to this question: "The sorting of students into ability groups has come under increasing fire recently. Should schools end the practice of grouping students by ability?"

> A decision to assign a child to an ability group or track will have far-reaching consequences, as grouping decisions made at one point in a child's school experience greatly influence later grouping decisions.
>
> Students assigned to lower groups or tracks are less likely to graduate or go on to college than students of the same ability assigned to higher tracks. Their

teachers have lower expectations for them and may teach at too slow a pace. In integrated schools, tracking usually creates racially identifiable groups, which can create inequities along racial or ethnic lines. For these reasons, grouping by ability should be avoided as much as possible and used only where there are clear educational justifications.

There are several situations when grouping may be justified. At the elementary level, there is no research to suggest any benefit of between-class ability grouping, but within-class grouping (e.g., reading and math groups within the class) can be beneficial. There is research supporting the Joplin Plan, in which students are grouped for reading according to reading level but regardless of age. At the middle school level there is still no known benefit to ability grouping but acceleration programs for mathematically talented students may be effective. High school students should be able to choose courses according to their interests and skills, but counselors must be careful to avoid steering students into low ability courses. While ability grouping may sometimes be necessary, we should avoid it as much as possible.

The practice of grouping students by ability for instructional purposes is not supported by research. Even though a majority of teachers believe that ability grouping improves the effectiveness of schooling, the studies reviewed suggest that the practice has deleterious effects on teacher expectations and instructional practices (especially for students put into groups for lower ability), student perceptions of self and others, and academic performance of lower-ability students. It interferes with opportunities for students to learn from, and learn to accept, peers of different socioeconomic backgrounds and may perpetuate the notions of superior and inferior classes of citizens. The practice is especially antithetical to the goals and objectives of the restructuring high school.

CHANGING THE SCHOOL CLIMATE

Several researchers have noted the "negative culture" of high schools in general (Sizer, 1984; Goodlad, 1985). Peter Drucker (1991) emphasizes that schools must focus on the strengths and talents of learners so that schools can graduate students who know how to learn. However, says Drucker, schools "focus primarily on the weaknesses of students, from kindergarten right on through graduate school, and this turns students off" (Drucker, 1991).

Although the majority of high school teachers care about their students, too frequently their caring centers on the students' ability to learn and not on their well-being or self-esteem. Thus, schools present critical, fault-finding, and negative stimuli (Schlechty, 1990). Add to this Glasser's contention that schools are controlling and coercive in their mainly "boss-leadership" approach to students, and it is easier to see why schools unintentionally provide a negative and unwholesome climate for students (Glasser, 1990). Therefore, any substantive effort to redesign public high schools must emphasize a positive, dynamic, and nurturing school climate as the best learning environment for students.

There are a number of instruments that are available to school administrators to help them work with teachers to assess school climate.

Power of Positive Students

The Power of Positive Students (POPS) was developed by William Mitchell, who, as superintendent of a large, problem-filled school district, discovered that even by addressing problems with more money, personnel, programs, and resources, he could not effect any significant or lasting improvements in student achievement. Only when he and his staff developed a widespread effort to raise the morale, motivation, and self-esteem of the students were the results dramatic.

In brief, POPS is based on research that concludes that "there is a significant and positive relationship between a student's concept of himself and his performance in school. Students who feel good about themselves and their abilities are the ones most likely to succeed" (Mitchell, 1985).

This structured program involves five steps:

- Team building
- Development of a positive climate based on positive mental attitudes
- Positive reconditioning and conditioning (power of suggestion, self-suggestion, and habits)
- Modeling
- Positive reinforcement

When these steps are implemented by faculty members, staff members, students, administrators, and parents who have been trained for and involved in and therefore "own" the program, there is a greater chance that the school climate will be conducive to learning and building high self-esteem in students.

POPS is headquartered in Myrtle Beach, South Carolina.

Invitational Education

Developed primarily by William Purkey of the University of North Carolina at Greensboro, invitational education is based on the idea that "students learn best when placed in the care of educators who invite them to see themselves as valuable, able and responsible, and to behave accordingly" (Purkey and Novak, 1988). For this to happen, the school climate must have the ingredients of trust, respect, intentionality, and optimism. Furthermore, the school's people, place, policies, programs, and processes (the five Ps) must be evaluated so all five can become inviting to students. Here again, educators trained in invitational education infuse their schools with creative and dynamic ideas and activities that constantly upgrade all five Ps by making them more "inviting" to students.

The International Alliance for Invitational Education, centered at the School of Education, University of North Carolina at Greensboro, sponsors the program.

NATIONAL REFORM NETWORKS

The Coalition of Essential Schools

The Coalition of Essential Schools is a high school–university partnership that works across the country to redesign the American high school for better student learning and achievement. The Coalition was formed as a result of an inquiry into American secondary education conducted by Ted Sizer from 1979 to 1984 under the sponsorship of the National Association of Secondary School Principals and the National Association of Independent Schools. As part of its findings, the study identified five "imperatives" for better schools: (1) provide room to teachers and students to work and learn in their own appropriate ways, (2) make certain that students clearly exhibit mastery of their school work, (3) get the incentives right for students and teachers, (4) focus the students' work on the use of their minds, and (5) keep the structure simple and flexible. These commitments, if addressed seriously, have significant consequences for many high schools, affecting both their organization and the attitudes of those who work within them.

Member schools in the Coalition are diverse in size, population, program, and geographic location and represent both the public and private sector. In addition to member schools, the Coalition assists schools in the planning and exploring stages of reform. The Coalition offers no specific model or program for schools to adopt. What Essential Schools hold in common is the nine principles that focus each school's effort to rethink priorities and redesign its structures and practices. Each school develops its own program, suited to its particular students, faculty, and community—hence, no two Essential Schools are alike, not officially, at least. They do have common characteristics. The member schools serve as examples of a variety of thoughtfully redesigned schools.

Schools applying to the Coalition must present a plan for change consistent with the Nine Common Principles and must demonstrate faculty and leadership team support for extending the plan to the entire school. There is no fee to join the Coalition; however, most schools require at least $50,000 a year for three to five years during the initial study and redesign phases for release time, travel, and professional development activities. Schools are generally responsible for securing their own funds; however, in many cases, they have obtained these from their local board of education.

The Coalition conducts ongoing, interactive research into the impact of the Nine Common Principles on school change. Past research focused on "student as worker, teacher as coach," reducing teacher loads to 1:80 within budget parameters, and assessment by exhibition. Further information may be obtained by writing to the Coalition of Essential Schools, Box 1969, Brown University, Providence, Rhode Island 02812. The phone number is (401) 863-3384.

NETWORKS THAT PROVIDE ADDITIONAL SOURCES OF INFORMATION

Alliance to Enhance Teaching of Science
> Contact: Ira Hiberman, Director of Curriculum, Penns Valley School District, RD2, Box 116, Spring Mills, PA 16875. (814) 422-8824.

Association for Supervision and Curriculum Development High School Futures II Network
> Contact: Ronald Tesch, Principal, Highland Park High School, 433 Vine Street, Highland Park, IL 60035. (708) 432-6510 *or* Judy Jonson, Director, Schenley High School Teacher Center, Centre Avenue and Bigelow Blvd., Pittsburgh, PA 15213. (412) 622-8480.

Authentic Assessment Network
> Contact: Albert N. Koshiyama, Administrator, Local Evaluation Assistance, California Department of Education, 721 Capitol Mall, Sacramento, CA 95814. (916) 324-7147.

High School Networking for Change
> Contact: Jim Ford, Principal; Iyvonne Fasold, Teacher; or Gil James, Assistant Principal, Sheldon High School, 2455 Willakenzie Road, Eugene, OR 97401. (503) 687-3381.

Interdisciplinary Curriculum
> Contact: Benjamin P. Ebersole, Director of Hershey Academy, Hershey Public Schools, Box 898, Hershey, PA 17033. (717) 534-2501, ext. 252.

School–Business Partnerships
> National Alliance of Business, 1201 New York Avenue N.W., Washington, D.C. 20005. (202) 289-1303
>
> Women's Educational Equity Publishing Center, Education Development St., Newton, MA 02160.
>
> Business Roundtable, 1615 L Street N.W., Washington, D.C. 20036. (202) 872-1260.

References

Bailey, W.J. (1991). *School-Site Management Applied.* Lancaster, Pennsylvania: Technomic Publishing Co., Inc.

Carnegie Forum on Education and the Economy. (1986). *A Nation Prepared: Teachers for the 21st Century.* Washington, D.C.: Carnegie Forum on Education and the Economy.

Cawelti, G. (1994). *High School Restructuring: A National Study.* Arlington, Virginia: Educational Research Service.

Center for Collaborative Education. (1994). *Connections.* New York: Center for Collaborative Education. pp. 1, 7.

Clune, W.H. and White, P.A. (1988). *School-Based Management: Institutional Variation, Implementation, and Issues for Further Research.* New Brunswick, New Jersey: Center for Policy Research in Education.

Dade County Public Schools. (1991). Report on SBM/SDM: Phase 1.

David, J.L., Purkey, S., and White, P. (1989). *Restructuring in Progress: Lessons From Pioneering Districts.* Washington, D.C.: National Governors' Association.

Drucker, P. (1991). *The New Realities.* New York: Harper & Row.

Elmore, R.F. (1991). Innovation in Education Policy. Paper presented at the Conference on Fundamental Questions of Innovation, Governor's Center at Duke University, Durham, North Carolina, May 3–5.

Fullan, M. (1993). Innovation, reform and restructuring strategies. In *Challenges and Achievements of American Education: The 1993 ASCD Yearbook.* Alexandria, Virginia: Association for Supervision and Curriculum Development. pp. 116–133.

Glasser, W. (1985). *Control Theory in the Classroom.* New York: Harper & Row.

Glasser, W. (1990). *The Quality School.* New York: Harper Perennial.

Goodlad, J. (1985). *A Place Called School.* New York: McGraw-Hill.

Hallinger, P., Murphy, J., and Hausman, C. (1991). Conceptualizing School Restructuring: Principals' and Teachers' Perceptions. Paper presented at the annual meeting of the American Educational Research Association, Chicago, Illinois, April.

Hatry, H.P., Morley, E., Ashford, B., and Wyatt, T.M. (1993). *Implementing School-Based Management: Insights into Decentralization from Science and Mathematics Departments.* Washington, D.C.: The Urban Institute.

Malen, B. (1990). Evidence says site-based management hindered by many factors. *The School Administrator,* 47(February), 30–32, 53–59.

Mitchell, W. (1985). *The Power of Positive Students.* New York: Bantam Books.

Purkey, W. and Novak, J. (1988). Education by invitation only. *Phi Delta Kappa,* 268.

Schlechty, P. (1990). *Schools for the 21st Century.* San Francisco: Jossey-Bass.

Sizer, T. (1984). *Horace's Compromise: The Dilemma of the American High School.* Boston: Houghton Mifflin.

Smith, M. and O'Day, J. (1990). Position Paper on Education Reform Decade. Stanford, California: Stanford University Center for Policy Research in Education.

Taylor, D. and Teddlie, C. (1992). Restructuring and the Classroom: A View from a Reform District. Paper presented at the annual meeting of the American Educational Research Association, San Francisco, California.

Weiss, C. (1992). Shared Decision Making About What? Paper presented at the annual meeting of the American Educational Research Association, San Francisco, California.

New Roles and New Behaviors for New Approaches to Leadership

The focus of this chapter is on the ways that restructuring has changed the context for leadership in high schools. It also explains how principals and others can respond to the challenges posed by the new conditions in the schools.

THE ADMINISTRATORS'S CHANGING ROLE IN RESTRUCTURING SCHOOLS

Typically the first question asked by high school principals once a restructuring effort gets underway is "What's my role?" No job in schools is undergoing greater change than that of the school principalship. Although more information is available now than a few years ago, there is still a lack of clarity about what skills and capacities school leaders actually need to succeed in these transformed educational settings (Goldring, 1992; Leithwood, 1992).

A great deal is known, however, about principals' roles and functions in traditionally organized schools. Peterson (1991, p. 2) notes:

> ...where authority is based in central office superiors, principals usually engage in a large number of highly varied tasks, many of which are short in duration and frequently interrupted by demands, crises, or problems of school management and leadership. In addition, the school principal plays a crucial role in assuring that the basic management routines of the school function effectively, that discipline and school climate are supportive of an effective learning environment, and that instructional leadership by the principal or others is facilitated, nurtured, and enacted at the school level.

In restructuring high schools, those patterns are altered in certain important ways. The concepts of parental choice, shared decision making, teacher empowerment, school-based reform, and site-based management—in many cases, authority that includes full control over policy and budget—represent new organizational arrangements in which school leaders must now function. Goldring (1992, pp. 58–59) points out:

> Principals...face increasingly complex role definition. It is clear from an external management point of view these principals face very uncertain, complex environments. They are almost totally dependent upon external constituencies for their own survival, as well as the survival of their schools...Consequently, these

principals, under an extremely high amount of external uncertainty, are expected to create professional, pluralistic schools.

In some districts, the transformation of the principal selection process to involve committees of teachers, other building administrators, and, usually, parents to review applications, interview candidates, and submit the name(s) of their choice(s) to the superintendent and board of education for final consideration has also changed the nature of the job. Since the central office no longer has a role in the selection of principals in these restructuring districts, principals, in turn, no longer feel compelled to participate in the politics of the bureaucracy.

Giving the school community—primarily teachers and parents—an important role in principal selection also changes the accountability structure. One teacher in San Diego described it as "making the principal a school employee rather than a district employee." Principals chosen by the school community now see their primary function as advocating for school needs to the district, rather than transmitting district policy and mandates to the school community, which is the role they once played. For these principals, the arrow on the organizational chart is now reversed; they have become the schools' emissaries to the district instead of the other way around. Changes such as this (others are discussed below) force principals to reevaluate the way they spend their time and how they approach their traditional tasks.

These new externally derived pressures and expectations suggest that principals and other leaders will need capacities and skills that go well beyond those delineated in the effective schools research of the 1980s. Even the sacred cow of instructional leadership is coming under scrutiny. As Leithwood (1992, p. 8) notes:

> "Instructional leadership" is an idea that has served many schools well through-
> out the 1980s...But in light of current restructuring initiatives designed to take
> schools into the 21st century,"instructional leadership" no longer appears to
> capture the heart of what school administrators will have to become. "Transfor-
> mational leadership" evokes a more appropriate range of practice.

Transformational leadership—a popular buzzword these days—emphasizes the capacity of the principal to engage and develop others as leaders, rather than the once-valued ability of the principal to organize and direct the efforts of parents and staff. Although accurate, such an explanation is too abstract to be of use to someone responsible for the daily operation of an institution as large and complex as a high school. For the purposes of this book, actual examples of transformational leaders at work are more useful. It is important that the understanding of new concepts for leadership take into account the difficulties that are the constant companion of fundamental reform, as well as the means by which people in schools typically cope with the shifting ground on which they must now operate.

In a sense, the new role of the principal in a restructuring school is similar to the role generally associated with that of the superintendent in a school district.

Since the individual school becomes more autonomous, the principal must be the leader in developing a direction for the school. Further, the principal must assist the major school constituents to become involved in making decisions affecting the school's performance. Collaboration and consensus are vital to the success of this type of decision making, so that everyone truly has a stake or investment in the outcome.

Goldring and Rallis (1993, p. 134) identify five forces that they believe are changing the ways in which principals must lead and manage their schools:

1. Teachers' responsibilities are extending beyond their classrooms and their students. Collaborative problem-solving teams, site-based management, career ladders, and differentiated staffing structures offer new possibilities for teachers to be highly involved in school improvement processes.

2. Student bodies are increasingly diverse. This diversity is no longer limited to cultural, racial, or ethnic differences. Schools and their leaders are challenged with meeting the wide range of needs of all students...

3. Parents are more vocal and more involved in schools. Many reform efforts specify a parental involvement component. Even in schools where parental involvement is not driven by such reforms, parents as individuals or organized groups are increasingly acting as either advocates or adversaries. No longer are principals solely leaders of other professionals; they are now leaders of a wider school community.

4. The social, technological, and communal contexts of schools are more complex. Schools can no longer close their doors on their surroundings. They are expected to help meet the total needs of both the children and their communities...Principals are crucial links between schools and their external contexts.

5. ...the relationship between the state and the local district concerning educational reform is changing. While in the past states have often left matters to local districts, today they are mandating programs and standards in response to national education reports of the 1980s. Principals must respond to these state mandates while simultaneously cultivating school-based, local initiatives.

A preliminary understanding of the new concepts of leadership is revealed by comparing and contrasting the roles played by principals of two high schools in Minneapolis, a district that is currently engaged in the restructuring of all its schools. The goal of this illustration is to help the reader understand how any principal's perception of role, during a whole school restructuring or at any other time, has a major impact on the direction of the change process at the school. The experiences of these two principals over a period of three years illuminate the impact of changing organizational conditions on the roles played by the principal.

TWO PRINCIPALS: TWO VISIONS,
TWO ROLES, TWO RESULTS

Harlan Anderson became principal of North Community High School in Minneapolis at almost the same time that Robert Jennings became principal of East High School in the same city. (The name of the second principal and the name of the second school have been changed.) Both principals were charged with developing and implementing the new magnet programs that were to be part of the citywide open choice plan for the seven high schools in the district.

The contrast in the leadership style between Anderson and Jennings can be seen in the way each saw the new role of principals. Jennings commented to me that the new role was "more of a manager of people and more of a public relations artist." This was seen by him as meaning a greater sensitivity to the concerns and interests of parents, as well as a sensitivity to the complexity of involving and working with teachers and parents in new decision-making roles.

Jennings wanted to make certain that the district's new focus on stakeholder involvement would not compromise the basic integrity of East High School's core educational program. It was important to him that the school maintain its commitments to the state syllabus in each academic area. He saw the restructuring initiative as an opportunity to do the extra things, to enhance the program with features that would interest students and parents. He envisioned his job as working with all constituent groups to build upon the school's tradition of excellence. The school, after all, was doing a fine job for many of the students. The honors programs were attracting the children of the city's most affluent and successful citizens. For him, East High School's traditionally high levels of student performance influenced both the goal and the substance of the principal's role in any reform effort. He was determined not to let any curricular innovations take the focus off East's tradition of excellence. As he frequently noted at public gatherings, "East High School students placed second in the state in the recent essay competition. We're not going to give up the academic standards we have."

Activities designed to implement the district's magnet program initiative were primarily viewed as extras or add-ons during Jennings' tenure. It was unlikely that the basic curriculum or organization of the school or the predominant approach to providing for classroom instruction would change in significant ways. On the contrary, as already noted, one of his primary concerns was to protect the school's basic curriculum from threats of dilution and lowered standards. Therefore, under Jennings' leadership, the goal of the school's restructuring was to incrementally improve a traditionally successful instructional program by enhancing the school's offerings with new and appealing self-contained magnet and special interest programs that would, Jennings hoped, attract students from outside of the immediate zone and fill the classrooms.

As the leader of the school, Jennings was therefore cautious. He viewed his role as a buffer; he had to protect the integrity of the school's instructional program from people at the school and the central office who threatened to dilute it. He also saw himself as a renovator doing a redecorating job: examining how to adapt the district's enthusiasm for restructuring and change into the framework of the school's current program. The clearly compartmentalized and limited boundaries of Jennings' vision also represented a limitation in terms of the potential of the effort to retool the school's approach to teaching and learning.

Although East High School was only involved in restructuring for three years prior to Jennings' involuntary transfer to another high school in the district, two points are obvious. First, his vision for the school was substantially more circumscribed than the notion of transformed schooling voiced by Dr. Robert Ferrera, the district superintendent at the time. The superintendent, in particular, viewed restructuring as a key mechanism by which to engage teachers in reexamining educational policies and practices in the district. The superintendent's goal was to transform the school culture such that he could mobilize teacher energies in the successful implementation of more powerful and complex curricula and methods of instruction.

Second, the boundaries of Jennings' vision had a major influence on the implementation effort. Time for planning was available only sporadically, and little support was provided for teachers to engage in the type of curriculum redesign necessary for a full integration of the effort into the curriculum and instructional programs already operational at the school. The school was meeting the letter of the superintendent's mandate—the creation of citywide magnets at each high school to achieve racial balance—but not its larger intent, which was the transformation of the instructional program to raise achievement levels for all students.

Although experience has shown that many comprehensive change efforts begin slowly and that it takes time and capacity building before staff begin to engage the school's most important teaching and learning issues, one can see how Jennings' perspective on the nature of schooling and on his role in the change process limited the scope of the changes at the school. His values and his power bases among the more traditional faculty members seemed sufficiently strong to keep attention away from the core of the school's instructional program. It remained the same, cloistered by the stream of student applicants from the city's most affluent neighborhoods.

Harlan Anderson of North Community High School also had to make a substantial adjustment when he became principal. His training for the principalship did not prepare him for the many hours with teachers and parents, individually and in groups, that were required by the district's restructuring effort. His vision for the restructuring effort at North Community High School entailed fundamental changes in the way that curriculum and instruction were conceived. Rather than adding to the existing program, he viewed the school's restructuring as a tool to revamp the entire teaching and learning program. His vision for the school included a more holistic approach to curriculum development, rather than a framework increasingly bombarded by layers of add-ons. Therefore, he encouraged teachers to think about instructional strategies that included both cognitive and affective outcomes and the end to the artificial separation between the two that existed at North and currently exists in most traditionally organized high schools.

To enact his broader conception of restructuring, he attempted to organize the school's effort by framing and communicating a guiding vision on the whole school and not just the selective Summatech Magnet Program. He viewed the school's overall plan as encompassing all school initiatives, not just as the creation of new magnets to attract students from outside the attendance area. In his conversations with teachers he regularly expressed the hope that everyone in the school focus on making curriculum and program connections so that school objectives are linked. He facilitated departments getting together to explore and develop new types of collaborative efforts that connect teaching in the different subject areas.

Consistent with his beliefs, he functioned as a catalyst and enabler. He viewed his role as providing the resources necessary for staff to develop and then implement their restructuring efforts. He provided major support for the development of new skills and attitudes among teachers, as well as for the creation of new organizational arrangements; for example, he supported a new schedule with longer time blocks and common planning time for teachers that made it easier to implement new instructional efforts. Anderson drew on many of the traditional skills of a principal, but he saw his role differently: as a facilitator and balancer. More importantly, perhaps, he was also a learner, growing professionally along with the teaching staff. He took on these roles because he saw that the world was different and he chose to capitalize on these differences in building a new North High School. As a result, his school *is* becoming different as it engages in ongoing processes of change for improvement. The task of creating an improved learning environment for students at North is not completed. Despite progress and some successes, there have been and there will be setbacks and disappointments. Rather, North High School is in a transitional phase, thus making leadership a highly complex function.

A CHANGED ROLE FOR PRINCIPALS

The principal's role in Minneapolis high schools has been altered primarily in the two areas of climate and instructional leadership.

The Changing Climate Leadership Role

In a restructuring district, especially one like Minneapolis with a citywide open admission magnet program, there is a more direct relationship between the initiative taken by an individual school and the financial resources available to teachers than in the traditionally managed school system. In such circumstances, it seems logical that there will be greater pressure on principals to work with staff on entrepreneurial pursuits such as grant writing, development of private sector partnerships, the development of high-visibility magnets that come with substantial resources, and other fund-raising activities, all of which are highly labor-intensive activities. Again, the result is that principals end up having less time for other things.

In addition, by permitting schools to market their programs directly to students throughout the city, the stakes for the school have been raised. A new and direct form of accountability that has not existed in the past has emerged. If the programs are not attractive and they do not have drawing power, the magnet, as well as the rest of the school, is out of business. Other schools' magnet offerings might induce local residents to travel across the city and abandon their neighborhood high school. One Minneapolis high school watched its student population drop to less than 700 before it understood that the district would not guarantee student enrollment. When the school was in danger of closing, staff finally began to create programs that would be attractive to youngsters in other parts of town. When one takes into consideration the direct participation of parents in the school's leadership group, it becomes obvious that parent beliefs, values, and perceptions become more central in the lives of professional educators as they plan for the future of the school.

The new emphasis on relationships with constituent groups (explored in greater detail in Chapters 9 and 10) highlights capacities that are seldom included in most pre-service principal training programs. Similarly, concepts of customer orientation that have become so essential in profit-making organizations seem to become increasingly important to both the tasks and the strategies that principals consider in leading their schools (Vanderberghe, 1992). As parents acquire much broader options within public school systems, as they have in Minneapolis, it becomes more natural for principals and teachers to perceive them as consumers and the schools as providers of services (Weindling, 1992).

There is a message here for district-level training and development personnel: the focus must be on creating among school people a heightened awareness of and sensitivity to the importance of external constituencies, as well as some specific and practical tools for dealing effectively with them.

The Principal's Changing Instructional Role

While concepts of transformational leadership are attaining increased popularity in the literature and among school reformers (Schlechty, 1990), there is no consensus on how that changes the principal's leadership role in instruction. Some themes are becoming clearer, however. In Minneapolis high schools, as in the case of the Franklin K. Lane Career Institutes described in Chapter 3, implementation of a school's magnet programs requires a much higher degree of interdependence and consensus about overall goals than is typically found in most high schools. Either teachers in different curriculum areas work together or the program never gets going. The greater interaction produces a need for greater coordination within and across departments and with the school's external constituencies. In some cases, as with the Summatech program at North Community High School, it also means collaboration with the private sector.

At most restructuring schools, responsibility for coordination is shared by the principal and the school's leadership council. As teachers' leadership roles expand, the principal's role evolves into a leader of leaders. As Leithwood (1992) notes, there is a direct relationship between the decision-making context in which the principal works (in this case, a collaborative one) and the need for new skills. For those who lead restructuring schools, the need for new skills and functions expands beyond the highly technical and very specific abilities that principals were expected to exercise during the 1980s. Hallinger and Hausman (1993, p. 140) summarize these points as follows:

> The idea that principals will function increasingly as leaders of leaders accentu-ates the capacity of the principal to work effectively in group problem solving. The ability to manage complex change in collaboration with other school-based leaders—both parents and teachers—is a skill that seems to be of paramount importance. This leads fairly directly to a recommendation for training that develops the ability of principals to identify appropriate problems and marshal the expertise of faculty toward productive solutions.

During the early days of the restructuring movement, there were suggestions from many quarters that principals might simply function as managers (Carnegie Forum on Education and the Economy, 1986). A professionalized teaching staff involved in developing new instructional efforts, the argument goes, would take ever greater responsibility for organizational policy issues and would have the capacity to assume major responsibility for schoolwide instructional leadership. There are also those who predicted a decreased need for the school principal. These people point to shared leadership with teachers in the form of management teams and wonder why a principal is needed. The expectation is wrong. Although there is a greater distribution of the instructional leadership function at North Community High School and at other restructuring schools, this in no way has reduced the need for the principal's leader-ship, albeit of a different kind.

The high school administrator performs a variety of roles in a restructuring school. First, there is the task of working with others to transform the school into one that is effective for those who work and learn within it. In this new paradigm, the principal's leadership function is grounded in his or her knowledge and skills rather than simply the position and the power the title holds. As one of the teachers at North Community High School recently said about Harlan Anderson,

> He's in front of us and behind us at the same time. When we need him to pull us forward, he does, sometimes sharply, but always in a caring way. And when we venture into risky territory, we know he's right there to catch us if we slip. There's never any doubt in our minds. He may scowl from time to time when a problem develops, but we know where he stands: forthrightly on the side of change, firmly in our corner, supportive of those of us daring to do things differently.

Second, the principal must foster a sense of trust and security among the different constituent groups at the school so they can undertake the often risky, threatening task of changing the status quo. Third, the principal must have a compelling vision that inspires others to join in; people need to see a place for themselves in the school-to-be. Unless the principal has a vision of where the organization is going and why, he or she cannot possibly help others get there.

However, it is one thing to have the vision and understand what it means to the organization, and it is an entirely different thing to communicate it to the major stakeholders in the school. Communicating the purpose and vision of the school, through words and actions, is one of the principal's most important tasks. The principal must be able to communicate the vision to a variety of constituencies: parents, teachers, students, and the community at large.

Without providing a full discussion of strategies for effective communication, which is the topic of a later chapter, it will suffice here to say that the principal must be able to help each group interpret the vision so that they can buy into it and apply it to their own definitions. Such a role requires new and different communication skills. For example, the principal should

- Favor an interactive, two-way mode of communication over the directed, one-way style of communicating so typical in autocratic and bureaucratic systems

- Promote equal access and expression as it relates to ideas, issues, and proposals

- Be an excellent teacher who thoroughly understands the vision and uses a variety of techniques to take an abstract vision statement and make it concrete and understandable to all parties

- Understand the ramifications of a shared decision-making model that includes teachers, parents, students, and community members in guiding future decisions in areas such as goals, curriculum, and staff development

In fact, some of the leading restructuring reformers (Glickman, 1992; Sizer, 1992) believe that the abbreviated vision or mission statements used by most schools should be expanded to include the major accepted teaching and learning principles. The more explicit the mission statement is, and the more specific, the better. Given the deep-seated mindsets that mediate change in most high schools, it makes sense to get everything into the open up front to allay suspicions in different quarters.

Leaders must not only consider changes in role but must also be prepared to confront a series of mindsets that can derail the change process if not carefully managed. Any high school principal who undertakes a school-based reform effort must be conscious of and deal with a number of habits of mind that can impede the change process.

The next portion of the chapter deals with some rarely noticed perils and pitfalls encountered on the way to successful implementation of school-based reform efforts. The most important of these pitfalls and, historically, the most difficult to change are, as seen in Chapter 2, those that are part of people's mindsets. Some of these mindsets concern their approach to and their view of their jobs and the institution they are part of, others have to do with process, and still others are unique to the school-based reform concept itself. Later chapters in this book serve as road maps to guide readers past some of the obstacles. Each pitfall has implications for the school's change leadership as they consider the roles they will play in the school's restructuring. This chapter identifies some of these mindsets with the aim of raising the awareness of readers.

DEALING WITH HABITS OF MIND

The Power Mindset

A short while ago I received a phone call from a high school vocational education counselor who informed me that she and a group of teachers had made major modifications in the nature and structure of the school's large and isolated vocational education program. She invited me to come to the building because she and the other staff members were excited about what they had achieved in a relatively short period of time. This was a high school in the poorest section of a small city in Connecticut. The school rarely received any attention or visitors, except when there was trouble, such as during a recent investigation into the embezzlement of funds by a parent group, and they wanted to take me around and show me what they had accomplished. The changes brought about at this school were of particular interest to me because I had been searching for successful models of integrating academic and vocational education programs without stirring up loud protests by teachers of academic subjects.

I still remember the excitement I felt from teachers and students on the day that I visited. As I walked into the building and was welcomed by an animated group, who then accompanied me down the hallway as they shared details about the changes that were underway in their classes. They felt a part of the school and, for the first time, they said, felt like "real high schoolers." When we reached the area of the building reserved for their "unit" it was obvious that what was taking place for students, teachers, and parent volunteers was an educational design that had generated a feeling of ownership and enthusiasm among all participants. It had, I thought, all of the elements required for a successful integration with the school's academic program. They had achieved what we at Lane were unable to do with our Career Institutes. They had thought of everything—student support, staff development planning time for different groups of teachers, weekend trips of groups of students—for improved educational outcomes.

As I stood there marveling at what this group of adults and students had accomplished together and how happy they all were, the principal wandered over to join us.

He was an old friend of mine, and at one point in our careers we had taught social studies classes in adjacent classrooms. On the surface, he appeared to be pleased by what had been accomplished by students and staff in his school. I knew, however, that something was wrong.

Later on, in the privacy of the principal's office, I asked my friend what the problem was and why. Although his words conveyed pleasure, his sad and slightly preoccupied tone said otherwise. He was, as always, completely candid. I will never forget his response.

> My gut reaction was that this was my authority and responsibility and that these teachers had no need of my knowledge or help. They had created a wonderful program and I had hardly been involved beyond giving them initial approvals and supporting their concept and an early discussion with the school's leadership cadre. I had been involved in school-based management and shared decision making for over four years. I knew about new roles and responsibilities. I had read a pile of books on transformational leadership. I cognitively understood that power is significantly greater when shared. Yet, inside of myself, deep down, I continued to carry the vestiges of my former understanding of how schools are run, and my almost primitive feeling about power and territorial imperative. I felt that mine had been invaded. Frankly, I felt bypassed and insignificant because they had done all of this without me. It was their party, not mine.

Transformational leadership has at its root the empowerment of others. Translated into practice, that means letting go, something many principals find difficult to do. If principals retain control, others cannot take charge. Every time the principal makes a decision, (s)he denies others the opportunity to do so. Learning to stand back, but remaining supportive, encouraging, and resourceful, is challenging, but necessary.

The Win–Lose Mindset

I was meeting in my college office with a group of my Administration and Supervision students a while back when we got into a discussion about grades. I turned to one of the women and said, "What would you like to get as a grade in this course?"

She glanced over at the others, smiled, turned back to me, and said, "Nothing less than an A would make me happy. Yes, an A would be great."

I said to her, "What if you got the A on your class paper and were sitting at your desk looking at your final exam—a big, red-letter A in the upper right-hand corner? How would you feel?"

She responded, "Just great!"

I said, "Now you turn to your neighbor; you can see his paper. It has on it a large red A+. Behind you is another A+." I looked at her again. "How do you feel?"

She said, "Not so good. I'd wonder what I did wrong."

Most people possess a pretty clear understanding that this is a world filled with winners and losers. The win–win philosophy spoken of as necessary to build a community of teachers in a school is essentially a foreign concept. For the most part, the significance of an A is the assumption that someone else got less.

This particular mindset is deep and powerful, and, like the earlier example of the power mindset, it impacts people more than cognitively. Most school-based reform models nonetheless require of participants some movement toward consensus prior to initiating an action. There is a need to involve divergent groups of constituents with different political interests and approaches to education in arriving at that consensus. American society, unfortunately, has taught that confrontation, or even negotiations to eventual settlement, will lead in the end to one party claiming victory over the other. Collaboration and win–win, although essential to implementation of most school-based reform models, is really counter to a mindset learned in early children and reinforced constantly, for example, on Monday Night Football or at the local billiards parlor.

The Problem-Solving Mindset

Most district restructuring initiatives utilize a model that equips a small group of participants with skills so that they can eventually go back to their building and collectively create a vision and mission statement to guide the improvement of their school, asking questions such as the following:

- What is the ideal school that you would like to work in?
- What characteristics would it have?
- How would it be organized?
- What roles would people play?
- What would its educational program look like?
- What knowledge, skills, attitudes, and behaviors would graduates have?

This movement toward collective vision creation, if accomplished, is powerful, for it sidesteps the natural inclination to use problem solving as the mechanism for effective change. The very words "problem solving" sound at first like a good thing, and yet any group of diverse individuals, such as teachers from different subject area departments, working as a team that moves directly from vision creation to problem solving—as people at most schools are tempted to do—is in immediate peril. Solving the problem in the short term may in fact move a school away from the potential win–win consensus scenario that is needed to succeed.

Many school-based leadership teams have fallen prey to this well-disguised snare. Most schools have little experience with the implementation of whole school change through vision creation, information gathering, consensus building, focused planning, and then, finally, implementation. The natural inclination is to define a problem—usually superficially—gain support from those who agree, fashion a solution to the problem, and lobby to get the majority vote for the position. In the process, those who have lost are left behind, as seen in the next chapter in the example of Beacon High School. People who have been disenfranchised and left behind, in many cases, prepare to act in a way that ensures that the solution they feel has been imposed upon them will fail. The task for principals and other leaders is to keep the channels of communication open among all constituent groups and to keep the focus on progress and not on problem solving.

The Model Program Mindset

There is a great deal of lip service paid to the adage of the restructuring movement that ownership among those who plan and implement a program is important if it is to be long lasting. People's behaviors, however, say something different. They persist in the mindset that someone else's way, tried and tested, is best. As a result, people focus on replication of what they perceive to be a paradigm, rather than on the creation of something new and different. There is no need to reinvent the wheel, they say. That mindset seems to permeate restructuring high schools to the point where all but the strongest and most secure teachers concentrate on planning and working on efforts that follow prescribed designs. In most cases, however, someone else's wheel will not fit another's wagon. It is little wonder that so many of these efforts fail after two or three years. If school-based reform is to work, and the effectiveness of design is to be owned by those who fashion it, then it must be understood that the desk-produced program (someone else's ideas) may not be appropriate to all the variety of purposes to which others may wish to apply it. Moreover, it is important for those who would create the new program to know that what is produced is cherished, cared for, serves its purposes, and is unique to the needs of the children in the school for which it is designed.

Creating a New Reality

Several years ago, during my years as a principal, we were able to join a teacher leadership development program with a national organization. The program consisted of involving promising teacher–leaders with a nearby university. Staff at the school proceeded to identify a number of novice teachers who were then notified that they had been chosen to participate in this experience, if they desired to do so.

At this school, we had two teachers with similar names. I will call them Robert M. Jones and Robert S. Jones. One was an outstanding new teacher. Students seemed to be captured by every word he uttered. The second was a new teacher who was only minimally satisfactory, according to his supervisor. Through a clerical error, it was the second teacher who received the letter of invitation to join the leadership program. He accepted and went to the university that very weekend for the first seminar. Several weeks after the weekend, I received a phone call complimenting the school on choosing such a fine representative for the program. I was told that Robert S. showed, at this three-day program, the kinds of leadership qualities that those conducting the workshop truly admired.

I believe that Robert S. responded at the university based upon his understanding of their perception of him as a novice teacher with great potential. They, in fact, created a new reality for Robert S. If school-based reform teams are expected to create new visions for new kinds of high schools, then an environment must first be created that allows others in the school to more clearly understand that reality can be fashioned and changed. Reality is in large measure what people collectively perceive it to be, particularly as they act in accordance with that belief. Unless reality is seen to be malleable, the best that a school and the people in it can be will be dictated by the collective perception of what it currently is, which the people believe, for various reasons, cannot be significantly improved.

These mindsets are only a part of a larger number of mindsets that fashion the understanding of how schools are and can be. It is essential that those in leadership positions be aware of and guard against these stagnant perceptions. Training experiences for staff must incorporate exposure of these mindsets, for they are inherent pitfalls to successful implementation of any school-based reform design. They are a part of the very fabric of the bureaucracy in action. They fashion thinking and, unless revealed and dealt with, have the potential for undermining any effective and long-term change. They can prevent principals from reformulating their roles to facilitate the change process.

References

Carnegie Forum on Education and the Economy. (1986). *A Nation Prepared: Teachers for the 21st Century.* Washington, D.C.: Carnegie Forum on Education and the Economy.

Glickman, C.D. (1992). The essence of school renewal: The prose has begun. *Educational Leadership,* 1, 24–27.

Goldring, E. (1992). System-wide diversity in Israel: Principals as transformational and environmental leaders. *Journal of Educational Administration,* 30(3), 49–62.

Goldring, E.B. and Rallis, S. (1993). *Principals of Dynamic Schools: Taking Charge of Change.* Newbury Park, California: Corwin Press.

Hallinger, P. and Hausman, C. (1993). The changing role of the principal in a school of choice. In J. Murphy and P. Hallinger (Eds.), *Restructuring Schools: Learning from Ongoing Efforts.* Newbury Park, California: Corwin Press.

Leithwood, K. (1992). Images of future school administration: Moving on from "instructional leadership" to "transformational leadership." *Educational Leadership*, 49(5), 8–12.

Peterson, K.D. (1991). The new politics of the principalship: School reform and change in Chicago. In S.K. Clements and A.C. Forsaith (Eds.), *Chicago School Reform: National Perspectives and Local Responses.* Chicago: The Joyce Foundation. pp. 1–9.

Sizer, T. (1992). *Horace's School.* New York: Houghton Mifflin.

Vanderberghe, R. (1992). The changing role of primary and secondary principals in Belgium. *Journal of Educational Administration*, 30(3), 20–34.

Weindling, D. (1992). Marathon running on a sand dune: The changing role of the headteacher in England and Wales. *Journal of Educational Administration,* 30(3), 63–76.

7

Igniting the Fire: Getting the Change Process Started

Chapter 6 showed how restructuring at the high school level has influenced the context for leadership. Chapter 7 follows up by explaining the stages of the change process and then demonstrating how a new type of leadership, displayed over a three-year period at one high school, started the change process off on the right track. In this chapter, one approach is emphasized, which principals and other leaders can use to begin the restructuring process, and concrete examples of strategies, which they can employ to (1) build faculty involvement and (2) provide direction and intentionality to the proposed changes, are provided.

THE STAGES OF THE RESTRUCTURING PROCESS

The restructuring process may appear overwhelming and intricate, but can be broken into stages (Loucks-Horsley and Cox, 1984; Harvey and Crandall, 1988). These stages are intertwined; it is difficult to know when one begins and another ends. Taken as a whole, however, they build on each other to form a continuous, ongoing cycle of change. The six stages outlined below can serve as a guide for principals and other school leaders as they prepare to manage the complexities of the restructuring process.

Stage 1: Determine Problems or Needs

Before beginning the restructuring process, administrators, staff members, and the school community must understand the extent to which changes in thinking, policy, practices, and systems are required. Recall the thinking and planning barriers discussed in Chapter 2 and the potential perils and pitfalls explained in Chapter 6. These changes will vary greatly, depending on the history of improvements already made, how well students are achieving academically, and the inroads gained into reconfiguring entire systems.

Gathering and analyzing the following data may help determine present condition and future needs and help focus the subsequent stages of the restructuring effort.

- Traditional indicators of school or pupil performance, such as dropout rate, attendance rate, expulsion/suspension rates, performance on district-level or state-level testing, and levels of vandalism or violent acts, can indicate problem areas.

- Disaggregate data (breakdown of student and staff member data by gender, ethnicity, age, socioeconomic level, etc.) for use in analyzing information such as student attendance, school enrollment patterns, placement in advanced classes/programs, college acceptance, student grades, and scores on standardized national or state tests may reveal patterns of success or failure that require attention.

- Actual or anticipated trends or shifts in demographics, society, family structure, and economics may indicate that what is working today may not work in the future. Resources such as *Megatrends 2000—10 New Directions for the 1990's* (Naisbitt and Aburdene, 1990) will provide insight into these possible changes that may have a major impact on the school.

Some areas or stages within the restructuring process may require further attention. Although considerable time may already have been spent by the school in developing vision and mission statements and realigning curriculum and instruction, other areas may also need to be addressed (i.e., assessment, parental involvement, district policy) to reinforce previous gains and complete the restructuring effort.

Stage 2: Become Educated About Restructuring

Those involved in the process must become educated by learning as much as possible about restructuring in particular and the change process in general. This can be accomplished by studying information, articles, literature, and research studies. Some school faculties set up brown bag lunch groups to accomplish this. Others set up reading clubs that meet in a social setting on weekends. Still others hold seminar sessions in the teachers' lounge. Teachers drop in during planning or preparation periods.

Many educational organizations have resources available on restructuring, including the National Association of Secondary School Principals, the Northeast and North Central Educational Laboratories, the American Association of School Administrators, and the Association of Supervision and Curriculum Development. The study or reading groups can review and discuss these materials and learn more about such topics as shared decision making, principles of learning, alternative assessment, total quality management, and parent–community involvement.

In addition, people may benefit from reviewing the proposals of the 11 design teams that have been awarded grants from the New American Schools Development Corporation. Whether school administrators choose to initiate their own course of inquiry, utilize a professionally prepared series, or use a combination of the two, the goal is to equip school people to make appropriate decisions about their own school by expanding their knowledge base with information about changing high schools.

Stage 3: Determine Gap Analysis

The Business Roundtable coined this term to describe how individuals determine where they are, where they want to go, and the strategies they will use to achieve the desired goal.

In stage 3, the goal is to apply the principles and methods of restructuring to specific problem areas or needs of a particular school. Success depends largely on how realistically participants assess the present status of educational gains, the concreteness of anticipated student growth in learning, and the innovation and resourcefulness that can be utilized in gathering support for proposed changes.

Especially vital in this stage is the involvement of all stakeholder groups— teachers, parents, students, community members, administrators, and support personnel—who contribute their unique perspectives. Several components are included in this stage:

1. There must be a clear and agreed-upon definition of the learning desired for students by staff members, parents, students, and the school community. This will most likely include a description (including characteristics, knowledge, behaviors, and attitudes) of what constitutes a "successful student," together with specific learning objectives. This definition may be referred to as the instructional mission of the school and will reflect the direction that the school community wants to pursue.

2. It is important that there be an analysis of change to determine the degree of fit, or the degree of dissonance, between the vision or mission and the current conditions at the school. Utilizing the information gathered in stages 1 and 2 will help develop the comparisons that must emerge in stage 3. The analysis can be focused by specifying distinct student outcome measures (such as increased graduation rate for minorities, better ethnic/gender representation in high-level classes, etc.) that will demonstrate progress. Later, this will help determine the extent to which the vision or mission has been achieved and will help evaluate the progress on the school's restructuring.

3. It is important for all in the school community to consider the implications of this vision of learning or mission for all facets of the school experience, such as

    a. Organizational structure: implications for the vision relative to school district policy or procedures, such as waivers (essentially, identify what permissions are needed and for whom before the mission can be implemented)

    b. Technology of teaching: curriculum choices, diverse methods of instruction, and assessment for learning

    c. Professionalization of teaching and parent–community involvement: expansion or creation of shared decision making and advisory councils

In reviewing the implications for the vision, the array of barriers inside and outside the school that may conceivably arise, which could jeopardize or undermine the restructuring effort, should be identified. These should be kept on a list and reviewed periodically.

It is important to identify the resources for fundamental change. Locate sources of funding—private or public—to assist in carrying through the restructuring plans. Are there foundations that will provide material support for the effort? Are there other groups that can provide technical assistance? Collaborations among community, business, or university partners can be sought. Those collaborating, however, must understand that they will remain junior partners in a supporting role. They must be made aware of the need for the school itself to remain in charge of the important decisions about its future.

It is crucial to determine the school district's degree of support if site-based management and shared authority are to be used in issues related to budget allocations, staff development activities, teacher assignments, and scheduling. It is also useful to identify central office personnel and individuals in other schools that may be used as resources and to include these people in the planning.

Stage 4: Build Involvement

At this stage, the vision or mission guiding the restructuring effort must be organized into a plan of action guided by clear and distinct goals. In establishing goals, reference should be made to information provided by the gap analysis so that expectations for student success and outcomes can be established.

Goals for all other individuals and systems that will support the student goals should also be developed. The more concrete and detailed the goals are, the better.

At the minimum, the action plan should include the following information:

1. Activities, methods, and strategies needed to achieve goals and realize the vision or mission, including alterations to be made in the areas of organizational structure, technology of teaching, and professionalization of teaching and parent–community involvement

2. Identification and designation of personnel (district and school) and school community participants (students, parents, community members, university personnel), with their roles and responsibilities for certain activities, as members of decision-making and policy-making committees, consultants, or evaluators

3. A timeline with short-term (one year) to long-term (three to five years) gains and activities to be completed

4. Budget, including sources of revenue (private or public funds, existing or predicted sources), with expenses such as personnel, equipment, and supplies spelled out

5. Expected utilization of facilities and scheduling, especially the impact of the restructuring goals on facilities and length of instructional blocks or periods, school day, week, and year

6. Evaluation, specifying yearly and periodic gathering of student data to measure success

Stage 5: Implement and Evaluate

Once there are an endorsed vision and plan of action in place, and resources have been identified, it is time to start the processes that will enact changes. This is the time for the school's leadership to organize and manage and redeploy personnel, to assign responsibilities for monitoring progress, and to carry out the restructuring process.

Stage 5 focuses on the process by which the goals and activities specified in the action plan will be implemented, such as build staff skills and develop new curriculum or instructional methods. Most likely, the principal and other assigned leaders, such as the school's teacher leadership group, will be responsible for overseeing the implementation and timeliness of the action plan.

The change effort should be evaluated on an ongoing basis while it is being implemented, so feedback about the strengths and weaknesses of the changes is constantly available to everyone. This prevents the development of suspicion and distrust present in most traditionally organized high schools. In addition to using student outcome measures, such as achievement scores or graduation rates that tend to be long-term gains, educators should also gather data from classroom and school observations; surveys of parents, teachers, and students; activity evaluations; and interviews of participants in the restructuring process. Ongoing and yearly evaluations of the restructuring effort will create awareness of the next series of improvements to be considered.

Stage 6: Institutionalize

The school's vision for learning and plan for action should by this point be part of the fabric of the daily operation of the school. Because of the complexities involved in restructuring, it may take five to seven years from the initial awareness stage until a school has created new ways of thinking and acting for its entire education program. Staff must become as accustomed to the new paradigm as they are to brushing their teeth each morning.

Institutionalization also requires support and stabilization of new programs by administrators, thus ensuring long-term security within existing and newly created structures. The principal who mobilized skills in communication, leadership, decision making, and fostering a shared vision can increase the likelihood that significant changes will be long-lasting.

BEACON HIGH SCHOOL: A CASE STUDY

The case study that follows shows how the new models for leadership described in Chapter 6 and stages 1 to 3 above are built into the restructuring process. This example recounts the steps taken by Dr. James Forrest, principal of Beacon High School (a typical but fictitious school) to build support for a vision of a school that looks and works differently from the one he was originally selected to head. It answers the questions posed by many high school principals: "How can I prepare my school for restructuring?" and "What roles can I plan and what strategies can I employ to build widespread support for change among staff members and parents?" Restructuring requires forethought and planning. The process for establishing a climate and, more important, a framework that promotes collaborative decision making is complex and filled with potential pitfalls, as seen in Chapters 2 and 6.

The School and Its New Principal

Beacon High School serves 1800 students in grades 9 through 12. Dr. James Forrest, the principal since September 1988, is widely respected for bringing openness to school affairs and for involving staff and parents in the school's policy making and management. Two capable assistant principals handle the day-to-day operations of the school. Forrest succeeded Dr. Emma Green, who admitted to being a directive principal used to "making all decisions." The contrast between Green and Forrest reflects the wholesale changes in expectations under the new district policies.

Dr. Forrest came to Beacon from a high school of similar size in a nearby city that was located in a poor neighborhood and served the most economically disadvantaged children, where he served as principal. Although his former school did not have anywhere near the level of resources available at Beacon, Forrest was proud of having had a hand in turning his previous school around. Forrest attributes his success in his former job, in part, to the extensive involvement of the teachers in schoolwide educational decisions. This was, in fact, one of the characteristics that led to his selection as the new principal at Beacon.

Beacon High School, located in Chippewa County, is adjacent to, but a world away from, a large metropolitan area in the midwestern "rust belt." Chippewa County grew in population during the 20 years following World War II as middle-class white families fled the city's changing neighborhoods. Until 10 years ago, more than 90% of the school's students were white. During the early 1980s, large numbers of minority group members moved to Chippewa County. Like their white predecessors, they were also seeking a better life for their families and better schools for their children.

By 1975, Beacon High School enjoyed a national reputation for excellence. Teacher salaries were high, students consistently scored above national norms on achievement tests, and 90% of the school's graduates entered higher education, including many prestigious universities. Suddenly, with the change in student population, there was a flurry of racial incidents and severe, seemingly intractable, learning problems. Each year, scores on state-mandated standardized reading and math tests dropped. It became apparent that the school's traditional learning program was not working for the newcomers. Not surprisingly, many long-time residents began complaining that it was no longer working for their children either.

The Commission

In response to the growing dissatisfaction, Forrest, with the authorization of the superintendent and the Board of Education, convened the Beacon High School Commission, a panel of local civic, corporate, and educational leaders, to suggest what Beacon's educational program should be like in the year 2000. Simultaneously, the superintendent included the school in an initial effort to reduce the achievement gap between white and minority students. The effort underscored and acknowledged the need for the district to support different, locally determined approaches to meet diversified needs, while maintaining a common core of learning outcomes for all students.

This effort, the Effective Schools Pilot Program, gave impetus to the Beacon staff to explore ways to allocate some personnel and financial resources according to the school's need, rather than by the standard formula applied uniformly to all district schools. Staff members began to notice how the greater flexibility in the way they used resources eased the implementation of new, locally developed innovations within the regular budget allocation (Clune and White, 1988). They also saw that the school system was willing to decentralize decision making to school sites. However, teachers were lackadaisical about the opportunity presented by the Effective Schools Pilot Program. Staff members did not feel the urgency for change. Few Beacon teachers volunteered to participate in the school's new planning groups. Magic bullets that would solve the school's most pressing problems emerged with each new season at Beacon. Teachers were bored with their coming and hardly noticed their going. Something more was needed.

Building a Firm Foundation

The Beacon High School Commission report called on the school staff to prepare for the challenges of the twenty-first century by joining with the community in a fundamental restructuring of the school. The report was endorsed by the superintendent and the Board of Education.

Forrest opened the academic year by challenging all staff members to join him in carrying out the Beacon Commission's call for restructuring. He talked simply and directly about the inadequacy of Beacon's instructional program and the failure of his top-down directives to improve learning significantly, particularly among the minority students at the school. Forrest shared his vision for the school and expressed the hope that Beacon's restructuring initiative would, before long, fundamentally change the way the school carried out its mission of educating young people.

Forrest spoke about the lessons learned from the school's Effective Schools Pilot Program, specifically the minority achievement and school-site budgeting initiative. His address to the faculty contained four elements:

- It acknowledged the school's proud past.

- It offered the hope of a better tomorrow.

- It reminded everyone of their common values.

- It created a sense of urgency and lit a fire.

Teachers responded to Forrest's speech—a description of his new vision for the school—with anger that he seemed to imply that they had not been doing their best until that point, with suspicion that he was manipulating them, and, some teachers, admittedly a minority, with confidence that the revolution was now at hand. Four years earlier, Green, the former principal, had vowed to rely on uniformity as a way of maintaining control over what was going on in each classroom. The school's administrative operations would be "lean and mean," charged with enforcing compliance with state, district, and school policies. All decision making had resided with the members of the school's administrative cabinet, to which only assistant principals and department heads belonged. Green and her administrative staff had dominated and run every aspect of school life. Now, the new principal was making an about-face and abandoning the approach used by the former principal.

Developing a Vision

Forrest knew it was important for him to develop a clear vision and then to employ it consistently in all his interactions with staff, parents, and students. He would use his links to staff members and parents to create opportunities for others to adopt his vision and make it theirs. An energizing, inspiring vision is critical to generating staff and parent support. The vision must be the clear, unmistakable picture that drives all action. Forrest used his vision to direct attention to the elements he believed would produce higher levels of achievement for all students. He focused staff members and parents on the mission of the school, and it inspired and stimulated them to find out more about the change efforts at the school.

Soon after his September speech, Forrest began to take steps to empower staff members to carry out his vision for his school. He enlisted the support of the superintendent and the Board of Education for the adoption of a statement endorsing the restructuring initiative at Beacon High School.

The board's resulting resolution contained a commitment to shift the authority and responsibility for making educational decisions from the central office to the school.

It reflected the understanding that implementation of a restructuring initiative involving the rethinking of rules, roles, responsibilities, routines, and results would be gradual and long-term. It would also require patience, and it would include mistakes. Included as well was the opportunity for school staff to attend periodic working sessions with the superintendent and the members of the board to apprise them of progress, hear suggestions, and generally review the change process underway at the school.

Generating Interest

Following approval of the board resolution, Forrest discussed with faculty members the need for the formulation of a long-range plan for reform at Beacon. He proposed that the issues be thoroughly analyzed and that school practices that were promoting or impeding collaborative decision making at the school be surveyed.

To further the process of building knowledge and interest, Forrest invited parents, teachers, and school and central office administrators to attend monthly seminars to examine various approaches to whole school reform in high schools. Participants discussed case studies prepared by people from other high schools with restructuring experience. Principals and teachers from other restructuring high schools spoke about their experiences; Beacon High School staff members who had visited other districts shared their observations and impressions. The monthly seminars expanded participants' knowledge about new instructional and organizational possibilities and created consensus among them about the need for change at Beacon.

Within six months, the seminars began to serve a second purpose. Participants coalesced into a tightly knit core group of knowledgeable people committed to a change effort that fit the unique conditions at Beacon High School. This group proposed that Forrest take steps to stimulate interest in change among teachers by shifting decisions about basic items, such as the allocation of funds for instructional material and office supplies, staff development, substitute days, and out-of-district travel, directly to the faculty.

Although not immediately obvious to the outside observer, the school built the foundation for fundamental reform during this initial period. Beacon High School was able to learn from the mistakes experienced by pioneer restructuring schools. For example, the school recognized the importance of creating clarity of terminology and expectations and the need to develop a proposed definition and system for change that would draw on the expertise of all parties at the school.

Creating a Framework for Change

The first step in building this framework involved creating a list of characteristics that would typify the school in the year 2000. This list would provide a yardstick against which day-to-day decisions could be measured. Step 2 involved holding interviews with Beacon High School staff, students, parents, and community representatives to create a profile of the school's current climate for change that would include an analysis of decision-making practices. Step 3 involved the creation of an action group representing the spectrum of interest positions at the school. This group would be charged with coordinating the change effort at Beacon.

Step One: Developing a Vision Statement of Organization Characteristics

After a series of discussions at workshops attended by staff members and parents, there was agreement that, one day, they would like the Beacon organization to be characterized by:

1. A clear sense of mission, i.e., a vision

2. Clearly stated expectations of performance and a sense of individual account-ability and responsibility for the education of each student

3. A performance-based rewards system for students and staff

4. Fairness and honesty in dealing with staff, students, and parents

5. Clear internal and external communications

6. High levels of performance and measurable results and outcomes

7. Responsiveness to student and community needs

8. A "can-do" attitude and energy in the system to achieve goals and objectives

9. An environment that encourages creativity and rewards risk taking

For Beacon High School to acquire these characteristics would involve everyone in any way associated with the school and would be hard work. The process would require continual examination, evaluation, planning, and implementation of change (Senge, 1990).

Faculty and parent agreement on a vision statement was only the fist step in a long process of generating support and commitment for the change process. It was important that everyone associated with the organization espouse the philosophy and, more important, use it to model their behavior and their approach to developing new learning and management systems for the school.

For example, "a clear sense of mission" suggests not just that there is some written mission statement, but also that everyone in the organization knows what the mission is and shares the vision of what the organization is trying to accomplish. It also means using the vision to set and communicate performance expectations for students and staff. Constant monitoring and evaluation of the school's performance are required, as well as feedback on "how we are doing." Many schools have vision or goal statements, fewer have an accountability system, and still fewer have a system designed to support the ongoing, long-term achievement of the organization (Schlechty, 1990).

Step 2: Developing a Profile of Current School Characteristics

Over 200 Beacon High School staff members, students, parents, and community members participated in the data-gathering process through individual interviews and small focus groups. Emerging themes were recorded. The interview data revealed overwhelming agreement that the administration essentially followed classic hierarchical management practices and that there was a stultifying climate at the school.

1. The school was organized hierarchically with top-down decisions, resulting in detailed rules and regulations that constrained innovation and flexibility.

2. Teachers perceived that administrators knew more and had a broader view of issues and that they thus questioned the ability of teachers to make responsible decisions on important educational issues. Teachers felt undervalued, with severely limited opportunities for input.

3. While the principal said he valued innovation and flexibility, he used standardization and uniformity to maintain control. Whereas the principal believed he had been loosening regulations during recent years, teachers felt that they had less flexibility in meeting the needs of students than they did in the past.

4. Most interviewees acknowledged a perceived mood of frustration and distrust at the school. There was no trust between teachers and administrators.

5. Most teachers and parents were skeptical of the principal's commitment to reform. They perceived that previous reform initiatives had come and gone. Some stated that they would "wait this one out." Others wondered "how long this fad would last." Participants were reluctant to invest time in planning. Many had worked on school task forces that ended up on the shelf.

6. Parents in the minority community and teachers were concerned that if more decisions were in the hands of local schools, it was possible that the needs of underrepresented students (minority students or special education students) could be overlooked.

7. Teachers expressed concern that not all areas would be included in the instructional program of each school if decision making took place at the local school.

8. Teachers not interested in change were concerned that reform would be mandated: schools would be required to conform to new practices even if they did not wish to.

The interview data sustained what almost everyone at Beacon already knew. The characteristics, traditions, and organizational dynamics of the school were lethal obstacles to reaching even modest improvement goals.

This type of data survey is very important. It may be disheartening for principals, especially those who have been successful in creating orderly learning environments by tightening controls, to read such a dispiriting description of the school's characteristics. However, such a list is not a manifestation of failure, but is a validation of the principal's vision that more of the same is not enough. Something different is needed. Information embedded in such a list points the way toward achieving the principal's vision: building a new school culture that is more nurturing of risk taking and change.

Step 3: Assembling a Group of People Interested in Coordinating the Change Process

The staff and parents who attended the monthly seminars recommended that an interim action group be formed. This group would informally oversee the change process. It would identify bottlenecks and outstanding issues and would be temporarily charged with managing and fine-tuning the school's restructuring. This group, which over time came to be called the Schoolwide Planning Committee (SPC), included people from the school's different job positions (administrators, teachers, paraprofessionals, and guidance staff) and from parent and community organizations and reflected the racial/ethnic diversity of the school's population. It was important that SPC members not view themselves, or be viewed by others, as representatives of specific job titles, since that view would contribute to fragmentation of purpose and operation.

The selection process for the SPC members was the first public test of the principal's commitment to his new vision for the school. School and district staff worked together to gather suggestions for the SPC selection process from staff and parents. The development of a process for choosing an interim SPC took two months because of the pervasive climate of distrust at the school. The unanticipated delay raised a significant point: the importance of a flexible planning process. Activities and time perspectives must be governed by institutional realities; they cannot be inflexibly determined beforehand. Any calendar-driven restructuring plan is doomed to failure. When reform is planned, especially one as comprehensive and fundamental as restructuring, each successive activity depends on the outcome of the previous activity. It is not advisable, at the outset, to plan sequentially.

Beacon High School Consensus Decision-Making Process

The goal of all proposals and decision making must be greater student academic success

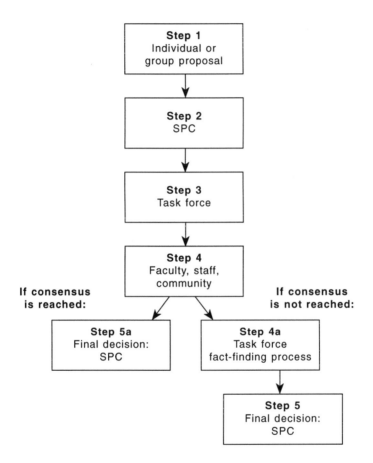

Step 1:   Day-to-day operational processes are the responsibility of the principal. The SPC is the school's elected shared decision-making, managerial, and policy-making body. Proposals for schoolwide policy changes may be submitted to the SPC by individuals or groups of staff, students, or community persons at least ten days before the regularly scheduled monthly meetings.

Step 2:   The SPC will discuss the proposal(s) and may decide to submit it to a task force, ask for more information from sponsor(s), or ask for changes to be made by sponsor(s).

Step 3: Once a proposal is assigned to a task force, it is the duty of the task force, through notices and other means, to make all constituencies aware of the proposal and how it will serve the goal of student success.

Step 4: The task force will conduct a formal consensus-gathering session with all faculty, using the following four-question format:

1. How will this proposal contribute to student success?
2. What disadvantages may result?
3. What resources are needed?
4. Will you agree to pilot the proposal?

Step 4a: If consensus is not reached, the task force moves to a fact-finding process that develops data (observable, measurable, factual) for and against the proposal. The fact-finding session is open to all constituencies. Results of the fact-finding session are forwarded to the SPC for a decision.

Step 5: A consensus decision to pilot the proposal goes to the SPC for final approval.

Step 5a: Final decision by SPC.

The SPC

The first SPC activity at Beacon High consisted of a three-day retreat to define the group's role and operating rules and to develop the broad outline of a flexible planning and implementation process for the school. These items would be submitted to the staff for approval.

The principal's active participation in the workshop sent a powerful message to the entire school. The restructuring effort had top priority. SPC members vividly recalled this first opportunity to work closely with Forrest and how important it was to hear him talk about his vision for the school.

Previously, Forrest had worked directly with only members of the school's administrative team. His infrequent visits to classrooms were formal supervisory occasions when there was no opportunity to discuss important issues with teachers and other staff. Forrest hoped that his new approach toward working with staff would prove dramatically and visibly that the old order was passing and that a new one was coming.

The Principal's Leadership Role

Forrest also found the retreat to be rewarding: "Attending the retreat allowed me to share my ideas with people and allowed me to hear their concerns. It was a new type of leadership experience for me." Some SPC members stated afterward that the principal's forthright manner in discussing his hopes for the school's restructuring effort renewed their spirits about the importance of their work. The enthusiastic reaction of SPC members to Forrest's participation at the retreat encouraged him to pose two important questions to those gathered around the fireplace one evening: What type of leadership did the faculty want from him and how would they like him to carry it out?

Teachers were forthcoming in their responses. They had thought about it and discussed it among themselves. Teachers wanted the principal to use a hands-on approach. They felt that in order to achieve a major change in school culture, they needed his help. They wanted him in the thick of things, physically present at important events. They wanted him to repeat his vision for change when their spirits were flagging, and they wanted him to work directly with them in changing the reward system to favor those who responded to the challenge.

Some principals have delegated important change process roles to an assistant principal or project director. Some have trouble understanding that change by fiat or policy pronouncement is only the first and easiest step in the change process. Such a statement sets a process in motion. When the change is consistent with the school's mode of conducting business, a subordinate, such as an assistant principal, can manage the process. Restructuring, however, involves a fundamental change in the school's orientation toward reaching its goals. It contravenes the traditional belief system and customary posture. Thus, it creates anxiety, doubt, and skepticism. New ways of doing and thinking require the utmost attention from sensitive, responsive leadership at the highest level. The principal must be an active participant in urging, persuading, and making it clear how important the changes are to those affected, as well as to the administration. It is important not to confuse change in policy with change in practice. Aligning practice with policy takes hard work. It creates opportunities for miscommunication, because those most important to the change effort do not see what is occurring or do not talk directly with each other regularly.

Forrest continually reminded people that he was counting on them to make changes. With his active support and participation, the SPC developed the scaffolding for the school's long-term effort to reach the goals outlined in the vision statement.

During the retreat, through plenary and small group work sessions, the conferees began developing a framework for a consensual process that brought together the different interests at the school. Forrest helped the process by modeling the behavior he wanted others to copy. In other words, he enrolled others in the effort by demonstrating the behavior that supported his vision.

For example, Forrest wanted to allow decentralized decision making at the school. Thus, it was important for him to look for ways to assign to the SPC high-visibility decisions, currently made centrally, and then make the information known to all at the school. Forrest knew that people followed all his moves and would watch for clues about what he really valued. He was clear about the actions that exemplified the vision; he learned how to demonstrate these actions dramatically in visible situations, and he was aware that if he did not model the behaviors he wished embedded in the organization, his efforts would fail.

SPC Results

At the SPC workshop, Forrest encouraged participants to generate specific concrete actions that would translate the school's vision statement into action. He helped this effort along by formulating his own action steps. For example, in response to a request for improved staff communications, he announced that he would publish a weekly newsletter containing information on the school's change activities, in order to bring all staff members into the information loop.

The participants in the retreat succeeded in creating a climate of open communication and acceptance. They raised hope that genuine trust and mutual respect might be possible one day, showing what could result when professionals and community members collaborate with a common focus.

Support for Reform

The SPC met weekly until they agreed on a set of operating principles grounded in the concepts contained in the school's vision statement. All actions and practices would need to be consistent with these beliefs. These operating principles would have to be submitted to the entire faculty and, if approved, would drive the change process.

The next step for the SPC was to extend support for the restructuring initiative through the school to the people who did not participate on school committees or task forces—the people who traditionally were at the end of the information chain. To create widespread commitment for a process of shared decision making among these people, there would have to be tangible evidence that this was not just another of a series of passing fads to be abandoned when the next fad arrived. It would be necessary for teachers to see tangible results. At the outset, therefore, the SPC would focus its efforts on the achievement of short-term goals that could easily be made known throughout the school.

The SPC shifted roles as teacher interest grew and the momentum for change increased. It began serving as a clearinghouse, a sort of brokering service, for staff development and workshop requests. Teachers responding to the annual teacher satisfaction survey administered by the district described the SPC as both "driving" and "fueling" the change process at Beacon, creating, within six months, a higher degree of professional and personal job fulfillment than ever before. They hoped that before long, the planning and implementation of new efforts at the school would accomplish the real purpose of the restructuring initiative: higher levels of achievement for all students at the school.

Dr. Forrest at Beacon High School succeeded in stimulating broad faculty involvement and support for restructuring. There are situations, however, where no matter how hard a principal or other school leader tries, faculty and staff simply refuse to respond. In many cases they do not see a need for change. In some places, things are so bad that teachers will go so far as to sabotage the efforts of others, even if they themselves are unaffected by the change. To these people, reform of any type anywhere on the school premises poses a threat. One teacher I know recently described his school as follows:

> ...there is no evidence of interest on the part of most teachers to develop new and more effective programs. This school is chock full of people marking time till retirement. The classrooms are boring, stifling places where instruction—using the term loosely—is targeted exclusively on kids who are motivated to get high marks. It's easy to forget about the rest. They just disappear and teachers consider their disappearance to be lack of interest in education rather than the result of inadequate instruction. This school forgets about this last group of students. Providing the teachers with information about its performance—that 50% of the Hispanic males drop out before completing high school—arouses a lengthy and disinterested yawn from most on the faculty. Change simply won't happen here without dropping a bomb in the middle of the campus...

Management team meetings at this school are dominated by discussions about insufficient security personnel in the faculty parking lot. Efforts to stimulate interest in change, such as workshops and retreats, become instead a seemingly endless series of gripe sessions that have as their primary theme the expectation that someone else is responsible for teaching and learning conditions at the school. This is a place where most of the faculty's emotional and intellectual energy is reserved for blame-placing directed toward anyone and everyone—the principal, innovative teachers trying to work differently, the central office, the superintendent, the Board of Education, students, parents, the State Education Department—anyone but themselves.

What options are available to principals who are ensnared in a thicket of reaction? What can a principal or other school leader or third-party advocate for change do to create pressure for change at a school that stifles innovation and treats reformers the way sharks treat wounded swimmers?

In situations such as the one just described, there are other strategies that a principal or other leader can employ. For example, principals can work with the Board of Education and those teachers in the school who support change to create a mandate and, more important, a framework for change. One example of this strategy in action comes from a high school in New Mexico.

In this case, the Board of Education, with the principal's encouragement, enlisted the assistance of its long-term restructuring partner, the Panasonic Foundation, to organize a High School Summit, focus groups, and a broad community survey that would provide opportunities for the teachers, parents, and community to offer input on the type of high school education they would like in Santa Fe. The first step in the process was to hold the High School Summit at the local convention center. The summit consisted of a keynote address presented by Dr. Dennis Littky, then principal of Thayer High School in Winchester, New Hampshire. He focused the 800 attendees on the importance of changing the thinking that served as a conceptual basis for high school education.

Following his talk, participants had an opportunity to hear a panel of students discuss their experiences at the school. In order to create desire and interest in change, it is important for people to see new models as possibilities. This is what Dr. Forrest did at Beacon High School when he organized the monthly seminars as a first response to the Commission Report. The seminars created interest in change at Beacon. Likewise, the High School Summit in Santa Fe elevated community interest in change, thereby creating pressure on teachers to respond. The resolution created by the pubic schools in Santa Fe is included here in Appendix 7.1 as a useful example for readers.

A useful framework for principals and others to use as they consider possible approaches to stimulate interest in restructuring appropriate to their own situations is *The CASE-IMS School Improvement Process* (Howard and Keefe, 1991) by the National Association of Secondary School Principals (NASSP). The CASE-IMS School Improvement Process is a common-sense design for the diagnosis of a school's status that utilizes a series of important descriptors. It gives the members of a school community important information, in a nonthreatening way, about the school's need for restructuring and provides a framework for starting the change process. The steps identified below grow out of the six stages of the change process outlined earlier in the chapter.

Step 1: **Forming the school restructuring coordinating team:** At Beacon this group was called the SPC. The function of the school restructuring coordinating group is to plan, coordinate, and manage the school change process. The restructuring group's function is not to be advisory, but to be the coordinating body for school restructuring. In some schools, an existing leadership group such as the principal's cabinet may be expanded to serve this role. The problem with the latter approach is that frequently the cabinet is dominated by subject department heads who feel threatened by the restructuring. It is important that this group be representative of all shades of faculty opinion. Often, groups of this sort see their function as maintaining the status quo, thereby impeding the change process.

Step 2: **Raising awareness:** At Beacon High School, the SPC sponsored a series of awareness-raising activities before conducting any formal assessment or building school vision and mission statements. Activities such as these serve to acquaint all school stakeholders with the need for fundamental reform and the importance of developing a future-oriented vision and mission statement.

Step 3: **Assembling baseline data:**   Data are collected on key outcomes identified by the SPC in conjunction with stakeholders. Targets can include student academic achievement, student behavior indicators (disciplinary referrals), students' course-passing rates, numbers of students excelling, student self-efficacy, students completing the school year, or student satisfaction. There are also a number of indicators that reflect teacher morale and commitment to the school's change process. Among these are teacher turnover/transfer/resignation rate, faculty attendance (particularly on Mondays and Fridays), faculty involvement with students beyond classroom instruction, and many others.

Step 4: **Comprehensive assessment:**   Focus groups, surveys, interviews, and discussion forums should be held with students, teachers, and parents to identify needs, goals, perceptions of current status, and reactions to school change issues.

Step 5: **Interpreting the data:**   The SPC at Beacon High School summarized the data it accumulated from its surveys so the results were in a format useful to staff members, student and parent leaders, and others for setting priorities and planning timelines and activities.

The NASSP has CASE-IMS software that can provide printouts with the following interpretive information: (1) a profile of 34 school variables, (2) a categorical listing of school strengths and weaknesses, (3) a what-if analysis that estimates useful changes in selected variables, and (4) alternative interventions for each variable perceived as a priority.

Step 5 also includes the application of the systems approach to school restructuring. The school restructuring coordinating committee, or any other faculty-authorized group, should coordinate a review of three basic and eight systems components of the school to prepare a formal, written design statement. Data from the CASE-IMS assessment, ideas from a search of the school restructuring literature, and school-developed specifications can be used to prepare a proposal to the school community for a change process that will address the concerns, needs, and hopes identified in the assessment.

Step 6: **Priority setting and planning:**   At Beacon the SPC scheduled workshops to identify and gain support for a limited number of high-priority goals that, by general agreement of all stakeholders, should receive attention from school task forces. Workshop participants ordinarily identify three to six short- and long-term interventions that have potential to help the school achieve each priority.

Step 7: **Task force organization and coordination:**   At Beacon the SPC appointed members to task forces. At Lane, we relied on volunteers. If one is using the CASE-IMS, it makes sense to organize eight task forces, one for each of the eight systems components of the school design statement as specified in the NASSP format. Another way would be for the school to adapt the model to its own needs and convene task forces as needed. The task forces prepare a list of specifications for their particular systems components, determine to what degree the selected priority can be implemented in the near and long term, and then present the coordinating committee, and ultimately the entire faculty, with the data.

Step 8:   **Evaluation and reporting:**   Every few months, the school's coordinating committee collects data on the target goals, including the six CASE-IMS student outcomes. The results are reported to the school staff, students, parents, district personnel, and members of the school community. A complete reassessment of priorities should be conducted within three to five years.

An important component of the CASE-IMS approach is the School Redesign Statement. The School Redesign Statement outlined below makes it possible for any school to be restructured using a systems approach.

School Design Statement:

Three basic components:

1. **Mission statement:**   A relatively brief statement summarizing the purpose of the school.

2. **Philosophical, psychological, and organizational assumptions:**   Those assumptions about the nature of learners, learning, motivation, the purposes of schooling, and school organization and budgeting that are considered basic to the school's design.

3. **Student outcomes statement:**   Those broad competencies that are seen as essential for effective participation in the emerging twenty-first century society and economy. These outcome descriptors form the basis for the school's curriculum and assessment systems.

Eight systems components:

1. **Instructional programs and curricula:**   These should be short, descriptive paragraphs that define the kinds of curriculum content and learning opportunities that will be offered by the school. These specifications should be aligned with the student outcomes statement prepared by the school. It is always important to make certain that the instructional process is consistent with what one wishes to achieve. In the past, that has often not been the case, and that is one of the reasons why restructuring schools that continue to use standardized norm-referenced tests which rely upon low-level knowledge and

short-answer responses produce lowered test results. Simply put, in those places, planning, implementation, curriculum, instruction, and assessment are not coordinated, nor are they rational.

2. **Instructional techniques:**   These are short paragraphs defining those teaching techniques that have been demonstrated to be successful in accomplishing the desired student outcomes. This information should be research based. Too often, schools use instructional approaches because they are convenient, because someone on the staff is enthusiastic about one or another approach, or because there are materials around that make implementation easy. None are good reasons. It is important to make certain that an approach to be used has proven validity in achieving the desired outcomes. If that is not the case, and the approach is still experimental, then it must be clear that the program will be monitored, that there will be periodic reviews, and that progress, tied to the desired outcomes, will be looked at on a regular basis.

3. **School structure and organization:**   Any school design plan should have a section describing how the school will be structured so that the proposed student outcomes can be accomplished. There is no such thing as a "good" or "bad" structure. Structures exist to achieve a school's educational objectives. Some structures facilitate the achievement of some goals; others are more appropriate to accomplishing others. The point is that usefulness and appropriateness have to drive decisions on structure and organization. The section might include statements describing the characteristics of the desired school schedule and social structure.

4. **School culture and climate:**   School culture in CASE-IMS is defined as "the characteristics, norms, and traditions of a school and its community." Climate is defined as "the shared perceptions of the characteristics of a school and of its members." Climate is a measure of school culture. If people in a school are not aware of the culture and its impact on instruction and on the change process, little progress can be made.

5. **School leadership, management, and budgeting:**   Descriptors specify how the planning, decision-making, and communications processes are to be managed. This section may include a description of how the school's site-based management will function.

6. **School staffing and staff development:**   The development of a genuine professional role for teachers, the creation of purposeful working conditions that provide teachers with fulfillment in their jobs, school-based teacher interviewing, hiring and induction policies, and staff development priorities and strategies must all be planned for.

7. **School resources, physical plant, and equipment:**   Document descriptors in this portion of the profile specify the characteristics of the physical plant, the equipment needed to support the envisioned curricula and instructional design, and provisions for coordination of school and community resources.

8. **Evaluation plan:**   The school's evaluation and reporting systems are specified. The plan is designed to inform all members of the school community of
the extent to which the design is being implemented and the desired student
outcomes are being accomplished.

For further information, contact the National Association of Secondary School
Principals at 1904 Association Drive, Reston, Virginia 22091.

Going through the type of thorough assessment and analysis described above can
result in a much better understanding of the steps that must be taken to ensure that
proposed reform efforts have a significant and lasting impact.

Louis and Miles (1990, p. 30) identify three forms of action that "seem to be
important in motivating a school's staff to engage in significant change—articulating
a vision, getting staff to believe that the vision reflects their own interests, and the
use of evolutionary planning strategies." That is what Dr. Forrest did at Beacon. That
is what must be considered before the newly ignited fire of restructuring can burn
brightly.

References

Clune, W.H. and White, P.A. (1988). *School-Based Management: Institutional Variation, Implementation, and Issues for Further Research.* New Brunswick,
New Jersey: Center for Policy Research.

Elmore, R.F. et al. (1992). *Restructuring Schools.* San Francisco: Jossey-Bass.

Fullan, M. (1991). *The New Meaning of Educational Change.* New York: Teachers
College Press, Columbia University.

Goodlad, J. (1985). *A Place Called School.* New York: McGraw Hill.

Goodlad, J., Klein, M., et al. (1970). *Behind the Classroom Door.* Worthington, Ohio:
Charles A. Jones.

Hallinger, P. (1992). School leadership development. *Education and Urban Society,*
24(3), 300–316.

Harvey, G. and Crandall, D.F. (1988). *A Beginning Look at the What and How of
Restructuring.* Andover, Massachusetts: The Regional Laboratory for Educational Improvement of the Northeast and Islands.

Hertzberg, F. (1966). *Work and the Nature of Man.* Cleveland, Ohio: The World
Publishing Company.

Howard, E.R. and Keefe, J.W. (1991). *The CASE-IMS School Improvement Process.*
Reston, Virginia: National Association of Secondary School Principals.

Howard, E.R. and Keefe, J.W. (1993). The CASE-IMS School Improvement Process: Suggested Components of a School Design Statement. Position paper for CASE-IMS Mini-Project. Reston, Virginia: National Association of Secondary School Principals.

Lewis, A. (1989). *Restructuring America's Schools*. Arlington, Virginia: American Association of School Administrators.

Loucks-Horsley, S. and Cox, P. (1984). It's all in the doing: What recent research says about implementation. In G. Harvey, S. Loucks-Horsley, P. Cox, and D.F. Crandall (Eds.), *Implementing the Recommendations of the National Commission and Studies of Education, Or What They Failed to Mention*. Symposium presented at the annual meeting of the American Educational Research Association, New Orleans, Louisiana.

Louis, K.S. and Miles, M.B. (1990). *Improving the Urban High School: What Works and Why*. New York: Teachers College Press.

Michaels, K. (1984). Caution: Second-wave reform taking place. *Educational Leadership*, 3, 14–19.

Naisbitt, J. and Aburdene, P. (1990). *Megatrends 2000—10 New Directions for the 1990's*. New York: Morrow Publishing.

North Central Regional Educational Laboratory. (1990). *Restructuring to Promote Learning in America's Schools*. Elmhurst, Illinois: North Central Regional Educational Laboratory.

Schlechty, P. (1990). *Schools for the 21st Century*. San Francisco: Jossey-Bass.

Schneider, B. and Coleman, J.S. (Eds.). (1993). *Parents, Their Children, and Schools*. Boulder, Colorado: Westview.

Senge, P. (1990). *The Fifth Discipline: The Art and Practice of the Learning Organization*. New York: Doubleday.

Sizer, T.R. (1989). Diverse practice, shared ideas: The essential school. In H.J. Walbert and J.J. Lane (Eds.), *Organizing for Learning: Toward the 21st Century*. Reston, Virginia: National Association of Secondary School Principals.

Appendix 7.1

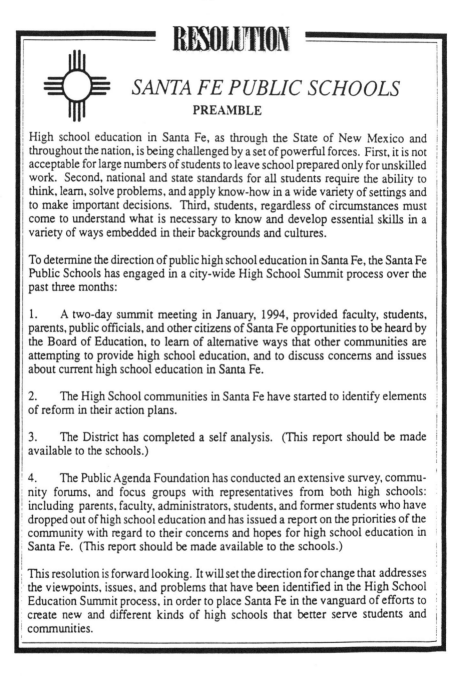

RESOLUTION

SANTA FE PUBLIC SCHOOLS
PREAMBLE

High school education in Santa Fe, as through the State of New Mexico and throughout the nation, is being challenged by a set of powerful forces. First, it is not acceptable for large numbers of students to leave school prepared only for unskilled work. Second, national and state standards for all students require the ability to think, learn, solve problems, and apply know-how in a wide variety of settings and to make important decisions. Third, students, regardless of circumstances must come to understand what is necessary to know and develop essential skills in a variety of ways embedded in their backgrounds and cultures.

To determine the direction of public high school education in Santa Fe, the Santa Fe Public Schools has engaged in a city-wide High School Summit process over the past three months:

1.   A two-day summit meeting in January, 1994, provided faculty, students, parents, public officials, and other citizens of Santa Fe opportunities to be heard by the Board of Education, to learn of alternative ways that other communities are attempting to provide high school education, and to discuss concerns and issues about current high school education in Santa Fe.

2.   The High School communities in Santa Fe have started to identify elements of reform in their action plans.

3.   The District has completed a self analysis. (This report should be made available to the schools.)

4.   The Public Agenda Foundation has conducted an extensive survey, community forums, and focus groups with representatives from both high schools: including parents, faculty, administrators, students, and former students who have dropped out of high school education and has issued a report on the priorities of the community with regard to their concerns and hopes for high school education in Santa Fe. (This report should be made available to the schools.)

This resolution is forward looking. It will set the direction for change that addresses the viewpoints, issues, and problems that have been identified in the High School Education Summit process, in order to place Santa Fe in the vanguard of efforts to create new and different kinds of high schools that better serve students and communities.

Appendix 7.1 (continued)

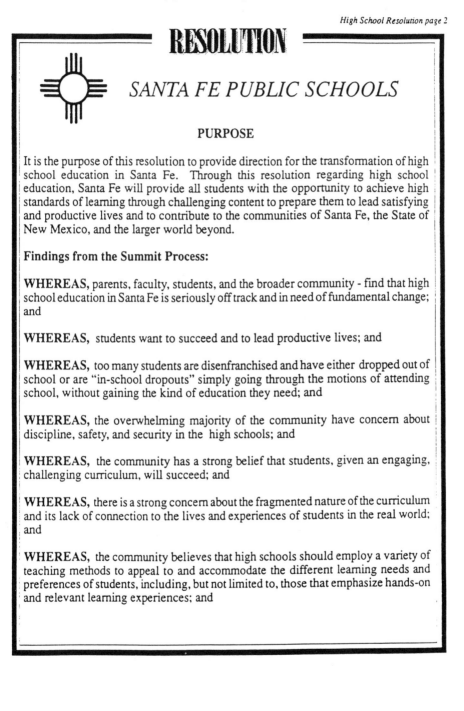

RESOLUTION

SANTA FE PUBLIC SCHOOLS

PURPOSE

It is the purpose of this resolution to provide direction for the transformation of high school education in Santa Fe. Through this resolution regarding high school education, Santa Fe will provide all students with the opportunity to achieve high standards of learning through challenging content to prepare them to lead satisfying and productive lives and to contribute to the communities of Santa Fe, the State of New Mexico, and the larger world beyond.

Findings from the Summit Process:

WHEREAS, parents, faculty, students, and the broader community - find that high school education in Santa Fe is seriously off track and in need of fundamental change; and

WHEREAS, students want to succeed and to lead productive lives; and

WHEREAS, too many students are disenfranchised and have either dropped out of school or are "in-school dropouts" simply going through the motions of attending school, without gaining the kind of education they need; and

WHEREAS, the overwhelming majority of the community have concern about discipline, safety, and security in the high schools; and

WHEREAS, the community has a strong belief that students, given an engaging, challenging curriculum, will succeed; and

WHEREAS, there is a strong concern about the fragmented nature of the curriculum and its lack of connection to the lives and experiences of students in the real world; and

WHEREAS, the community believes that high schools should employ a variety of teaching methods to appeal to and accommodate the different learning needs and preferences of students, including, but not limited to, those that emphasize hands-on and relevant learning experiences; and

Appendix 7.1 (continued)

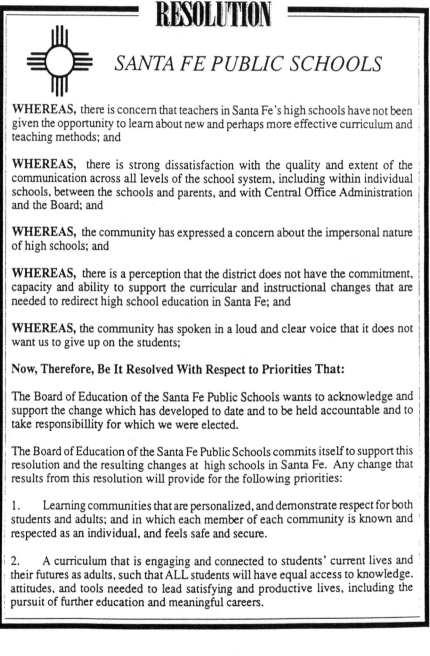

High School Resolution page 3

RESOLUTION

SANTA FE PUBLIC SCHOOLS

WHEREAS, there is concern that teachers in Santa Fe's high schools have not been given the opportunity to learn about new and perhaps more effective curriculum and teaching methods; and

WHEREAS, there is strong dissatisfaction with the quality and extent of the communication across all levels of the school system, including within individual schools, between the schools and parents, and with Central Office Administration and the Board; and

WHEREAS, the community has expressed a concern about the impersonal nature of high schools; and

WHEREAS, there is a perception that the district does not have the commitment, capacity and ability to support the curricular and instructional changes that are needed to redirect high school education in Santa Fe; and

WHEREAS, the community has spoken in a loud and clear voice that it does not want us to give up on the students;

Now, Therefore, Be It Resolved With Respect to Priorities That:

The Board of Education of the Santa Fe Public Schools wants to acknowledge and support the change which has developed to date and to be held accountable and to take responsibillity for which we were elected.

The Board of Education of the Santa Fe Public Schools commits itself to support this resolution and the resulting changes at high schools in Santa Fe. Any change that results from this resolution will provide for the following priorities:

1.   Learning communities that are personalized, and demonstrate respect for both students and adults; and in which each member of each community is known and respected as an individual, and feels safe and secure.

2.   A curriculum that is engaging and connected to students' current lives and their futures as adults, such that ALL students will have equal access to knowledge, attitudes, and tools needed to lead satisfying and productive lives, including the pursuit of further education and meaningful careers.

Appendix 7.1 (continued)

RESOLUTION

SANTA FE PUBLIC SCHOOLS

3.   New curricula and alternative approaches and strategies for learning that meet the needs of students, with emphasis on personalization.

4.   High standards for academic achievement and behavior for all students, and the assessment of learning through professionally accepted performance measurements.

5.   High standards for all faculty, administrators and staff, and assessment through professionally accepted performance measurements.

6.   Programs that pay particular attention to students who are disenfranchised, that is, those who have already dropped out of school or are at high risk for dropping out.

Now, Therefore, Be It Resolved With Respect to Policies That:

1.   The Santa Fe Board of Education, as part of its commitment to site-based shared-decision making, invites and authorizes but does not direct teams of faculty, students, parents, and community members to submit proposals for the creation of smaller learning communities within the existing high schools if the existence of such learning communities would meet the needs of students. These learning communities may be self-managing, self-governing entities, and will be designed to meet the priorities stated above as well as the state's requirements for high school education.

2.   The Santa Fe Board of Education, as part of its commitment to site-based budgeting, authorizes the district administration to work with each learning community to establish its own site-based budget system.

Now, Therefore, Be It Resolved With Respect to the Process That:

1.   The high school principals will work with their staff and school communities to support the development of learning communities and facilitate the transition.

Appendix 7.1 (continued)

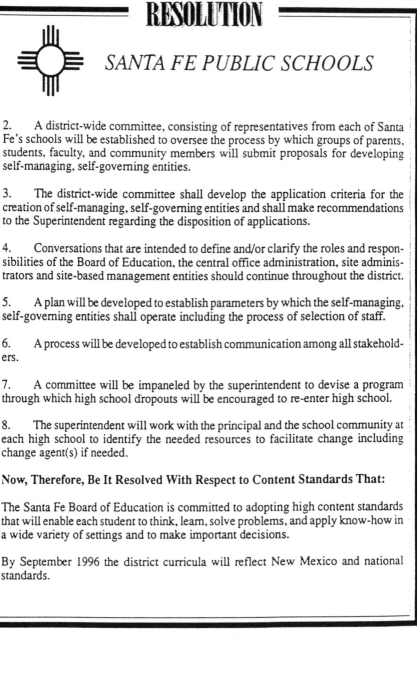

High School Resolution page 5

RESOLUTION

SANTA FE PUBLIC SCHOOLS

2.   A district-wide committee, consisting of representatives from each of Santa Fe's schools will be established to oversee the process by which groups of parents, students, faculty, and community members will submit proposals for developing self-managing, self-governing entities.

3.   The district-wide committee shall develop the application criteria for the creation of self-managing, self-governing entities and shall make recommendations to the Superintendent regarding the disposition of applications.

4.   Conversations that are intended to define and/or clarify the roles and responsibilities of the Board of Education, the central office administration, site administrators and site-based management entities should continue throughout the district.

5.   A plan will be developed to establish parameters by which the self-managing, self-governing entities shall operate including the process of selection of staff.

6.   A process will be developed to establish communication among all stakeholders.

7.   A committee will be impaneled by the superintendent to devise a program through which high school dropouts will be encouraged to re-enter high school.

8.   The superintendent will work with the principal and the school community at each high school to identify the needed resources to facilitate change including change agent(s) if needed.

Now, Therefore, Be It Resolved With Respect to Content Standards That:

The Santa Fe Board of Education is committed to adopting high content standards that will enable each student to think, learn, solve problems, and apply know-how in a wide variety of settings and to make important decisions.

By September 1996 the district curricula will reflect New Mexico and national standards.

Appendix 7.1 (continued)

High School Resolution page 6

RESOLUTION

SANTA FE PUBLIC SCHOOLS

Now, Therefore, Be It Resolved With Respect to Community Involvement That:

The Santa Fe Board of Education reaffirms its commitment to involving the larger Santa Fe community in matters affecting the district's education programs.

Now, Therefore, Let it Be Resolved that the Board Of Education of the Santa Fe Public Schools does hereby acknowledge and proclaim this document as its Official Resolution For High School Education In Santa Fe.

Signed this _____ day of _____, 1994, by the Board of Education of the Santa Fe Public Schools:

_____
Linda Kellahin, President

_____
Michael E. Vigil, Vice President

_____
Marcel Legendre, Secretary

_____
Richard Gorman, Member

_____
Jimmie Martinez, Member

Peak Performing Schools Need a New Model for Human Development

Reforms in teaching and learning in our high schools do not come about by accident. They happen only when members of the school community combine thoughtful program development with hard work. For the school's professional personnel it means developing strategies that are powerful enough to change even the most entrenched classroom practices and bureaucratic habits.

Restructuring high schools requires major shifts of attitudes and behaviors that can only be accomplished by educators who are open to change, ambiguity, and challenge—people who are growing. Many principals, if they are themselves ready for the challenges of restructuring, will find many staff members who are not. Only one way can prepare them, and that is by motivating substantial growth and renewal. In order for change in schools to be sustainable, teachers must become equipped to deal with issues such as standards, assessment, and student performance. They must be able to think through the process of transcending the organizational patterns that maintain the current mediocre performance and cripple school improvement efforts. That is why high-quality, relevant, and ongoing professional development is a key factor in explaining why some restructuring initiatives work well and why others falter and fade.

The obvious conclusion is that attention must be devoted to the development of the school's human resources. The greater the transformational effort, the greater the need for professional development. Professional development as used here means the variety of individual and collective experiences that enable educators to enhance their professional competence in teaching students, leading and/or serving as members of a professional community, and/or assuming changed roles demanded by a changing educational context. These experiences may involve inquiry, analysis, skill, and knowledge development and may be offered on or off site through a variety of strategies. Professional development is fundamental. Wise leaders invest substantial resources in the growth of people because training can help teachers and other staff members surpass previous levels of performance.

For teachers to nurture students' personal, social, and academic development, as well as their diverse cultural background and learning styles, teachers themselves must understand the relationship between these factors and teaching and learning. For teachers and administrators to restructure curricula and assessments, deal effectively with external partners, and participate in school governance, they must have broader and deeper understandings of and ongoing experiences with these issues.

However, the fact that opportunities for productive learning by educators are, as a general rule, infrequent and insubstantial is well documented. All too often, professional development consists of one-shot workshops aimed at imparting specific skills to teachers, over which educators have little control, after which they receive little follow-up support, and which are seldom linked to clearly articulated goals for schools.

The type of professional development advocated in this publication emphasizes intellectual inquiry and reflection about classroom practice as well as new teaching strategies.

As illustrated in Chapters 2, 3, 4, and 7, eliminating teacher isolation and fostering the development of a community of professionals who are anxious and eager to learn must be a characteristic of the schools to be created. The conventional staff development approach considers the individual teacher working alone in a self-contained classroom as the basic learning unit. It reinforces isolation and prevents teamwork that is grounded in cooperation and interaction.

Thus, in those places where schools are already forming teacher work teams that stay with students for multiple years in some cases, it is important to make these teacher teams the basic professional development unit. There are restructuring schools that form teacher teams and then weaken them by creating learning programs that provide for individual rather than team learning. Sometimes these are subject-area–based workshops held at the district or state level; other times, they are school-organized experiences that group teachers by grade, official class assignment, or teaching schedule. Frequently, in these situations, teachers working on the same team learn at different places and at different times. Principals and other school leaders can build teamwork by fostering experiences that facilitate *team* learning and making such learning a core part of the organizational structure.

This chapter focuses on new approaches to professional development that assist in building the capacity of teachers and other staff members to implement new and different ways of teaching students. It describes the ways that principals and other school leaders can provide the support necessary to make a new approach to teacher learning a successful component of the school's restructuring.

A NEW MODEL FOR PROFESSIONAL DEVELOPMENT AT HARRISON HIGH SCHOOL

The restructuring effort at Harrison High School is a good example of how teaching staff and administrators are working together to design an effort that fosters such changes. Harrison teachers have designed a new professional development model that provides new skills and knowledge for the teachers of a troubled high school in dire need of total and comprehensive reform. The following examples are illustrative of the progress made at Harrison, four years into the restructuring process.

- On a sunny May afternoon, small groups of students in a combined ninth/tenth grade class in integrated math/science are involved in a group experiment. At one point, the teacher reviews agreed-upon standards for scientific evidence and requires students to explain the projects they have completed that meet the standard. The teacher asks each student in the group to evaluate their own performance and those of their peers. Students in the class have become a peer assessment and support group.

- Two teachers have teamed to create an interdisciplinary humanities curriculum on the imaginary realm. Today, one of the students in their class is making a multimedia presentation about the Renaissance involving video, drama, literature, and history.

- The librarian stays at school through the late afternoon to work with a support group for the five foreign language teachers. Her role is to help them integrate social studies concepts into their teaching. A secondary goal is to minimize the use of texts in foreign language classes. The librarian is assisting them in planning for a series of workshops, each to take place at a location outside of the building. It reflects her commitment to assist teachers as they move away from standardized learning materials to a wide variety of sources, thereby encouraging students' projects to be more relevant and concrete.

Scenes such as these are occurring more frequently at Harrison, mostly as a result of the school's redefining its approach to professional development as a means for effecting whole school reform. Prior to beginning its new professional development effort, Harrison was having trouble with its restructuring efforts.

In the district, 57% of the students are eligible for free or reduced-price lunch; in the school, upwards of 80% of the 1500 students were eligible. The school's dropout rate was soaring. Its register included large numbers of students who were overage for their grade placement and, consequently, at risk for dropping out at any moment.

The school also had a reputation for a climate defined less by the goal of educating students than by containing them. Suspension rates were among the highest in the city, taking a toll on students and teachers alike. The teachers' motto at Harrison had become "close your door and hope for the best." Finally, many educators in the school had limited confidence in the ability to teach all students. For example, a survey conducted at the start of the restructuring effort found that only 55% of the teachers responded "yes" to the statement, "Teachers in this school feel they can make a difference," and only 54% agreed that "Faculty and staff have high expectations for all students." Most troubling of all, only one out of eight teachers responded "yes" to the statement, "All students are capable of learning." Clearly, such beliefs constituted barriers to mobilizing staff to develop programs that would result in high achievement for all students.

Problems with the Current Staff Development Model at Harrison

Restructuring was in trouble at Harrison. The district's standard approaches to high school restructuring and professional development, though helpful, seemed insufficient for the task of transforming this school after many years of neglect. One problem was that no one in the district had defined the purpose of the restructuring in terms of producing student achievement gains; neither were curriculum and instruction central to the restructuring effort. This circumstance prevails in many places. Moreover, changing internal structures, such as implementing teaching teams, is meaningless unless the work that teachers assign to students is changed concurrently.

Likewise, the conventional short-term in-service training normally implemented by high schools had failed to produce desired academic gains. No matter what the school did, the student achievement indicators remained the same. Although some teachers enjoyed individual professional development workshops, they did not necessarily apply strategies from in-service sessions in their classrooms. Individual workshops may have been excellent, but teachers working alone could not bring about widespread implementation.

Indeed, research bears out the experience at Harrison. It suggests that approaches that define teachers as individual consumers in a marketplace of workshops do not yield lasting change in school or student performance. For example, noting that most school districts "leave professional development to chance or to individual preferences," Joyce Epstein and her colleagues (1991, p. 40) warn:

> Most teachers who have been "in-serviced" in workshops, clinics, or short courses do not change their practice. They are not expected to do so, not rewarded for trying, and not guided in their efforts. If this pattern of staff development continues, there will be little notable improvement in...education.

A Professional Development Committee Explores Issues of Involvement, Expectations, and Support

A specially convened subcommittee of the school's restructuring leadership group began a discussion of specific tactics of reform to fit changing perceptions of the needs of the school, students, and teachers. No one at the meetings had a foolproof recipe for high school transformation, but they were certain that if authentic reform were going to take hold, it would have to involve teachers in a variety of roles. They also sensed that teachers would have to expand their pedagogical repertoire to create classrooms where teaching and learning could compete for the attention of adolescents against a compelling peer culture and demanding social circumstances. With these thoughts in mind, they developed a dual focus on professional development and curricular reform directed toward improvement in student achievement.

The professional development subcommittee's mission was to institutionalize broad involvement and to draw out the best ideas available from school staff. The committee's membership consisted of three teachers, the principal, and a department head. It met on a regular basis to think about and plan for ways of expanding faculty knowledge and capacity as the school proceeded with its school-based change process. The committee considered what teachers needed to help implement and deepen the school's restructuring.

The committee undertook the coordination of the new opportunities for professional development that would be offered. The committee found that as soon as the restructuring efforts were well underway, the need for professional development became obvious to a large proportion of the staff. Teachers began to realize that "add-on" enrichment, mentoring, and programs for high-risk youngsters would go only so far. Still, not all teachers at the school welcomed what they perceived would be more in-service training. Night workshops did not fit their exhausting schedules, and many had developed the feeling that they had "heard it all before." Lacking faith in themselves or the system that was supposed to support them, teachers often turned to blaming students for poor academic performance as a way of revealing a deep sense of hopelessness about reaching the most disadvantaged students.

Recognizing that the traditional district efforts had been inadequate to boost teachers' confidence in themselves and their students, some members of the subcommittee speculated that acquainting teachers with exemplars from outside the district might have a better chance of alleviating their discouragement. Accordingly, they did so. That, too, went just so far. Teachers, however, could not absorb any more options or suggestions about new strategies. Teachers already felt overwhelmed with the choices available to them. From the principal's perspective, making time available presented administrative problems, including that of arranging for and supervising substitutes when teachers left for professional development workshops. Being away from the classroom was also of concern to teachers; they wanted to spend more time with their students. At the end of the restructuring effort's first year, spirits were good, but results were meager.

Discovering the Power of Professional Development

At the early stages, few of those involved in the subcommittee fully understood the exact direction the school's restructuring would ultimately take. Increasingly, however, teacher teams began to understand that if they were to see meaningful results, they would need to focus resources more directly and more strategically.

The subcommittee gradually came to a consensus that the restructuring needed a more pointed focus on building those teacher skills that would foster student achievement. With this focus, school-based teams could begin to encourage as many teachers as possible to develop skills in a few strategies like cooperative learning so as to bring consistency to classroom norms and interactions.

The subcommittee decided that the school's restructuring effort should focus even more intensively on professional development. First, the professional development would be tied to two main premises of the school's reform philosophy:

1. High school reform would mean little if it did not change the teaching and learning that occurs daily in each classroom.

2. High school reform would mean little if it did not strengthen the school's capacity to mobilize all resources so that curriculum and instruction routinely become the foundation for learning.

Second, recognizing that higher expectations for student outcomes warranted a more intentional approach to professional development, the planners gave school-based teams of teachers the latitude to investigate issues of importance to them. Such an approach was predicated on several assumptions:

1. Teachers work best on problems they have identified for themselves.

2. Teachers become effective when encouraged to examine and assess their own work and consider ways of working differently.

3. Teachers help each other by working collaboratively.

4. Working with colleagues helps teachers in their professional development.

In short, professional development at the school would be a means to strengthen school performances overall, rather than simply to "develop" individual teachers. As Epstein et al. (1991, p. 37) note:

> Most staff development falls short for large numbers of teachers mainly because it is not designed to help teachers feel more professional, work together with other teachers, or improve individual skills...most staff development pays little attention to the ultimate impact of the staff development activities on student skills, attitudes and successes.

Such assessments suggest that professional development for the school should depart from current traditional models. To underscore the commitment to professional growth at Harrison as a means for reform, the subcommittee made a recommendation to the school's leadership group that it invest heavily in the people who could implement change—those already working on teams and those interested in collaborating with colleagues in the future. The school used its authority under school-based budgeting to convert staff units into dollar equivalents to allow the school to provide teachers with the support they said they needed to implement the proposed changes.

With high school reform at Harrison defined in terms of improving teaching and learning, professional growth opportunities had to be set up to provide teachers with powerful pedagogical tools commensurate with the task of teaching some of a school's hardest-to-reach students. Thus, the Harrison High School staff development subcommittee developed the following framework:

- Instead of being developed from the top, professional development would be designed by and for teams of teachers from the school.

- Instead of focusing on organizational processes and structures, professional development would focus on student achievement and teaching higher-order skills within content areas.

- Instead of offering short-term workshops, professional development would be long term, offering teachers training in summer institutes and semester-long experiences, with school-based follow-up also available.

- Instead of leaving choices for professional development to individual teachers, professional development would address the needs of teams of teachers from the school so that new learning could be sustained by teachers meeting collegially at the school.

In short, there was an understanding that change at Harrison High School required a major investment in the teachers responsible for implementing the classroom changes that could improve student performance. Taken together, these features communicated a significantly different message from that of a more traditional "cafeteria" approach to professional development. Expectations at Harrison were changing, not only for student performance, but for teacher performance. Teachers would now have access to expanded opportunities to broaden their roles and sharpen their skills. In turn, they would grow as professionals in a professional community of learners. This was the concept that the subcommittee would recommend to the school's leadership group. It would become the scaffolding for all that was to follow.

The First Summer Institute

It was clear from the lessons learned from other restructuring schools and districts that intensive, school-based professional development had to take place in a setting where teachers were undistracted by daily obligations. Fill-in time between classes or add-on time at the end of the workday were not effective. Teachers needed extra time to observe new pedagogical approaches and develop classroom strategies that they could claim as their own. They also had to gain an understanding that meaningful professional growth required ongoing support from colleagues once they began to apply new approaches in the classrooms.

The teachers' first experience with the new approach was to be a summer institute focused on interdisciplinary curriculum in the humanities and math/science. The planning subcommittee, in consultation with teachers in the school, fashioned plans for a summer institute during which functional teams of teachers would explore research related to interdisciplinary curriculum and would then design strategies for implementation.

Teacher teams from the school would meet six hours each day for ten days during the early part of the summer, to be followed by one full-day workshop in late August, just prior to the opening of school. A second full day would be set aside early in September. After that, there would be monthly one-hour sessions for follow-up and support.

The first week of the summer institute would focus on creating communities of teachers who were committed to working on interdisciplinary curriculum in a team framework. Each day would include a morning presentation by consultant teams of teacher practitioners from other schools and then afternoon working time.

During the second week of the workshop, teachers would spend most of their time working with colleagues on developing interdisciplinary units for use in their classrooms the following year. The guiding principle undergirding all decisions was that good professional development must be long term and it must be particularly focused on instruction in the classroom.

Institute results that first year surpassed the expectations of the subcommittee. Teams of teachers worked together to write curriculum and design activities that incorporated professional insights developed during the institute's first week. Teachers also designed rubrics to identify criteria for student evaluation. At the end of two weeks, teachers had produced enough activities to fill a spiral-bound guide for three interdisciplinary units, including activities that would allow for group and individual student projects. Teachers also spent part of their time identifying theme-based questions that could frame intellectual issues for their students and sharpen dialogue to foster improved learning in each classroom.

It was important to the school's leadership group and the professional development subcommittee—the school's change managers—that momentum for change not stop at the end of the summer period. To ensure that teachers actually used the activities developed during the institute, ongoing support was arranged with the practitioner/consultants who worked with the teachers during the summer. This ongoing support is key to maintaining progress, giving teachers confidence, and providing feedback to each school's leadership team on those structures and routines, including the school's schedule or grouping practices, that might undermine implementation and progress in the effort. This last item is critical: feedback meetings must be scheduled with school leadership groups and administrators. It is important to make things easier for those involved in innovation. Outsiders, such as consultants, can play an additional role by acquainting school leadership with bottlenecks and barriers to change; it is then up to the leadership to get the bottlenecks out of the way.

It is difficult for teachers to improve in isolation. They need a supportive network where they receive guided practice and coaching over an extended period of time. Professional development will only have a lasting effect when principals, central office support staff, and others roll up their sleeves, join the teachers in their classrooms, and help them to process their successes and their failures.

During the course of the year following the institute, teacher participants began to apply new approaches in their classrooms. New strategies quickly produced results in terms of teachers' sense of improved efficacy and student motivation. Improved student achievement indicators, naturally, would take longer.

PROFESSIONAL DEVELOPMENT STRATEGIES FOR CHANGING TEACHING AND LEARNING

The change process at Harrison is moving along nicely, much of it attributable to the new professional development strategy. Change is most evident in teachers' expectations for students and in classroom instruction. In addition, as teachers formulate new roles for themselves and shape new school routines and procedures, the school is becoming a place where all organizational features support teacher professionalization.

Expectations and Standards

Much of the blame-placing that commonly characterized teacher conversations at many schools is disappearing at Harrison. The new professional development model is addressing the once pervasive problem of low expectations for student performance by strengthening teachers' classroom efficacy. The belief is that professional development, which increases teachers' grasp of learning theory and engages teachers in designing and using a challenging curriculum, results in higher expectations for student learning. In fact, although some teachers still express concern that their students may arrive at the school with weak skills (i.e., blaming students' circumstances for poor academic performance), it is a rare activity in this school. This is not to say that teachers are unaware of the personal and social challenges students face; rather, they are not seen as insurmountable barriers to learning at high levels.

Changed teacher expectations translate into new norms, structures, and routines that reflect these expectations on a day-to-day basis. For example, some teachers are now willing to experiment with multi-ability classrooms so that less confident students interact academically with their more successful peers. In fact, teachers now not only have a higher level of expectations for all children, but also new kinds of expectations for more students. These new expectations, in turn, foster a reconsideration of the kinds of activities that might enrich student learning. Teachers are no longer surprised to find that kids are fascinated by opera, ballet, and Renaissance art.

Authentic Curriculum and Assessment

Central to the belief of the new professional development model is that improved learning depends on teachers who are knowledgeable about academic content and able to employ a variety of teaching methodologies to help all students master that content. The purpose at Harrison is to create curriculum and instruction that offer more meaningful school experiences to high school students.

This focus on higher-order thinking also crops up in teachers' new understanding that difficulty in basic skills mastery should not bar students from attempting to grapple with the universal concerns of the humanities. Teachers are developing new skills that increasingly engage students in extended dialogue for understanding based on close reading of challenging original source materials like *The Congressional Record*. Such materials challenge students to look for evidence that supports different perspectives and complex points of view.

Connecting School and Real World Learning Through Interdisciplinary Thematic Curricula

As teachers begin to organize interdisciplinary content around themes such as justice, violence, bravery, and courage, students have opportunities to explore ideas in depth. For example, themes that teachers develop during the summer institute lend themselves to multiple readings about particular historical events and about such topics as diversity and growing up. Teachers take more time to complete a theme, and their work reflects, according to staff members, higher standards. They have more time on a topic, so they get an opportunity to delve into different points of view. When teachers work on interdisciplinary thematic learning and the librarian or guidance counselor, for example, is linked to the team, students have available a wider variety of supplementary materials. Sources such as audio tapes ranging from sitar music from India to songs of the Civil War engage students who want to explore the theme even more deeply.

Many teachers know intuitively that their students would benefit from activities that connect school learning to their daily lives, yet they often lack the wherewithal to develop the skills or knowledge to implement their plans. A professional development approach such as the one at Harrison gives teachers an opportunity to validate these intuitions and offers them tools to design activities connected to students' life experiences. In many classrooms, teachers now employ strategies to help students expand and structure their own knowledge around personal concerns. Students in grade 9 now construct books about such issues as child abuse and family violence, and they research family histories, producing family trees for display in school hallways. Activities like these foster a deeper understanding of broad, underlying concepts within content areas.

A Climate of Support for Student Achievement

In many districts across the country, teachers point to a perceived lack of support for learning in the wider environment their students inhabit. Harrison High School has begun to put into place a variety of social supports for learning, both within and outside of schools. Advisor–advisee programs now offer all students the opportunity to learn the self-development and decision-making skills that accompany success. As part of the professional development effort, teachers and administrators are developing a new advisory curriculum. The school's professional development program allows them to put in the time that such an effort requires.

Teachers in the school see multiple effects of the professional development effort as they focus on student needs. In fact, school routines like scheduling and grouping are changing to maximize learning. For example, English teachers realize that implementing new teaching strategies to effect the greatest possible benefits for students means they must plan the day so that English, reading, and research periods are scheduled back to back, allowing for a double or triple period. In turn, a rescheduled school day such as this eliminates the need for bells, and hallways seem almost empty when students from only one or two teams at a time are changing classes.

The school has also moved assertively to involve parents in supporting their children's school performance. Teams of teachers (rather than the school as a whole) involve parents in their children's education. One team initiated new procedures to make monthly awards to parents for their contributions to learning, with recognition based on students' own nomination essays. Not only have parents turned out in large numbers for the awards ceremony, but they have subsequently become volunteers at the school, strengthening the bridge between school and home. Moreover, many teachers are now communicating more clearly to parents about homework and are asking parents to sign off on required assignments. Taken together, these examples suggest that Harrison High School is moving irreversibly toward building a school climate characterized by what Oakes (1989) has called a "press for achievement." Along with equal access to knowledge and a climate for professional practice, a school's commitment to make the push for achievement manifest in all its activities is a key enabling condition for improved learning schoolwide.

A NEW PARADIGM FOR PROFESSIONAL DEVELOPMENT AND PROFESSIONALISM

Professional development that includes teacher discussion, follow-up learning, classroom observations, and personal feedback has been thoroughly welcomed by teachers at Harrison High School. They report a much stronger sense of professionalism as a result of their experiences. Indeed, the extent to which teachers have thrown themselves into new opportunities for professional development alone is testimony to teachers' willingness to engage in activities that strengthen their skills.

A redefinition of professional development has been an unintended but critically important result of the effort. When the school's restructuring began, teachers at Harrison were so thoroughly disillusioned with the standard fare of in-service training that they doubted the value of *any* professional development for improving student achievement. Three years later, these teachers will never again be satisfied with traditional approaches to professional learning. They have created a new model for professional development that includes teacher involvement in decision making, a focus on student achievement, the development of new teacher-directed networks across schools, and the expectation that teachers will assume expanded roles to promote best practice in professional settings.

Teacher Involvement in Decision Making

With the initiation of a democratic, collegial planning model, teachers at Harrison have established that opportunities for teachers to serve in decision-making roles are, by definition, opportunities for professional growth. As one teacher noted,

> From the first meeting we had with the planning subcommittee, teachers have had the same authority as the principal in voting. The initial group and the others that have developed since have given us a method of formalizing shared leadership at our school and has enabled administrators and teachers to get together about something "real" in moving toward a common goal. In turn, teachers who have served on the initial planning group have been first to advocate similar decision-making structures and establish the expectation that teachers would be asked to stretch themselves into new roles. Moreover, as the planning group itself expanded, more and more teachers have been exposed to decision-making roles that develop the leadership skills they can put to good use in the school as a whole.

Professional Development for Student Achievement

Increasingly, professional development nationally is moving to emphasize student outcomes directed toward improved performance, not just greater job satisfaction. Teachers at Harrison now want to know if the new strategies are resulting in improved learning outcomes. Thus, teachers and administrators alike have developed a thirst for data they can use to affirm, modify, or reject new approaches.

Teachers as Instructional Leaders

Teachers are actively experimenting with a variety of ways to share their new knowledge and skills with colleagues. Many of the teachers on the subcommittee have become leaders in the school at large. As teachers have entered instructional leadership roles, they have spawned a variety of teacher networks to support the application of new teaching and learning strategies.

These networks institutionalize continual, learner-centered, school-based professional development for teachers who want to try new methodologies in specific content areas. Peer feedback and coaching available through the networks also encourage a confidence that supports risk taking.

With new skills, more and more teachers are ready to take on roles in other schools as teacher consultants, experienced in strategies such as cooperative learning. In fact, the expectation that teachers trained in new strategies will become staff developers for others is explicitly built into the school's effort. They feel that helping others will continue the learning process for Harrison teachers.

Sharing New Knowledge in Professional Settings

Teachers who have become instructional leaders at their schools have also increasingly taken on responsibilities for disseminating new knowledge and skills in professional settings outside the district, such as at regional and national conferences. Harrison teachers are workshop presenters for other restructuring schools. Teachers also assume responsibility for writing proposals to support their own ideas for classroom innovation.

AN IMPROVED PROFESSIONAL CLIMATE AT HARRISON HIGH SCHOOL

An important result of implementing the new approach is an improved professional climate at the school. One illustration is the teachers, administrators, guidance counselors, librarians, paraprofessionals, and other classified personnel who gather voluntarily after classes for their monthly "brown bag" reading group. In addition to discussing a common reading, they use these meetings to reflect on and discuss issues pertaining to school climate, community relations, and student performance. In this relaxed and friendly forum, staff members engage each other's ideas. In the process they design innovative approaches to improve student engagement and achievement in school and create incentives for student and staff improvement and parental involvement. Over refreshments, participants informally air grievances and voice concerns about schoolwide problems that go beyond the boundaries of the regular team. Thus, even an informal reading group becomes yet one more opportunity to strengthen staff interaction and to generate additional ideas to further improve the school.

This is but one example of ways in which teachers are increasingly interacting with one another to create a more collegial atmosphere. One teacher put it this way:

> The biggest change is that we can now look beyond the teacher contract for solutions to our problems. This is not something this faculty could have done three years ago when we were citing the contract provisions as a reason not to change.

Signs of student achievement gains, teacher professionalism and empowerment, and positive school climate at Harrison High School are cause for optimism about the potential for reform in high schools.

The restructuring effort at Harrison was not thought of as a professional development initiative at the outset, but over time it has evolved in that direction, as staff have tried various approaches to high school reform, listened to teachers about what worked, and refined the most successful programs. This evolution paralleled a growing realization among staff and administrators that if the school could not effect changes in teaching, they would not bring about desired changes in learning.

As teachers at Harrison have discovered their own direction, they have concluded that professional development must target school-based teams of teachers. When teams of teachers participate in intensive, long-term professional development with a focus on student achievement, these teachers develop a strong sense of camaraderie nurtured by a shared experience and goals. In turn, this camaraderie enhances the likelihood that teachers will actually use new strategies, not only to add life to their classrooms but to energize the entire school.

As a result, teachers who had grown cynical about professional development now see its power for reform in their school. If the catalytic role of the subcommittee and the involvement of teacher teams in planning and implementing professional development are strengths of the Harrison effort, they are also factors that principals must think about. Once there is a decision to involve and listen to teachers, there is little choice but to endorse professional development that is flexible, school-based, practical, and long term with follow-up.

A second issue for principals to consider is time for reform. School reform takes time! When reform revolves around professional development, schools face the challenges of devoting hours in the day to it from the limited amount of time available to teachers. For example, there is no one good, set time to do the training and planning that are needed. On one hand, after-school and summer workshops or institutes cause teachers to feel overextended and overworked. On the other hand, school-day programs present problems in finding substitutes.

The dilemma of finding time for reform becomes even more wrenching as teachers begin to execute broader roles and responsibilities inside and outside the school. For these new roles, they need time for up-front advance planning, reflection and in-depth conversations, and follow-up with and attention to individual teachers. Moreover, although many teachers want to respond to the higher expectations inherent in new roles, they do not want to abandon their classrooms entirely or sacrifice the follow-up component and the attention given to each individual teacher.

Principals face similar dilemmas in reallocating time for reform, both their own and that of the teachers. On one hand, principals must provide administrative support for reform by arranging for substitutes and scheduling time for teacher teams to be away from their classrooms. They must also support peer observations and coaching by creating time and space for regular discussion of classroom activities among teachers. On the other hand, principals also need opportunities to strengthen their own skills to keep pace with their teachers. Indeed, if principals do not understand the potential of new instructional strategies for improving achievement, they may fail to set aside time for the study groups and peer coaching that are essential to implementation.

Finding time for reform is an ongoing challenge at Harrison. The solutions devised by teachers facing this challenge across the country suggest that until additional resources and staff are available, schools can resolve this challenge in only temporary and piecemeal ways.

The restructuring initiative at Harrison has taken a direction that reflects more closely the knowledge of what constitutes effective practice at the high school level. Additionally, it is more compatible with the real needs of teachers and is more immediately applicable to classroom practice than the school's earlier efforts. In taking a direction that was clearly school-focused and developed with and for teachers who participated in both planning and implementing, the effort has begun to demonstrate the possibilities for comprehensive reform at Harrison. The teachers at Harrison would be the first to admit that the job of reforming the school in general and helping teachers retool for success in particular has just begun. At the same time, it is clear that the teachers at Harrison will never again confuse a four-hour workshop with meaningful professional growth.

References

Epstein, J.L., Lockard, B.L., and Dauber, S.L. (1991). Staff development for middle-school education. *Journal of Staff Development,* 12(1), 36–41.

Oakes, J. (1989). What educational indicators? The case for assessing the school context. *Educational Evaluation and Policy Analysis*, 11(2), 181–199.

9

Building the Capacity of Middle Managers: Assistant Principals and Department Heads

Every so often an event occurs that serves as an indicator of just how profound the impact of a restructuring effort can be on a school and its staff. One such event occurred recently when I was facilitating a workshop for high school middle-level managerial and supervisory staff (department heads and assistant principals) approximately six months after the onset of a restructuring initiative. Although workshop participants had requested the opportunity to meet and had planned an agenda that consisted primarily of skill-building experiences, something else took place. What began as a quiet discussion about revised job descriptions quickly gave way to a volcanic eruption of resentment over new responsibilities and altered working conditions at the school. Logic and reason were tossed to the wind as expressions of powerlessness, alienation, and exasperation built in intensity. The psychological fallout of the restructuring process was paralyzing the school's middle managers just when they were most needed. They felt that no one at the school was listening or helping.

The roles and responsibilities of middle-level school managers in restructuring high schools are undergoing such enormous and rapid change that staff members, such as the assistant or vice principal, department head, special education coordinator, or subject area supervisor, are reinventing their functions as they go. Right before their eyes, the traditional school hierarchy is disappearing and the clear distinctions of title and role are becoming blurred. Their traditional sources of power are changing, and their leverage with teachers has taken on new dimensions.

The cause is clear: the restructuring initiative. Participatory decision making means that middle-level managers must begin acting as a source of expertise to support these decisions. Some do not know how to do this. The result is a major shift in channels of activity, communication, and power at the school. Horizontal ties and cross-departmental collaboration are replacing the traditional compartmentalized and isolated subject area department organization of the traditional high school. Some schools are literally turning themselves inside out as teachers acquire the option of working as semi-autonomous and autonomous teams, with the authority of hiring outside consultant help if they wish, instead of utilizing the expertise of the department head or assistant principal.

Thus far, the educational community—including those involved in high school restructuring—has given little attention to the dramatic change that occurs in the working lives of those in middle-level management positions in restructuring high schools.

Most middle managers currently view the new work as loss of power because they have seen much of their authority as coming from hierarchical position. Now that everything is shifting, and roles, reporting lines, and job descriptions at the school are blurred, they are confused about their working relationships with other school staff members and with their colleagues. Most cannot imagine the ways in which the shift in roles and tasks can become an opportunity for greater personal influence and professional satisfaction.

The dynamics precipitated by high school restructuring are important for principals because they affect the way people do their jobs and, no less important, the way they view and work with the principal to achieve school goals. Restructuring messages get filtered through various interpreters as they move from a principal through assistant principal and department heads on their way to teachers. Even though a principal may communicate directly with teachers as often as possible, (s)he cannot be everywhere at once and must rely on middle-level managerial staff to transmit the message. The filtering of the restructuring message as it passes through the school's bureaucratic layers diffuses, and may even fundamentally change, the message if the principal and the department heads do not speak with one voice.

This chapter describes what happens to middle-level administrators and supervisors as high schools restructure to become more participatory, less bureaucratic, and more entrepreneurial. Principals and others should first understand why middle-level managers are struggling with the restructuring effort before they consider strategies for overcoming managers' resistance during the extended period of time required to bring about a new high school organization. The dilemmas and frustrations of the change process are illustrated below by the experiences of Ms. Helen Brandon, the English chairperson at a high school in New York State. The second half of the chapter provides principals and other school leaders with an approach toward winning the support of middle managers, while at the same time providing them with the skills they will need to work differently with their teachers. Finally, the chapter offers a model for empowering middle-level managers and keeping them engaged while pursuing the restructuring process. It also suggests strategies for reducing resistance, generating support for the change process, and helping vice principals and department chairpeople to see the restructuring process as a "win" rather than a loss.

THE OLD RULES ARE GONE, BUT WHERE ARE THE NEW ONES?

When Helen Brandon was promoted from security coordinator to English Department head, she felt she had acquired everything a teacher could want. Her title and rank were undeniable, and she was responsible for the English, speech, reading, and Chapter I programs with a staff of 37 teachers. She expected to bring about improvement in the classroom by instructing people in the right way to do things as she had when she was in charge of security. She developed a system for monitoring and overseeing what was going on in the classrooms. She saw to it that all teachers followed procedures and that books were distributed and collected on time. Helen Brandon provided the marching orders; the others followed. That was the way she wanted it.

Then the sand seemed to shift beneath her. The principal announced a restructuring initiative. "This will be a fundamental and comprehensive transformation of the way we work together and the way we are organized to teach our students," he said. Some people at the school, however, took the principal at his word and grasped the opportunity presented by the principal's announcement. They began to develop new approaches to instruction and school governance. There was to be a new faculty-dominated leadership council to oversee policy and management issues. There would now be autonomous teams of teachers working on interdisciplinary curriculum with a self-contained group of youngsters; each autonomous team would have control of their own staff development money and could hire whomever they wished to assist with program development. Before long, teachers were asking for assistance with change-related tasks that Brandon was not sure she could provide without first learning new skills.

Soon afterward, the principal met with Helen Brandon and her colleagues to state his expectations that they reinvent their roles to focus on support, facilitation, and encouragement for the newly empowered teachers. "The change process is fragile," he reminded them.

> I would like you to spend time with teachers to help hasten the pace of change. I want you to find out what the barriers are and help when bottlenecks develop. I would like you to let them know by words and deeds that they are now in charge of the school's future direction. Moreover I would like you to remove the word "no" from your vocabulary with teachers. Your job is to help them figure out how to implement their plans for their students.

To complicate matters further, Brandon, as part of a reorganization of responsibilities, was placed in charge of spearheading the development of the school's framework for the emerging role for technology. She felt that because she had no direct control over the data processing secretaries or the computer education teachers, she should not be held accountable for every facet of program design and implementation. After all, she had been a high school English teacher before anyone ever thought about computers in writing classes or computer-assisted instruction. What did she know about the development of technology at the school level? Not much. How could she be held accountable if she had no direct line of authority over the people involved in the effort? These were people she hardly knew, people in other departments, and she had never worked with them. However, she was to be fully accountable.

To make matters even worse, just as she was now forced to work across traditional departmental organizational lines, the people in her department were working with other department heads on projects such as special education inclusion and the development of learning outcome standards. The members of Brandon's department were often away on cross-department teams and task groups just when she wanted them to help develop the English program.

Brandon became increasingly distressed as the school's restructuring effort progressed. Instead of chairing a tidy compartmentalized unit—a real department—the way that her predecessor had, she now presided over what looked to her like chaos. The principal frequently reiterated his wish that the department heads join him in a "leadership rather than managerial" role, but Brandon did not know what that meant. How could she exert any type of leadership when she had obviously lost control over her subordinates' assignments and activities? She resented her perceived loss of position power at a time when the pressures were greater and unlike anything she had ever experienced. Brandon became increasingly bitter as time passed and her feelings of powerlessness grew.

FRUSTRATION AND ASTONISHMENT

The principal understood that restructuring meant change of roles, relationships, and responsibilities of every stakeholder group in the school. His goal, insofar as the department heads were concerned, was to transform a tradition-bound organization divided along subject area lines into one focused on facilitation and support, a customer orientation, significantly higher levels of performance, and the capability of continuous improvement of organizational processes.

The principal began to notice, however, that along the way the school's restructuring caused some unusual, unanticipated side effects on the ability of department heads to work. Different areas of responsibility overlapped. Teachers found it advantageous to request classroom space nearer to others working on the same team, even if it meant separating themselves from their own subject department members. Most unusual of all, task groups and project teams consisting primarily of teachers had a great deal of contact directly with the principal.

The principal became increasingly despondent during the grueling weekly meetings with Brandon and her colleagues. Each session was filled with a barrage of their complaints. They could not continue with their traditional tasks and also invent new ones at the same time. They did not always know what their teachers were doing, but they still believed they ought to know. They no longer had sole input into staff performance appraisals; other people had a voice as well, and some of them knew more about teachers' activities.

At first the principal thought that perhaps the department heads' upset and resistance was just the normal noise associated with any change. Then, over time, he began to realize that something more profound was going on. The school's restructuring initiative was challenging people's traditional notions about their roles and power. Moreover, the changes were affecting feelings of self-worth. He began to understand that he was leading people into a world in which the old rules no longer applied and the new rules had not been written.

UNDERSTANDING THE NEW ORGANIZATIONAL DYNAMICS IN A RESTRUCTURING HIGH SCHOOL

Helen Brandon and the principal had very different views about the changing nature of the administration's role in the newly reorganized school. However hard it is for principals to remake strategy and structure, they themselves will, in all likelihood, retain their identity, status, and sense of control. For those below them, in this case assistant principals and department heads, change is often much harder. Had the principal been able to anticipate the real meaning of the change process on the school's middle-level managerial staff, he could have broken down the impact into four areas:

1. There are an increasing number and variety of channels in the school for initiating action and exerting influence.

2. Primary working relationships are shifting from the vertical to the horizontal, from the traditional hierarchy to networks of teacher teams.

3. The distinction between job titles and status at the school is diminishing, especially in regard to control over the assignments of teachers and classified staff.

4. Relationships among subject area departments are increasingly important as sources of power and influence.

It became obvious to the principal that he had to find new ways to help the middle-level managers confront the changes in their own bases of power and provide them with a framework for finding their place in the new organization. After all, he relied on them to bring the teachers along.

The changes in roles that accompany a fundamental restructuring can be frightening for people like Helen Brandon who were trained to know their place, to follow orders, and to do things by the rules. The rules are gone. In the new order of things at the school, all staff members must learn to operate without the crutch of hierarchy and have only themselves to rely on. Teachers are encouraged to think for themselves, and department heads and assistant principals have to learn to work synergistically with others. Success now depends on figuring out whose collaboration is needed to act on good ideas. In short, the new work implies very different ways of obtaining and using power and influence.

Hierarchical organizations in many restructuring schools are not only flatter, but they also have many more channels for action. Interdisciplinary projects, joint ventures with other agencies, collaboration with parent and community groups, and activities outside the mainstream reporting lines contravene the traditional organization chart and ignore the chain of command.

The existence of new channels for action has several important implications. For one thing, they create more potential centers of power in the school. As the ways to initiate action increase, the ability to command diminishes. Alternative paths of communication and access to resources inside and outside the school erode the authority of those in the chain of command. Simply put, the opportunity for greater flexibility undermines the traditional school hierarchy. As more and more action takes place in these new channels, the tasks that take place within the traditional subject area departments decline in significance (Lawler, 1987).

In the traditional high school organization, rank and formal structure used to limit people's access to information and, consequently, to the power that information provides. Information was often confined to the few authorized individuals (usually the principal, the vice principals, and heads of departments) who could communicate between departments and with outside agencies and individuals.

It was traditionally the job of these department heads and other administrators to survey the terrain for new ideas and resources. In a restructuring high school, this kind of environmental scanning is now an important part of everyone's job at every level of the school organization. The environment to be scanned includes many potential outside partners, including the private sector. At the same time, all staff members are encouraged to think about what they know that might have value elsewhere. It is not unusual to find security or guidance personnel working with teacher teams to develop interdisciplinary units of instruction that involve other classifications of staff in the classroom activities.

Every member of the school staff must think cross-functionally because everyone has to play a role in dealing with schoolwide as well as departmental problems. In fact, in the new high school organization, the ability of department heads to get tasks accomplished depends more on the number of team networks in which they are involved than on their position in the hierarchy. This new strategic and cross-functional collaborative role is particularly important as middle-level managers shift their roles to become integrators and facilitators, not watchdogs and interventionists. They need to see that their services justify them to the other people in the school, that they are literally competing with outside service providers. For example, one district in Canada recently placed all central office personnel, with the exception of the superintendent, on a pay-as-you-go basis. Schools can hire central office consultants at set per-hour fees, or, if they wish, they can contract with private consultants or consulting agencies. Now these people must prove to the satisfaction of schools that the services they provide have value. They can now compete with school department heads.

As school managers spend more time working across boundaries with peers and other school staff members over whom they have no direct control, their interpersonal and negotiating skills become essential assets. Power evolves from personal strengths, not from organizational structure. At the same time, more staff members at more levels are active in the kind of external relationships that only the principal or selected administrators or supervisors were previously authorized to conduct (Kanter, 1989).

In the cross-department teams and task groups, staff members become more personally exposed. Since these ventures often bring together people from different professional communities, good deal-making depends on the capacity to step into other people's shoes and appreciate their goals in order to work together effectively. As one social studies department head stated after a few months of working as a member of a cross-department task group,

> I'm gaining experience anticipating the reactions and responses of the other people on my team. While we still occasionally disagree about important issues, we no longer have the destructive conflicts that erupted during our first few meetings. Before I present the social studies point of view, I'm learning to ask myself what others will say. Sometimes I alter my proposal before I present it.

An increase in the number of channels for contact means greater opportunities for people with ideas to stimulate action. Innovative suggestions for resolving schoolwide operational and managerial problems blossom among school staff members who traditionally felt it was their obligation to carry out orders and implement the ideas of others. Department heads who begin spending more time serving on cross-department task forces are forced, because of lack of time, to delegate more responsibility to teachers and others who, over time, feel greater authority to chart their own direction. However, teachers charting their own direction have implications for the principal. When task force reports are presented to the principal, they frequently bypass the chain of command: they are not passed through the traditional management levels, first to department heads, then to assistant principal, and finally to the principal.

The principal who receives a report that did not trickle up through the traditional hierarchical channels is suddenly confronted with a new task. He now has to juggle different constituencies rather than control a set of subordinates. Department heads, in particular, feel bypassed and find reason to oppose change efforts that reduce their ability to work independently of others in the school.

The principal's task in such instances is to work with everyone inside and outside the school to get people past power and turf issues. This makes it possible to build a network of cooperative relationships among all those people and groups that have something to contribute to the implementation of an action plan proposed by a task force report (Walton, 1985). The principal at Helen Brandon's school observed that

> It's been much harder to gain consensus in a restructuring high school. More people and more groups speak up. It takes a great deal of balancing. Knitting together a variety of stakeholder groups is very different from controlling the traditional high school bureaucracy. The new way gets more done, but it also takes more time.

The restructuring process clearly places great additional burdens on the principal during the organizational transition, as discussed in Chapters 7 and 8 with the principals at Beacon High School and the two Minneapolis high schools. The new organization exists on a chart in name only and is not really functional. Although the old organization no longer exists on paper, it continues to haunt the minds, habits, and performance of staff.

Understanding the topsy-turvy world of the middle manager in restructuring schools is one thing; making them comfortable in a rapidly changing organization is quite another. As in the example above, a participatory decision-making structure, new conceptions of school governance and organization, changing roles for teachers and other staff members, and the greater involvement of parents and community turn the world of the middle manager upside-down and inside-out.

To successfully apply a new and different participatory leadership model, middle-level school administrators and supervisors must adopt a new management and supervisory style that is consistent with the way the principal and the district are now working. As with people in other job titles, principals must play a major role in helping these people become comfortable in the evolving organization. This is best done through experiencing a new way of working, having a support system to encourage further steps, and having the time to reflect upon new practice. People frequently have trouble imagining what new roles and relationships and ways of working will look and feel like before they experience them. Lists of new responsibilities prepared at workshops or retreats tend to overwhelm people who cannot yet see a place for themselves in the new organization.

How critical is it for principals to bring these middle managers along and to win their support? It is the highest priority. Teachers cannot become convinced that there is real commitment among the school administrators to making collaborative decision making work if different members of the administrative and supervisory team give mixed messages or are inconsistent in their responses. These mixed messages interfere with the development of higher levels of trust in the school and slow down the change process. As at Beacon High School (in Chapter 8), during the change process teachers scrutinize every move made by administrators and supervisors. They search for the slightest indication of lack of sincerity. Middle-level administrators and supervisors will be responsive to new ways of working only if they know they have the wholehearted support and encouragement of the principal.

Providing them with support does not have to become a time-consuming enterprise that is separate from the principal's regular work in supporting the change process. It can be built right into the principal's overall plan for moving the restructuring agenda. Multiple goals can be accomplished at once. For example, one way to build staff confidence with decision making, provide assistant principals and department heads with experience, and move the school forward instructionally is to develop a framework that represents a new way of working in which everybody in the school is dealing with real school problems and issues. The practical insights gained from successfully implementing this approach can be particularly useful to principals who are aware that they can alter the traditional supervisory and managerial format by creating new problem-solving structures in the school, but thus far have only heard and seen theoretical constructs and wonder what such an effort can look like in actual practice.

Participatory concepts utilizing the leadership role of department heads were combined and applied at Lane, as described in Chapter 3, in an attempt to build supervisor confidence with new strategies and techniques. The hope was that the approach would help them work across department lines to develop the interdisciplinary Career Institutes, an important component of the redesign plan. It did not work for a number of reasons that are discussed later. Since that time, I have had the opportunity to experiment with the approach at other restructuring high schools. The experiences of one of those schools in New York State is described below.

Wheaton High School (a real school with a changed name) is a suburban school serving 2000 students. Wheaton launched its restructuring effort two years ago. Nothing like it has ever been tried before at this school, which is still traditionally organized with the usual subject area departments. The principal works with eight department heads and two assistant principals. The department chairmen—and they are all men—like their counterparts across the nation, see their responsibilities as tending to the needs of teachers within their jurisdiction.

THE IMPORTANCE OF TOP MANAGEMENT SUPPORT

The first priority in getting such an effort underway at Wheaton was to enlist the interest, or at least the minimal (however grudging) cooperation, of the vice principals and department heads. The appeal was direct and truthful. The principal told them that he was counting on them, that they were members of the same team no matter what happened, and that he needed their leadership exercised in new ways in order to make a success of the school's new participatory decision-making framework. Without their support, he said, no effort to alter the school's governance, planning, and management structure could ever succeed.

The goals and objectives of the problem-solving program, the theoretical background, and practical strategies for involving teachers in decision making were introduced to the school's department heads at a retreat, where they had time to reflect upon the outlines of the plan and make modifications in those areas where they were not yet comfortable. The real heart of the program was a continuous cycle of meetings, initially involving teachers from each subject area and their immediate supervisors. During each meeting, the group would identify organizational or institutional problems, assign responsibility for implementing proposed solutions to one or more members of the group, and hear reports from members about progress in addressing issues identified in earlier meetings.

To get this type of department problem-solving process off the ground, department heads and middle-level administrators must be willing to accept and use a new managerial style, and teachers must accept a considerable amount of responsibility that they might not have had before. These role changes, as learned in Chapter 2, are often difficult to make, and progress may initially be slow. One way to build support for the process is to provide teachers with a vision of how the model can work by setting up a pilot program. One of the first tasks taken on at Wheaton was to help department heads get comfortable with the new approach. A major component of this task was a reeducation and retraining program, designed by the department heads, to equip them with concepts of leadership, new facilitative and other process skills, and strategies to help them and the teachers in each of their departments hold effective problem-identification sessions. Since the actual process was to be entrusted to department heads, it was essential to focus on behavioral details such as leadership methods suitable for use in working with teacher groups, a skill most lacked when the program began.

Many hours were spent at these workshops, as participants compared and contrasted the roles of the assistant principal and department head in the traditionally organized high school with the new collaborative facilitative style sought in a school undergoing restructuring. For example, in the traditional role, the department head sets goals for subordinates, defines standards, and monitors performance. In the new role, (s)he participates with staff members in solving problems and setting goals and works with teachers to set up a process by which they can evaluate their own performance.

For some department heads and assistant principals who were long comfortable in tradition-bound schools, this new style was hard to accept; it required an about-face on their long-standing attitudes toward their work and the people they worked with. Some department heads rejected collaborative decision making because it seemed to threaten them personally. Those who were reluctant to accept the general idea of a collaborative decision-making model and were unable to alter their attitudes usually stalled the progress at the workshops with quibbles and complaints that closed off discussion and group explorations.

The importance of establishing a positive approach cannot be overemphasized. For example, the chairman of one department was so impressed by the enthusiastic reports he heard about the pilot project that he immediately began on his own to conduct meetings to set goals and solve problems, without waiting for his colleagues. Much less successful was the chairman of a second department, who admitted that he considered teacher involvement in decision making about policy, operational, and instructional issues to be a worthless enterprise. The question-and-answer approach he used in his department meetings was not suitable for problem identification, and his lack of understanding was obvious in such questions as "Are there any more gripes?" Furthermore, he believed that teachers in his department were only interested in dealing with issues that took place inside the classroom walls. In fact, he believed that was the way it ought to be. He felt that their opinions would intrude on his administrative and supervisory prerogatives and that the teachers would resent any additional work arising out of the new program. A third department head gave his teachers a multiple choice questionnaire as a substitute for a discussion at a meeting. Needless to say, he was no more successful than the second department head.

After the initial retreat, the principal began to work with three small groups of department heads on a regular basis, giving them in-depth training in leading problem-solving groups and alerting them to potential pitfalls. The principal made an attempt to formalize a leadership training program by scheduling these workshops to take place weekly. The chairmen, however, did not respond to settings in which they were formal "learners." Informal sessions with individual supervisors worked out better.

The positive feelings voiced by those who participated in the pilot program convinced the principal that a schoolwide effort was worthwhile. The program's potential for improving the school's learning climate while reducing teacher and middle manager alienation and its surface symptoms (e.g., burnout, early retirement) prompted him to recommend that the effort become a part of the citywide staff development and training initiative for administrators and supervisors. This enabled the program to receive district funds permitting the hiring of outside consultants to assist the principal in the training process.

PROMOTING A NEW MANAGERIAL STYLE

An important phase of implementation was the reeducating and retraining of subject area department heads to equip them to hold their issue-identification and problem-solving meetings with their departments. The training program designed for the department heads included a deeper exploration of the skills and experiences initially introduced at the retreat. Since the actual conduct of the project was to be entrusted to the department heads, they were now offered more specific strategies, such as leadership methods that are suitable for problem-solving conferences.

Before long, teachers in different departments were grappling with important issues. In one instance, a math teacher suggested to other department members that the more experienced teachers teach the ninth grade classes. Until this time, veteran teachers had traditionally been assigned senior classes, and those with least experience had been given ninth grade classes, which were often more difficult to teach. The department head asked the group to discuss the issues and personal feelings involved in altering the system of assigning classes. After the discussion, the department head explained the equity protection built into the class assignment system. Teachers soon realized that any new policy would require much thought and planning. Moreover, the issue crossed the boundary of the math department: it was a schoolwide issue. A subcommittee was formed to meet with the principal. It advocated for the convening of a task force consisting of people from different departments to develop a new policy. The math teachers were subsequently very effective. They met every two weeks for three months and identified and solved a variety of problems that had plagued the department for years.

The lesson for department heads and other supervisors and administrators is that they must focus the group's attention on problems its members can help solve. It is all too easy to let meetings get sidetracked into unprofitable discussions or a gripe session. At the initial stages, group members are likely to divert the attention of the group by citing worst-case scenarios as reasons for not following one or another approach. The minute an idea is presented, they can be counted on to present the "what if" response. In such situations, it makes sense to alert the entire group to what the nay-sayers are doing. Principals can state clearly:

> When ideas requiring substantial change and risk are presented, our tendency is to focus on the most extreme examples of what could go wrong. I think that we ought to prepare for what could go wrong; however, it makes more sense for us at this point to devote our attention to the potential of the idea and then build in the protections for reasonable risks. We can never prepare for every eventuality. And, by the way, current practice doesn't make provision for every eventuality. Things go wrong now. If the new idea is at least as good as what we are doing now, we ought to try it.

Once a department head became committed to collaborative decision making and problem solving and developed a sense for opportunities and pitfalls, the principal and the individual worked together to set up a program, starting with a format for the initial meeting with teachers. It was the one-on-one meetings between principal and supervisor that guided and molded the process.

THE FIRST MEETING WITH TEACHERS

The first meeting for problem identification is the most critical part of the effort, as it brings the administrator or supervisor face to face with the entire group, in this case, the subject area department. For some at Wheaton, this was the first attempt at interacting with the people with whom they worked in a collegial way. The successful implementation of this part of the effort required the following guidelines:

1. The principal should pave the way for the middle-level manager who will work directly with the group.

    The principal began this meeting by describing the effort as a component of the school's restructuring initiative and how the school could be enriched by broadening the problem-solving and decision-making processes. He emphasized the opportunity within the new framework for attaining individual as well as schoolwide goals. The principal pointed out that often the real expert at identifying and solving problems connected with teaching was the person closest to the scene—the teacher. The principal addressed those faculty members who were skeptical of the administration's commitment to improving teaching and learning by involving teachers in genuine decision making. For example, he stated:

> Many of you—especially long-term faculty members—have seen school improvement programs come and go over the years. Some of you, no doubt, may be saying to yourselves "Here it comes again," or "What did he say the improvement program or the 'magic bullet' will be called this time?" Well, this time, we're really serious about a new approach and we want to see it work. We're going to devote ourselves to it. But you're the ones that have to give it a chance to work. You will have to see whether we are serious by challenging us each time there is an inconsistency or we fall back into old ways. This is hard work and we will make mistakes and I would like us to help each other through the errors.

2. The department head should help the group identify problems and assign responsibility for solving them.

The meeting was then turned over to the department head, who asked, "What problems do you have that make it difficult to succeed with your students?" Typically, at this point, there was a protracted silence. Prior to the meeting, the principal had advised the department head not to break the anticipated silence, even though (s)he felt quite tense in the role of group leader. Eventually some group members would describe what they felt were their major problems. When this happened, the department head listed them on a flip chart, avoiding discussion other than that needed for clarification.

Groups tend to deal initially with "safe" factors, or what Hertzberg (1966) termed "hygiene" factors (heat, light, ventilation, cleanliness, and textbooks). In general, groups with lower morale spent more time on these items than groups with higher morale. After 30 minutes, most groups at Wheaton High School had moved the discussion away from these items and toward issues more directly related to teaching, such as developing classroom policy and initiating new instructional programs. Some groups at Lane, however, remained on "safe" topics throughout the term. One group discussed noise in the street (always a nuisance, but once taken care of hardly worth seven or eight conversations) for an entire year. At each meeting, they listened to a report on the noise situation. They assessed the decibel level when windows were shut, when they were open, in good weather, when it was raining, when a security guard was on patrol, and when students were on their lunch break and unsupervised. Noise, some said, was the reason they gave students busywork.

Principals would be well advised not to spend an inordinate amount of time on groups such as this. Their time is better spent on those groups that are more responsive to the concept of group decision making on behalf of improving teaching and learning.

Some department heads encouraged their groups to discuss teaching-related items immediately by specifying problem areas for group concentration. The latter approach worked best in the career, trade, business, and technical departments, where most teachers had previously held blue-collar jobs.

Shortly before the first meeting was scheduled to end, or when the group felt it had pinpointed an adequate number of the key problems, department heads asked that volunteers offer possible solutions. Because it is often difficult to get volunteers, supervisors sometimes suggested assignments as a last resort. To begin to build trust and promote participation, the supervisors would take responsibility for solving those problems needing administrative resources. Initially, meetings ended with scheduling a date for the second meeting. Most groups wanted two to three weeks to work on their initial problem-solving assignments.

3. Between meetings, those responsible for solving the problem should work on its solution.

Sometimes problems can be solved as soon as they are raised. This is generally not the case for issues related to curriculum and instruction, which require more intensive exploration, planning, and discussion. Frequently, coordination with other school departments, such as programming and guidance, are needed. In some cases, it is unwise for the department to proceed on its own; it should collaborate with other departments.

Since most teachers are accustomed to working in isolation and being directed by a vice principal, department head, or other manager, they rarely, at first, take the initiative to deal with broad, schoolwide organizational issues. Especially at the outset, department heads should follow up on assignments between meetings in informal discussions and casual meetings with teachers. They should use the model developed by the principal: working one on one with the department head in his effort to create comfort with the process. In those instances in which the department head failed to work one on one with group members in such areas as fact finding or developing connections with other administrators, some groups came to the second meeting equipped only to raise additional problems. They were stalled because they had not yet clarified the problems and issues identified in the first meeting. Thus, it is important for supervisors to hold short but frequent scheduled and unscheduled meetings to review progress with those responsible for accomplishing tasks.

In addition, department heads must successfully resolve the problems they agreed to handle. By doing so from the beginning, they show that they are serious about collaboration and wanting to become a contributing member of the group. When confronted with evidence of procrastination, for example, some teachers readily admitted they were dragging their heels because they did not yet believe their department head would follow through on his own assignments.

Another pitfall is the teachers' uncertainty about others' authority and responsibility in the changing school organization. When grappling with a problem, they are often afraid of stepping on the toes of those who have traditionally handled it: the principal, assistant principal, and other department heads. Some groups overcame this hurdle, and simultaneously strengthened their own positions, by integrating representatives of the school administration into the problem-solving team or planning group as needed.

FOLLOWING UP: MEETING II

Department heads usually opened the second meeting by summarizing the problems identified in the first meeting. They candidly reported on the status of the issues they had taken responsibility for, emphasizing the action they took and the results of that action. Their report used criteria that the group understood and that were consistent with the criteria the group was developing for self-evaluation. It was noted in the minutes or decision sheet if action was not taken.

Next, department heads asked for progress reports from group participants. Without such reports, people would feel little was being accomplished or that their accomplishments were not being recognized. Hence, such reports should be faithfully made, even if the information contained is somewhat complicated. If the report includes topics such as progress on a component of the school's restructuring, they should be tied to the agreed-upon goals for the group. Department heads should also ensure that relevant data are updated on a periodic basis and disseminated to group members in a timely manner.

GOAL SETTING

When groups have reached the point at which they can assess the impact of their actions, they are ready to set their own short- and long-term goals. By the second meeting, some department groups were at this level. It took other groups six months to arrive at this level; some never got there.

For example, one group of art teachers set a goal of decreasing the number of students who failed courses because of absence. After six months, they became discouraged when the figures had not improved appreciably. They felt they had wasted great time and energy in trying to improve the passing percentages. Analysis of the situation by the principal and the department head helped the teachers recognize that their goal was long-term and difficult to accomplish, given the school's social setting and the complexity of the reasons for pupil absences. However, the art teachers had unknowingly affected two other variables, which were pointed out by the department head. Class cutting had decreased, and the number of high-risk students attending class on a more regular basis increased. By initially selecting a measure over which they had little control, the group members felt frustrated and were on the verge of disbanding, even though their efforts had resulted in substantial improvement in different areas. Once they recognized both their success and error, the group moved ahead to successful goal setting.

CONTINUING THE CYCLE

In Meeting II and every meeting thereafter, department groups identified new problems and kept track of the success of their solutions and planning processes. This approach sets up a continuous cycle of activity that incorporates some of the managerial work of the traditional supervisor with a collaborative decision-making style that includes shared management responsibilities, both on the part of the department head and on the part of the teachers.

Figure 9.1 contrasts these two styles graphically. Note that the traditional style explicitly shows leadership as a separate entity. In a collaborative framework, leadership is absorbed into the work cycle itself. Thus, unlike the traditional, linear approach, the continuous cycle described in this chapter is not mechanistic or formalistic; rather, it is a fluid and dynamic approach that each department or other group can mold to suit its needs.

To illustrate this point, two groups at Wheaton High School scheduled meetings only when they felt there were enough problems to warrant it, and others scheduled meetings to take place at regular intervals. In either case, meetings were held less frequently as time passed because the team had developed enough candor and canniness to hone in on its "real" problems and quickly establish meaningful criteria and goals. In addition, faculty members felt that over time there were fewer key problems to address.

Another important factor was at play. At Wheaton, teachers said that progress in the school's restructuring meant that the school's department organization was being replaced by semi-autonomous clusters of "houses" or self-contained mini-schools. These, rather than subject area departments, became the unit of primary identification for teachers. Since houses developed their own problem-solving cycle of meetings, there was soon no real need for the department groupings as problem-solving units.

Two departments never attained this continuous cycle and discontinued the process for different reasons. One department attained its initial goals after just a few meetings, and the department head saw no need to continue. It may have been that the scope of the goals was too limited. It also may have been due to the way the

---

FIGURE 9.1 TRADITIONAL VERSUS COLLABORATIVE STYLES

In the traditional style, the supervisor	In the collaborative style, the supervisor
Defines the goals and the basic methods for achieving them to subordinates; defines the standards for quality and for results.	Works with subordinates to identify and resolve teacher-related problems; guides and assists them in setting the standard and goals.
Uses forceful leadership and persuasion to move or push subordinates ahead.	Helps subordinates set challenging goals for themselves by channeling and molding their own motivation.
Checks up on subordinates' performance and evaluates it; judges a performance as an achievement or a failure.	Educates subordinates to check on their own performance and promotes self-evaluation; encourages their achievements and counsels them on how to learn from their failures.
Develops subordinates' abilities and prepares the successful ones for promotion or alternate assignment.	Provides opportunities for subordinates to pursue and move into areas of growth and development.

---

department head discontinued the process. One supervisor at Wheaton became disillusioned after the second meeting when the group concentrated on maintenance items or only discussed problems arising in other departments. The pressure of responsibilities for extracurricular activities at Wheaton High School kept another department from meeting on a continuing basis, although this group accomplished its goals.

Other groups established a continuous cycle of the problem-solving meetings. Where this happened, the candor and openness of the group members increased. For example, members of one group that had been meeting for eight months confronted the department head with the statement that they could do a more effective job of scheduling coverage for absent teachers than he, since they could pool information and knew which teachers enjoyed the additional assignment or wanted to earn extra money.

CONCLUSION

Five years of work using this model with 300 teachers at Lane supported the general soundness of problem solving within a collaborative supervisory framework. The program was not a complete success; it followed an all-or-nothing pattern. Departments that made gains often did so in spectacular fashion; those that failed usually did so in less than three months.

Greater success was achieved at Wheaton. First, the department heads displayed a greater willingness to experiment with new approaches. Second, teachers in the department groups were ready to transfer primary affiliation to cross-department groups. Third, they were able to establish relationships with the new teacher clusters and house units. In other words, they made a successful transition by carving out a new and significant role for themselves in the new organization. Department heads at Lane were unable to make this transition.

There are a number of lessons to be learned from the experience of both schools. First, having the principal work with assistant principals as the school's top managers helped everyone fully understand the different concepts and techniques. This proved to be a vital step, not only in the assistant principals' understanding of the concepts, but also in earning their commitment to the program. Once the assistant principals realized that this type of effort resulted not only in increased job satisfaction but also in increased willingness of teachers to get involved with educational innovation, they generally endorsed the program, conveyed their support to the department heads, and provided the administrative wherewithal for the effort to succeed.

Second, it is critical to choose the right people for training. The principals worked individually and in groups with the department heads who conducted the problem-identification and problem-solving sessions with teachers. Given their central roles, the success of the program depended on the attitudes and behavior of the supervisory staff. Those with more traditional outlooks on their responsibilities found the collaborative style of group work onerous and rejected it, resulting in disappointment for themselves and their teachers. Such failures dealt a setback to the schoolwide restructuring effort. Others experimented with the process. Some found the experience personally rewarding. Success was much greater with the latter two groups.

Third, when meeting with teachers, it was important for the department heads to set the stage for involvement by explaining the philosophical approach and the strategy for the effort, its potential, and how it would work. They stressed the teachers' role in identifying problems by asking them to remember that they knew the problems associated with their teaching better than anyone in the school because they were closer to those problems, that they were relied on to identify the problems and issues, and that everyone would work together in solving them.

The supervisors also informed teachers of the new commitment of the school administration to expand the decision-making process. This is a very important point. Teachers will be mystified if a department head suddenly does an about-face in his or her approach toward people in the department. The motivations for that change will become suspect—it will perhaps be seen as a "hidden agenda"—unless the department head is forthcoming with information and clear about his or her goals.

As the groups became increasingly adept at problem identification and the development of approaches for dealing with them, they identified additional teaching-related problems, set goals, probed for solutions, and achieved their goals. Department heads and teachers reported that morale improved. Concomitantly, there was a significant increase in the number of new instructional efforts. It seemed as if the effective groups became self-motivating, taking on more and more managerial functions as they evolved a continuous cycle of activity.

Naturally, there are difficulties inherent in this new managerial approach to school-based collaboration and planning. The most important problem was resistance by department heads, especially during the early phases of the effort. Also, some problems have no immediate solutions, e.g., the limitation on the use of federal funds targeted toward students with special educational needs. Given the net gain in terms of individual and organizational improvement and the popularity of the effort with teachers, supervisors, and administrators, these problems were not enough to stymie the program at either school where it was tried. Instead, it was seen as purposeful and effective in solving school-based problems. It helped teachers feel better and more confident about their role in school decision making. It also won the support of the assistant principals and department heads. It gave them the capacity and the skills needed to play a leadership role in the school's restructuring effort. They found their place in the organization that was being created, and they were able to contribute in bringing it about.

The ingredients for success are easy to list. The principal enhances the chances for success if he or she obtains the commitment of the other members of the administrative team to the concept of a collaborative and inclusive management style. The members of the school's administrative team must then obtain the commitment of department heads and program coordinators. Together, the principal and his or her administrative team must devote the time necessary to educate supervisory and managerial staff in collaborative management practices. The administrative team must also help staff to figure out how to get the teachers started on a continuous cycle of problem-solving and goal-setting meetings.

Department heads or program coordinators, in turn, must structure group meetings and individual conferences to encourage teachers to help identify problems and then consider approaches and solutions, record successes and improvements, and set realistic departmental goals. Other important tasks include:

1. Making sure that in each case the whole problem is solved

2. Making certain that the goals set are both attainable and challenging

3. Working with teachers to develop meaningful criteria for measuring its impact

4. Reporting conscientiously on their own projects

5. Making sure that the teachers report on their projects as soon as possible

Ingredients for failure include:

1. Emphasizing short-term factors to measure program or planning effectiveness (this leads to concentration on short-term goals and neglect of the school's deeper and more complex problems)

2. Not immediately countering staff views that the new process is "just another program" that will soon pass

3. Superficially training supervisors

4. Concentrating on problems over which the team has no control, e.g., school board policy

5. Setting goals that are unattainable in the near future, given the resources and authority available

6. Not intervening to stop early disappointments from discouraging teachers

The real effect of the approach discussed in this chapter can best be understood by the following incident. Two teachers were overheard talking in the hall. One, a member of a group in which the process was successful, described the great involvement of teachers in the collaborative problem-solving process to a second teacher from a group in which the program was not working. The second teacher responded:

> You may not be turning the school into St. Augustine's *City of God* but you're bringing about small improvements and planning even bigger ones. More important, you're excited about your job and you enjoy coming to work again. At the very least, supervisors and teachers are now treating each other like professionals.

For some schools with a history of consensual decision making, a restructuring initiative is the logical next step in the maturation process. It continues the school's commitment to quality comprehensive education for all students by maximizing the opportunity for teachers and school administrators to participate more fully in educational decisions. For other schools, it requires no less than a philosophical about-face in the way business is conducted. The old adage that the greater the change, the greater the support needed certainly applies in this case.

Did Helen Brandon finally change her ways? It's not certain. When last heard from, she was still struggling. None of this is easy. Although high school administrative and supervisory staff have acted in the past to preserve the power of the bureaucracy, they have the capacity to reverse course and work collaboratively with teachers and the principal to create the kind of school that works better for all who work and learn within its walls.

References

Hertzberg, F. (1966). *Work and the Nature of Man.* Cleveland, Ohio: The World Publishing Company.

Kanter, R.M. (1989). The new managerial work. *Harvard Business Review,* 67(6), 85–92.

Lawler, E.E. (1987). Transformations from control to involvement. In R.H. Kilmahn, T.J. Covin, et al. (Eds.), *Corporate Transformation.* San Francisco: Jossey-Bass.

Walton, R.E. (1985). From control to commitment in the workplace. *Harvard Business Review,* 63, 76–84.

10 Building New Relationships with Teachers: Listening, Problem Solving, and Communicating Tools to Facilitate the Change Process

A colleague recently remarked that the restructuring initiative at her high school was a cupful of agony and a teaspoonful of ecstasy. For teachers, restructuring can be an opening to try out new ideas, or it can be an unwelcome disruption of well-seasoned and comfortable practices. It can provide professional growth opportunities, but it can also impose yet more work in an already overloaded and stressful workday. It can engender exhilarating exchanges of new ideas and suggestions or instigate endless, enervating meetings that accomplish little or nothing. It can liberate teachers' hopes and dreams and creativity or stifle their spirits and create a siege mentality that reduces the likelihood of reform.

Any restructuring effort worth the name is usually not one or the other, but a combination of both positive and negative elements. The extent to which it becomes a positive force in the lives of teachers depends to a great extent on how well the change process is managed, primarily by the principal, but also by the rest of the administrative team and the teacher leadership. These leaders are in a position to guide the progress of the entire effort by the approach they employ to build new and more productive working relationships with the teaching staff. Teachers on school leadership teams have the mistaken notion that only principals have to work hard at relationship building. They are wrong. A restructuring effort rebuilds not only the school, but many of the interpersonal relationships within it: persons on both sides of the relationship must contribute to its reconstruction.

High school teachers are neither the universally conservative obstacle to change that many principals and school reformers identify, nor are they the potential revolutionaries and anarchists who are eager to change for the sake of change, about whom the public and nervous school board members frequently worry. As with any large and diverse group, it is dangerous to lump them together with a single characterization. Some of them will almost always resist change, some of them will almost always be eager to try new things, and some of them will be cautious and hesitant about attempts to explore new ways of working before deciding whether to join in or hold back. Some in each group will approach change thoughtfully, some will be mindless in resisting a new effort, and others will be equally mindless in jumping on board a new venture—they will try anything that is different. No matter how obviously advantageous a particular reform might be, there will be those who will find a personal reason to oppose it. At one school, a proposal for teaming was defeated by the leadership council because it interfered with the lunchtime bridge and canasta groupings. Characterizing any particular group or subgroup within a school as "opponents" or "resistors" places them in permanent opposition, freezes political lines in the school, and reduces the likelihood of winning them over at any point in the future.

How flexible scheduling, interdisciplinary instruction, teamed heterogeneous groups, and such changes eventually affect students depends in large part on the lenses teachers use to view those changes and how teachers translate their ideas into daily practice. The issue is not simply whether or not a reform will be implemented. It is, rather, what form the reform will actually take in the classroom and what its impact on the teacher–student relationship will be. High school restructuring cannot be managed effectively without paying attention to the cauldron of beliefs and values into which change efforts are being mixed.

How can leaders of restructuring schools acquire deeper knowledge about the values and beliefs of the teaching staff? Once they know what these values and beliefs are, how can they work more effectively as they facilitate the overall change process at the school? An added question is how leaders can then convey to a faculty through their words and actions their own values, beliefs, thoughts, and ideas about the future of the school.

Even in advanced restructuring districts where the professionalization of teaching ranks as a priority, high school teachers are for the most part marginal participants in overall discussions about restructuring that take place at the system level. In many places, they are not involved at all. To include a teacher or union representative on a districtwide committee does not include teachers in an important way. Moreover, although some teachers are becoming empowered to rearrange the way things are in their particular school settings, they are not empowered to rearrange the way things are at the system level, even those events that directly affect the school and their working lives.

There are some district officials at every level, on the other hand, who feel no compunction about making extensive changes in schools. They frequently talk about "their" schools as if they own them and make decisions without consulting anyone who works at or is associated with the site. Thus, even though some teachers' voices are heard on certain issues in some districts, those voices do not necessarily represent teachers as a group, nor do they carry a weight equal to other voices in the system. This circumstance is perplexing, because teachers are crucial to whether or not restructuring actually makes a difference for students. They are the ones who determine whether a school reforms in a cursory or cosmetic manner or in a creative, truly new way. They determine whether the classroom is reconstituted based upon old and time-worn educational practices or altogether different and refreshing visions of the teaching and learning process.

It is up to the principal—more so than other leaders—to help connect teachers to the system by transmitting information from the district to the school and vice versa. Although teachers may not have a significant voice at the district level, principals who take the time and make the effort to listen and genuinely understand them can more effectively advocate for them and for the school.

More important is the role of the principal and other school leaders as advocates for change inside the building. They can create the circumstances by which teachers feel heard, understood, and acknowledged inside the school. This last role is not an easy one. It requires new knowledge and new skills. In schools undergoing change, there are higher stress levels and greater conflict among teachers and between teachers and administrators than in schools that are maintaining the status quo. The reasons are obvious. High school change leaders, particularly the principal, must deal with teachers who, under stress, appear to be angry, sometimes even irrational. That is just part of the job of a principal at a restructuring school. It is easy to be put off by the intemperate behavior, especially if there is a long and unpleasant history of such outbursts, and never address the real issues causing the distress. Learning to listen to the real issues and then work together to improve the situation is difficult but, in the long term, potentially more rewarding for the change process, for the education of students, and for the school at large.

Before formulating solutions to resolve the conflicts with teachers and among teachers themselves that accompany change, leaders must take the time to understand the real, often unstated and disguised underlying problems that cause the behavior. Otherwise, it is easy to fall into the trap of focusing energies on solving the wrong problem. The key is *listening*. The task for leaders is to develop better listening skills. Will the time spent by leaders honing listening skills help the school achieve its educational and social mission? Walton (1969, p. 109) says yes:

> When one finds that despite efforts to explain himself he is not understood, he tends to feel frustrated with the situation, angry toward those who do not understand him, and defensive about his views. These feelings contribute to the conflict. If and when he finally discovers he is more correctly perceived, he becomes more relaxed; he feels somewhat more accepted by virtue of his being understood; he is more likely to critically review his own position and to modify it in ways which are responsive to the other person's views.

This section of the chapter examines three aspects of working in conflict situations. It provides school leaders with a guide for listening and a model for using this information to reduce levels of disagreement as the school moves ahead with change. It also provides a framework for elevating listening to a higher level. Used in combination with nonjudgmental, reflective listening, respect for others' feelings, and a belief that each party to a dispute can learn from the other, the data gathered through focused listening can help resolve disputes with the purpose of better serving children and implementing programs to accomplish the school's goals.

BECOMING A BETTER LISTENER

Listen for Fears

Teachers frequently fear that events or decisions will unjustly harm them, their ability to reach their career objectives, or perhaps even earn their livelihood. When their fears are realized, their anger is exacerbated by feelings of "victimization" or "violation." The greater the magnitude of perceived fear and loss, the greater the intensity of anger (Beck, 1976). In Chapter 7, some teachers at Beacon High School were greatly alarmed at the thought of losing the independence of the self-contained classroom. They directed their anger toward the principal, as well as toward the school's leadership group, the SPC.

Prior to responding to anger, leaders must ask themselves a series of questions to help them get beyond the teachers' descriptions of particular problems. They must search for and identify the underlying fears that are causing the anger. How much better it would have been for the change process at Beacon High School if the principal had addressed the fears expressed by staff members early in the process. If the principal can visualize and understand the "horrible things" or long-range consequences the teacher thinks might befall him or her, it will help to build the trust required to collaboratively develop solutions attractive to all parties.

For example, at a school in New York City, Ms. Bressler erupted in rage when the principal, in accordance with a resolution of the leadership council, proposed that she join a newly organized teacher team at the school's annex nine blocks from the main building. The school was reorganizing itself into self-contained units, but the building could not accommodate the increased space needs of the new groupings. The principal knew that she belonged to a small coterie of staff members who were opposed to the teaming effort and believed that her opposition to the move was primarily because she wanted to continue working by herself in her own classroom.

Ms. Bressler had had a series of interpersonal problems with colleagues in the main building, and efforts to resolve disputes had not worked out. Over the years, there had been individual and group attempts to resolve the disputes. There had been a number of school workshops on interpersonal relations, but there had been no improvement in the situation. Ms. Bressler nonetheless insisted that she remain at the main building. She accused the principal and members of the leadership council of using the interpersonal problems as an excuse to get rid of her and contended that she could work effectively with anyone.

Careful listening would have revealed that the underlying issue for Ms. Bressler was not, as the principal believed, the prospect of having to work with a team at the annex. In fact, she preferred the teachers who were working in that smaller building. She believed, however, that there was a plot by other staff members, the leadership council included, to get her out of the school and that assignment to the annex, far away from the school's power center, was a step closer to that goal.

During the meeting in the principal's office, the principal responded to Ms. Bressler's resistance by listing the many attempts already made by the teaching staff to resolve the disputes with Ms. Bressler. The principal defended her own involvement in providing support and ridiculed Ms. Bressler's contention that the leadership council was trying to get her out of the way. Not surprisingly, Ms. Bressler assumed that the principal had rehearsed her lines and was trying to avoid having to deal with interpersonal problems by transferring her out of the main building. Since the principal would not listen to her arguments that she was being pushed aside, Ms. Bressler believed that the principal fully intended to get the teacher out of the way and was simply going through the motions of a formal discussion. Compounding these negative perceptions was the principal's failure to offer adequate evidence that the efforts to resolve interpersonal differences among staff had succeeded. That Ms. Bressler interpreted these efforts as "a pro forma covering of the bases" did not help.

Ms. Bressler felt that transfer to the annex amounted to "exile," where she would be out of the mainstream of school activities. Her fine teaching abilities, she believed, would not be seen by central office officials who only spent time at the main building. Moreover, if she was working with a team, her work would be mingled with theirs. She would not get a promotion and would not be considered for the assistant principalship she wanted so badly at this or any other school. She believed that remaining at the main building was necessary for obtaining a promotion; no other option was satisfactory. She would go to any length, she stated, including a formal grievance or legal action, if necessary, to remain at the main building. The annex was definitely not for her, she vowed.

Unfortunately, the principal personalized the issue. She saw Ms. Bressler as an unreasonable, angry person trying to force the school administration to assign her to the main building without regard for the rights and interests of others. Had the principal listened carefully to the thrust of Ms. Bressler's arguments, and not defended her own efforts while criticizing each and every suggestion made by Ms. Bressler, she might have realized that the teacher was ready to work on a team and that she would support an alternative other than the one that had been suggested.

When listening for fears, it is important to consider the needs and aspirations that motivate people. Ms. Bressler was afraid the principal would keep her from satisfying her legitimate goals, i.e., her needs. She identified career success with teaching at a place where she could be noticed by high-level district officials. The main building was the place where visitors came; she was afraid that the principal stood in the way of her promotion by not allowing her to work in that building.

Glasser (1986) provides a model that is useful in identifying needs. Glasser identified primary psychological needs as (1) belonging, (2) power, (3) freedom, and (4) fun. People behave as best they can to control their lives and satisfy their needs. Glasser's model can help reveal the deeper meanings, the genuine sources of teachers' fears that surface at meetings such as those involving the principal and Ms. Bressler.

When listening for the fears of teachers, leaders should be aware that people fight to protect what is dear to them, as well as for what they believe is essential for their survival and prosperity, and that each person has unique ways of satisfying his or her needs. Consequently, behavior that seems "irrational" or "unreasonable" to the listener is highly rational and justifiable from the teacher's point of view. It is only by carefully identifying fears and objectives and dispassionately considering the legitimacy of the teachers' perceptions that leaders can help achieve mutually acceptable solutions to situations in which wide differences exist. This requires skill. The listener, in this case the principal, must suspend judgment of the teacher as (s)he examines the substance of staff members' perceptions. Ultimately, the leader needs to be an advocate for the new and emerging school that the faculty is committed to creating, regardless of organizational or interpersonal consequences. This requires becoming adept at listening.

Listen for Assumptions and Self-Defeating Thought Patterns

Everyone makes assumptions about people and the world and has self-defeating thought patterns. Both can exacerbate misunderstanding and lead to protracted, unnecessary, frequently destructive power struggles, which is the last thing anyone wants at any point in the change process. Teachers and school administrators approach each other with an array of assumptions they are unaware of. Persons on both sides assume that they see things the way they actually are, understand speakers precisely as the speakers intended, know right from wrong, and communicate effectively. One assistant principal remembered a teacher who thought he was cold, uncaring, and impressed with himself because he sat back and listened to the teacher express her views without offering any comment. In contrast, the assistant principal thought he had listened well and shown sensitivity by giving the teacher ample time to fully express herself. Only after the teacher finished did the assistant principal present his views on the teachers' ideas. He thought that he provided useful information in showing the teacher the weaknesses of her ideas. He was sure at the time that this was the role the teacher expected him to play. He was wrong.

At times, almost everyone engages in thought patterns that distort reality and inhibit problem solving, including:

- **Dichotomous thinking**   ("He's smart, I'm not.")

- **Overgeneralization**   ("This teacher will never do any better. He'll never get his kids quiet.")

- **Magnification**   ("He's late with his reports again. Another failure. He'll never manage to get his work in on time.")

- **"Should" statements**   ("This teacher should be realistic. He should understand I have eighty other teachers in the school. I can't devote all my time to one person's problems.")

- **Mind reading** ("She says she respects my ability to make fair decisions, but she really is trying to manipulate me.") (Margolis and Tewel, 1988)

Anger is heightened by the belief that the anticipated harm from a course of action is unjust or that it will prove catastrophic. The greater the anticipated consequences of perceived harm, the more intense the anger. Ms. Bressler was afraid that she would be assigned to a teaching location where her ability would not be noticed by the central office officials who could affect her ability to get a promotion. For her part, the principal felt boxed in, afraid of an outcry from the leadership council and the teacher teams at the main building if she backed down and assigned the teacher to one of their teams, since they didn't want Ms. Bressler.

Thus, the issues of both justice and harm must be addressed. Failure to provide a clear rationale for a proposed course of action that teachers find credible arouses thoughts of unfairness, capriciousness, and bias. This means that the leaders must present valid justification for and identify measurable benefits from a proposed course of action.

Once the teacher and the principal or other leader agree that a particular course of action may be warranted, its consequences need to be considered. A five-column chart (similar to the one in Figure 10.1), listing potential benefits, possible problems, criteria for success, signs of difficulty, and additional information needed, can provide a safe way for teachers and those in leadership positions to clarify concerns and to inform each other about what each considers important. This requires recording the information on a flip chart and encouraging the teacher to fully participate in its development. To avoid unanticipated problems, it is important to schedule periodic meetings with the teacher or group of teachers to assess progress. The five-column chart and agreed-to assessment meetings can reduce fears that a mistake that will prove calamitous will occur.

FIGURE 10.1

Potential benefits	Possible problems	Criteria for success	Signs of difficulty	Further information needed (specify the exact information needed)

Listen for Perceptions of Power

Power is the ability to get things done. Lack of power, combined with feelings of victimization, causes resentment. Very often, angry teachers have unrealistically low estimates of their power (justifiably so, given the reality of their working lives) and unrealistically high estimates of the power of school administrators to get things done "if they really want to." A goal for any leader must be to help aggrieved teachers formulate a realistic picture of the resources, or sources of power, they and administrators have.

Power should not be confused with brute force. French and Raven (1959) and Raven and Kruglanski (1970) discuss six sources of power that can help any leaders understand teachers' perceptions of them and how they themselves can unknowingly exacerbate conflict by ignoring or stressing their power, especially at a time when the focus in the school is on reconceptualizing roles, power, and decision-making authority. Lastly, they discuss ways to help teachers identify resources to improve the situation:

- **Reward power:**   The ability to provide teachers with what they want

- **Coercive power:**   The ability to hold back or take away that which teachers consider important

- **Legitimate power:**   The formal roles, responsibilities, and obligations of the building leader, traditionally the principal

- **Referent power:**   The attractive and unattractive attributes of a leader

- **Expert power:**   The expertise and motivation of a school leader, whatever his or her position, to help a particular teacher

- **Information power:**   The unique information possessed by the leader (e.g., how to manipulate the master schedule) to help a teacher

By careful listening, leaders can identify the types of power a teacher values most and the powers they attribute to the leader and themselves. This helps leaders think through the appropriate power sources conducive to conflict resolution. For example, if it becomes clear that Ms. Bressler values referent power, the principal might have asked her to work with a group of teachers or a supervisor whose style she admired and removed her from contact with teachers or administrators whose styles differ. Thus, it would be important to listen for the personal attributes of staff members Ms. Bressler admires or dislikes and identify who has high referent power for her.

Other teachers may have little concern for referent power but great concern about expertise. When such expertise is critical to resolving a problem with a teacher, the leader must acknowledge this and obtain the services of another person the teacher views as trustworthy. Failure to obtain such expertise prevents resolution of outstanding issues.

Listen for Mutual Understanding

Often what sounds and feels like conflict may be no more than pseudoconflict (Rhenman et al., 1970), which occurs when people mistakenly think they understand each other. Semantic difficulties, the insufficient exchange of information, and interference create pseudoconflict. For example, when the principal referred to Ms. Bressler as "prone to…," she actually heard "troublemaker." She never questioned the principal's actual meaning, but took it upon herself to be offended that the principal thought of her in such terms.

Insufficient exchange of information occurs because everyone forgets much of what they hear. To compensate, listeners accentuate an element or two and fill in missing information in ways that make sense to them but which typically distort the speaker's message. Interference is anything that interferes with accurately receiving the speaker's message. For example, Ms. Bressler had a concealed hearing problem and heard only bits and pieces of what the principal said. She also devalued the principal's suggestions. The principal, after all, had never been a member of a teaching team and did not understand how teaming prevented people from developing an independent reputation that could help with promotion.

Minimization of pseudoconflict requires full two-way communication, characterized by the free exchange of information and the mutual understanding that rank-and-file teachers and the school's leadership are both legitimately entitled to influence final decisions and outcomes. In some schools, this last idea is so new that it takes work to develop school capacity for sharing and being accountable for decisions. Free and open exchanges tend to precipitate misunderstandings, which makes it imperative that leaders continually check to assess the degree to which teachers understand them and they understand teachers. Sometimes reflective listening is enough. Other times, it requires gentle questioning (e.g., "What are your concerns about my recommendation that your team move to a different teaching location so that your students are away from cafeteria noise?"). Questions should be phrased to clearly communicate that they are meant to enhance understanding rather than criticize.

Summaries of *explicit* information help teachers confirm or correct what the leader has understood from the conversation. This, however, does not deal with the staff members' feelings, which are absolutely critical to resolving differences. Johnson (1990) provides three essential components for checking staff members' feelings:

1. The leader should describe his or her perceptions of the teachers' feelings.

2. He or she should then ask if those perceptions are accurate.

3. The leader must suspend judgment.

By not checking, leaders can get trapped into believing that what they see accurately reflects reality. By checking, misperceptions can be corrected before damage takes place. Fears, expectations, and feelings prejudice impressions. If leaders fear anger and expect a teacher to be angry, they may incorrectly see the teacher as angry. As Napier and Gershenfeld (1989, p. 14) noted,

> The fact is that people are a thousand things, but first and foremost in their effort
> to understand reality they are what we want them to be in relation to our own
> needs.

Because people frequently misperceive what others think and feel, school leaders
must verify their perceptions (Johnson, 1990).

Listen to Assess Teachers' Understanding of Problem-Solving Processes

When differences of opinion exist, teachers and leaders, particularly if they are
principals, often find themselves trapped in "positional bargaining" in which each
tries to impose its will on the other. Continuing to argue the advantages and disadvantages of one particular approach or service is "positional bargaining" (Fisher and
Ury, 1981), which limits options and quickly evolves into a win–lose power struggle.
Typically a "winner" emerges, who does not understand the other's heightened
alienation and resistance. It is critical that leaders prevent positional bargaining from
becoming a protracted, counterproductive power struggle between members of the
teaching staff and the school's leadership team. Such a struggle would be in conflict
with the basic tenets of the restructuring effort and impede, perhaps even destroy, the
entire change initiative.

A major cause of positional bargaining is not knowing how to solve problems. The
struggles with decision making that accompany a restructuring effort sometimes give
a teacher or a small group of teachers the opportunity to impose his or her will on the
school, without apparent interest in mutually acceptable solutions. Leaders should
listen and pose questions in order to understand the teacher(s) and the ultimate goals
of the teacher or group of teachers. After the teacher acknowledges that his or her
views have been well understood, discussion should sequentially consider (1) the
inevitable drawbacks of positional bargaining, (2) the benefits of problem solving,
and (3) strategies for systematic problem solving when two or more people are
involved. Naturally, the teacher should be informed that if problem solving proves
unsuccessful, (s)he retains the option of pursuing a particular solution through the
grievance machinery included in the local employee agreement with the Board of
Education.

APPROACHES TO PROBLEM SOLVING

Effective listening inevitably leads to the need for problem solving, a second important skill for those in leadership positions. Acceptable solutions frequently become
obvious and easy to implement once teachers, the teacher leadership group, principals, and other school administrators have a better understanding of each other's
views, beliefs, and interests. When resolution is not apparent, despite the teachers'
indications that they are understood, problem solving is needed. To avoid the inevi-

table confusion of haphazard attempts at problem solving, the approach must be systematic, should involve other school personnel (those not party to the dispute) as necessary, and should provide for full teacher participation.

Initially, the principal or other school leader, together with other invited staff members (such as the shop steward or staff member chosen to be an advocate for the complainant) and the teacher complainant should agree to follow a set sequence of problem-solving procedures. If not, participants might become confused about what ensues, creating lack of cooperation and alienation. Discussing and agreeing to a simple problem-solving sequence such as the IDEAL model (described below) generates understanding and commitment while minimizing confusion. The IDEAL process is highly structured, rational in nature, and easily applied to the types of disagreements that develop among administrators, teachers, and teacher leaders in restructuring schools. When working on resolving problems with angry, disappointed, or disaffected teachers, it is important to try to maintain a sequence of steps such as those in the IDEAL model, which moves from understanding, to seeking solutions, to evaluation, while remaining flexible and responsive to the staff members' immediate needs. Keeping the steps in mind provides a valuable road map for getting everyone to his or her destination. When combined with empathetic listening and trust building, the model improves the likelihood of success.

When using the IDEAL or any other problem-solving model, it is advisable to use a large visual stimulus, such as a flip chart, for recording all comments, concerns, and recommendations. This is important for several reasons. It focuses attention and avoids confusion. It reduces the necessity for repetition by assuring that all contributions will receive attention. It facilitates mutual understanding by simplifying questioning and editing. It acts as a common memory, assuring accuracy and maintaining focus, and it helps all participants at the meeting better understand what each thinks is important. It flushes out hidden agendas and builds trust, as each continues to more accurately understand the other, while considering the other's views in a rational, logical manner. It fosters feelings of safety and community as the group focuses on ideas rather than people. Compared to individual notes, material written on a flip chart is easier to refer back to for confirmation, correction, and questioning. In summary, it facilitates accurate communication and trust by assuring that everyone knows exactly what is happening.

Bransford and Stein's (1984) IDEAL model provides an easily understood guide for problem solving and action. The steps are:

1. **Identify potential problems.**   Carefully listening to teachers before formally attempting to solve problems helps build a better understanding of the real problem. It may well be that the problem presented by the teacher differs from the real, underlying problem. At this stage it is important to make a very preliminary hypothesis about the underlying problems and the staff members' underlying fears. Remember, however, that the word "hypothesis" implies "notion" and connotes the possibility of being wrong.

2. **Define and represent the problem.** Unfortunately, teachers' initial statements of anger or concern often mask the real problems or define them in terms too broad (e.g., "This school is bureaucratic and doesn't care about individual staff members.") or narrow ("Each time I try to do something that is different other staff members' complain.") for effective intervention. In such cases, the person in the leadership position needs to help the teacher define what (s)he considers the critical problems or high-priority concerns. This requires great care as definitions limit or expand the potential for effectiveness and creativity. Focusing on needs rather than advocating particular solutions increases chances of developing action plans that are satisfactory to all parties. The problem statement "This team needs assistance with planning and management to allow teachers to coordinate teaching strategies" will elicit more options and creativity than "You need help with getting student data files in order." The latter statement leaves little room for purposeful discussion. The former statement might well result in consideration of a variety of options that teachers might wish to consider. Because "different definitions…often lead to different treatments" (Bransford and Stein, 1984, p. 15), considerable effort should center on reaching agreement on a problem definition broad enough to satisfy all salient needs but specific enough to generate potentially effective solutions.

Writing proposed definitions on a flip chart for all to see and asking each person to circle words or phrases he or she finds vague or confusing promotes mutual understanding and trust while ensuring accuracy. Diagramming problems reduces complexity and misunderstandings. Typically, new information necessitates revision of the problem statement. Otherwise, it is possible the wrong problem may be addressed.

3. **Explore prospective solutions.** This stage emphasizes generating and cataloguing as many solutions as possible. It requires temporarily suspending evaluation to encourage the sharing of ideas. It is also useful to divide complex problems into parts and to investigate solutions others have applied to similar difficulties.

After everyone feels that he or she has been understood and an ample number of ideas have been put forth, criteria to evaluate suggested solutions should be agreed upon. Developing specific criteria further defines priorities and promotes reason while educating each participant about the other's concerns. Before agreeing to a solution, it is beneficial to discuss how to improve and combine ideas and to get the most from each.

Lasting agreements require consensus. Consensus does not mean unanimity that one particular idea is best or that a proposed solution is everyone's first choice. It does mean that all agree that their opinions have been seriously considered and the idea is at least worth trying. Forced decision-making strategies, like voting, typically miscarry. Teachers view such strategies as power tactics designed to force an agreement that is favorable to the school administration but not to themselves. Skillful use of a problem-solving approach frequently makes agreement anticlimactic. If, however, consensus is not reached, perhaps the problem was not adequately defined, teacher suggestions were not adequately understood, or understanding was not communicated in nonthreatening ways. It is also possible that more discussion may be necessary to reveal deeply concealed agendas. Perhaps sharp differences in values require resolution by a trusted third party, such as a central office official or a trained mediator.

4. **Act on agreed-upon solutions.** Before implementation, each person's responsibilities should be outlined, together with agreed-upon timelines. All important information should be written down to ensure accurate understanding and faithful follow-up. It is impossible to guarantee beforehand whether or not a proposed solution will work.

5. **Look at the effects.** The belief that once a solution is implemented it cannot be revised creates teacher reluctance to proceed. Scheduling periodic assessment meetings to help decide whether the proposed solution should be continued, modified, or abandoned before finalizing action reduces resistance and increases willingness to take risks. The more objective the data, the greater the probability of building trust and weakening resistance.

When problem solving, as with listening, it is important that all significant information be considered concurrently. Although the different components of listening and problem solving have been presented in this chapter as discrete components, in actuality "these activities do not occur in neat little compartments, perfectly distinct from one another. The boundaries between components are usually fuzzy" (Bransford and Stein, 1984, p. 11).

WHEN TEACHERS WILL NOT COOPERATE

Sometimes people resist problem solving. The deeper the fear and the greater the level of suspicion—personally or as a result of school culture—the harder it is going to be to gain cooperation. When teachers seem to be resisting problem solving, principals or other leaders should continue to listen carefully to them. In such circumstances, it is also useful to reflect upon the issues fueling the teacher's distrust. Perhaps it is the benefits the staff member might derive from continuing with positional bargaining or the existence of deeply hidden agendas requiring additional exploration. Sometimes, what appears on the surface to be fierce resistance is actually a plea for help in easing underlying concerns. Sometimes the teacher just needs more time to think through and assess his or her options. Sometimes a teacher will be dissatisfied no matter what the school's leadership does, and, in rare instances, despite skilled listening and effective problem solving, an impasse will be reached. A very small percentage of aggrieved teachers will simply demand that the school accede to their wishes, no matter how unreasonable they are. In such instances, the problem may require a discussion by the entire faculty leadership group or management team. The problem might also be referred to higher authority, or the formal grievance machinery may have to be invoked.

Most of the time, however, skilled listening coupled with the problem-solving approach will markedly enhance the likelihood of success. It can keep the school's restructuring from getting derailed or bogged down. In contrast, poor listening virtually assures failure. It increases stress, promotes teacher alienation, and foments mistrust. It undermines the ability of teachers to work together and diminishes the leader's role in the change process. Teachers in schools undergoing change frequently need assistance with solving problems. Poor listening by school leaders creates new problems.

Although listening and problem solving are critical steps, they are not, in and of themselves, enough to keep the change process on track. More is needed—much more. Listening and problem solving must be followed up by effective communication with teachers, students, parents, and the larger school community. Just as it is important to acquire listening skills to get beneath the words heard from teachers, it is also important, in order to really understand and to affect what is going on in the school, to structure the channels for listening so that all shades of opinion are heard. Therefore, the next section of this chapter is an exploration of ways in which principals and others in the leadership cadre can structure and expand their ability to listen so that they can receive and provide important information from and to groups of teachers and the entire faculty.

IMPROVING COMMUNICATION

As one retiring principal of a large suburban high school said to his successor, "Yesterday was the last day you heard the truth from your faculty." In many schools, often in spite of efforts to improve listening skills as a mechanism for better understanding, leaders are unaware of what is actually happening in the school. Sometimes teachers provide leaders, especially administrators, with what they think they want to hear, as demonstrated by the following humorous illustration:

THE PLAN

In the beginning was The Plan.
And then came the assumptions;

And the assumptions were without form,
And The Plan was completely without substance;
And darkness was upon the faces of the teachers.

And they spoke unto their department heads, saying:
"The Plan is a crock of shit and it stinks."

And the department heads went into the office
of the guidance director and said:
"It is a pail of dung and none may abide the odor thereof."

And the guidance director went to the assistant principal
and said unto him:
"It is a vessel of fertilizer and none may abide Its strength."

And the assistant principal went to his colleague and said:
"It contains that which aids plant growth and It is very strong."

And the second assistant principal went to the vice principal
and said unto him:
"It promotes growth and is very powerful."

And the vice principal went to the principal and said unto him:
"This powerful new Plan will actively promote
the growth and effectiveness of the school
and student learning in particular."

And the principal looked upon The Plan and saw that it was good.
And The Plan became Policy.

The intelligence that principals or teacher management teams receive through formal and informal channels is all too often incomplete or slanted. Compounding the problem is the fact that some leaders are incapable of accepting and assimilating information that conflicts with their personal values and predilections. Consequently, decisions and plans that are of critical significance to the future of the school and the change process are often made on the basis of incomplete, inadequate, or incorrect information. Without knowing it, leaders are in the perilous situation of the shipmaster who blindly sails uncharted seas, unaware of potential difficulties until confronted with them. There is a strong possibility that such lack of genuinely open communication may cause the failure of even small, presumably well-intentioned innovations, let alone those situations in which the entire school is involved in change on multiple fronts. It also may explain the fact that a principal who is forward looking, a change agent, and an innovator—the type of leader needed in a restructuring school—has the least job security of anyone in the district organization.

In order to assist principals and other leaders in dealing with communication issues that are critical to the success of the change process, this chapter explores the communication problem by examining: (1) the barriers that prevent leaders and others from knowing what's going on amongst others in the school community, (2) the sources of error hindering the change leadership's ability to communicate effectively with faculty, (3) the interventions that can meaningfully improve the flow of important information throughout the school, and (4) the personal conflicts which must be overcome in order to facilitate clear, comprehensive, and valid communication throughout the entire school community.

Failures in Communication from Faculty
to the Principal and Other Change Leaders

Many principals and teacher leaders are often lulled into a false sense of security regarding the quality of communication flowing in their schools. The first and most egregious error is to assume that assistant principals or department heads are providing a clear channel of vertical communication, either to or from the principal or the collaborative leadership group. Lateral communication among teachers in different departments within a single school building tends to be equally unreliable. Actually, most levels of management in the traditionally organized school are less communication centers than communication barriers, as observed in Chapters 3, 4, and 9. In addition, different departments are frequently less inclined to be cooperative *allies* with one another than to be competitive *rivals* for recognition. At one time, such recognition came from the principal; now it comes from the teacher management group as well. Hence, communication among department members competing for these forms of recognition is often poor. Although teachers are prolific sources of useful information, this does not mean that the data they provide is complete, accurate, objective, or generally valid.

Misleading Information

Much information provided to the school's leadership by faculty members can also be either intentionally or willfully and maliciously inaccurate. There are a number of reasons for this. First, no subordinate wants the school's chief administrator—despite perceptions that the position might not be as powerful as it once was—to learn of anything that may be interpreted as discreditable, either actually or potentially. Hence, there may be a conscious attempt to screen everything that is transmitted upward by filtering out those items of information that are potentially threatening.

Second, subordinates in any organization eventually discover what their superiors would like to hear. Therefore, they become adept not only at avoiding the unpleasant, but also at stressing the positive. If the principal or management group is to support one or another change effort, it is likely that they will hear reports that stress the positive elements of the initiative. Though the individual subordinate may consciously be sincere and accountable, personal anxieties, hostilities, aspirations, and systems of beliefs and values almost inevitably shape and color the interpretation of what has been learned and is expected to be transmitted.

Third, the traditional culture and the compartmentalized nature of high schools often create conditions in which each subordinate is desirous of impressing the leadership with the superiority of his or her contribution to the effort and, conversely, with the inadequacy of the contributions of rivals. How can the leader know which protagonist is telling the truth? In most instances, it is difficult to be sure. If (s)he depends solely upon his or her own judgment, (s)he will probably be wrong at least as often as (s)he is right. Thus leaders must work to extract the conditions that allow this to happen from the high school culture.

A fourth source of error arises from the fact that the position of principal, in particular, is one for which there is often substantial competition and rivalry, sometimes within the school. The incumbent, on taking office, is not surrounded by allies and friends, despite overt servility, obsequiousness, and dramatic protestations of loyalty. Although most assistant principals or teachers would not deliberately sabotage their principal, many are not at all reluctant to sit by and let him or her stumble and fall on his or her own during the upheavals of the restructuring process.

Finally, there is the problem that many in leadership positions are unable to comprehend and accept valid information, even when it is brought to their attention. No wonder some leaders are sometimes denied "the whole truth and nothing but..." by teachers and others on the staff.

Resulting Errors

In effect, the typical school principal or school leadership group is frequently a prisoner of position, as far as communications are concerned. He or she (or the group) is largely insulated from the everyday realities of the school and dependent on others for information. It is not surprising that under these conditions change leaders frequently make needless but costly, sometimes even fatal, errors such as: (1) the acceptance of misinformation concerning what is actually happening within the school on a day-to-day basis; (2) the institution and perpetuation of ill-advised policies and practices; (3) loss of contact with and misinterpretation of parent, community, and staff attitudes toward the school; and (4) the failure to be realistic about his or her own wishful thinking concerning the present state of the school and its future prospects.

Deficiencies in Communication Between Principal and Teachers

Failures are in no sense limited to upward communications. Many in leadership positions believe that announcements by assistant principals and department heads, supplemented by printed material such as newsletters and bulletin boards, suffice as channels to convey messages to teachers. It is assumed, moreover, that as long as the message is clear, concise, well illustrated, and dramatically presented, its reception will be satisfactory, whatever its message. This, unfortunately, is not true. There is much more to communication than merely the cogent presentation of a message. If the communication is not understood, believed, and regarded as having a positive value for its recipients, it will fail in its mission. The overestimation of the effectiveness of the communication media employed is one of the greatest sources of managerial error in dealing with staff.

Missing Feedback

In order for communication to be effective, it must be a two-way process. Ongoing and effective feedback from recipients is necessary to ascertain the extent to which the message has actually been understood, believed, assimilated, and accepted. Encouraging this kind of "give and take" is a process in which few school staff and administrative members engage. Economy of time is certainly one legitimate explanation; however, there may also be a latent fear of discovering how little of the message has actually been transmitted.

Thus, principals and teacher leaders are frequently isolated. Whereas this is merely undesirable in schools in which the status quo is being maintained, it is catastrophic in one undergoing reform. A restructuring school relies on effective channels of communication to garner faculty support needed to move the process forward. Principals and teacher leaders thus isolated are denied access to valid information about what is transpiring in the school, while channels for outward communication with other than a few immediate associates are severely circumscribed. As a result, the principal and members of the management team are often forced to make major decisions on the basis of unreliable data. Furthermore, as seen in the Lane case study, instructions to staff may be distorted or even blocked at the level of the assistant principal or department head. Consequently, it is not surprising that even an able, experienced, and well-qualified principal or a highly effective management team is often unable to cope with the problems such conditions create. This is especially true when there is a new principal brought in from the outside who lacks immediate, personal knowledge of local conditions. Under such circumstances, (s)he is almost totally at the mercy of subordinates in the area of communication.

These difficulties are not insoluble. There are two essential things that leaders can and must do if clear, comprehensive, and valid channels of communication with the school's teaching staff are to be established and maintained: (1) recognize the primary dangers to good communication and (2) periodically conduct a teacher poll or morale survey to determine the real impact of the reorganization on school personnel.

Recognizing Dangers

The establishment of clear channels of communication throughout the school hinges on the leader's recognition of the following primary dangers:

- The tendency for people to perceive only what they want to see

- The insufficiency of the school's supervisory and administrative hierarchy for conveying information both to and from the principal or teacher leaders

- The possibility of chronic and legitimate staff dissatisfaction caused by school conditions or administrative policies and practices

- The weaknesses of some middle-level school administrators and supervisors, which damage morale and efficiency

- The risk of staff misunderstanding, disbelief, or refusal to accept a factual statement about school issues or problems and the reasons behind them

Polling Staff

The second thing the leaders should do in establishing communication with others in the school is to seek their opinions. This can be accomplished initially by the administration of a special, three-phase opinion poll or morale survey. However, if those polled fear that their identities will in any manner be revealed, their responses will tend to be falsely positive: "Everything is just fine." Therefore, it is often advisable to utilize an independent, impartial outside agency or group to conduct the poll. This step need not be costly. There are pro bono groups in each community that can conduct and tabulate the poll results if they are provided with the survey instruments.

Survey Techniques

The initial step in conducting such a survey is to determine the organizational units to be polled. Ideally, within each school, each teacher team, house unit, or grade can constitute a discrete segment. Unfortunately, if there are less than five persons in one of the functional units, its members may believe that their identities still will not be adequately protected, even with an outsider conducting the poll. In such circumstances, it is advisable to consolidate related small groups into a single larger unit. This makes it difficult to pinpoint teacher attitudes toward the issue in question, but this shortcoming is preferable to risking the contamination of subject responses. The procedure not only provides faculty with a safe opportunity to voice grievances and problems, but it permits the determination of staff attitudes toward the school's administration as well.

Quantitative Questionnaire

The poll is a simple, multiple-choice questionnaire of 25 to 30 items. Separate sets of questions are used for each staff category in order to adapt the procedure to local conditions. Where it is advisable to distinguish the responses of men and women, different colored paper stock may be used for the two sets of questionnaires. The important thing is to convince each subject that his or her identity will be absolutely protected. This is accomplished by:

- Not asking the staff members to sign their names or provide identifying data of any sort

- Designing the questionnaire so that all questions can be answered by using check marks in lieu of writing

- Allowing the staff member to select at random the blank forms (s)he will complete from a pile, thus precluding the possibility of marking or keying any individual questionnaire

- Placing the completed questionnaire in a single ballot box so that the questionnaires are all mixed up together

In administering the first portion of the poll, every effort must be made to motivate staff to answer fully and frankly. All of these devices to shield staff members' identities can be pointed out before the study starts. It should be stressed that the findings will bypass all intermediate-level supervisors and administrators and go directly to the principal and the faculty leadership group.

Informal Leaders

While the poll provides much useful information and permits participation by differ-ent categories of staff members, it is, nevertheless, limited in scope. It provides a quantitative measure of the issues being surveyed, but contributes little information on why the circumstances are as they are. It does, however, offer an excellent springboard for a further investigation of factors affecting morale by means of follow-up interviews with selected staff. These personal interviews, designed to be conducted by the outside survey group or by an individual not tied to the school, may be held with the staffs' natural leaders: those individuals who hold no formal line or staff position but who exercise leadership among their peers. From these leaders— most of whom are articulate, knowledgeable about conditions in the school, and loyal—much valuable, detailed, and qualitative information can be obtained. These individuals comprise the school's informal organization.

Well in advance of the staff questionnaire survey, the informal leaders may be invited to participate in the process through engaging in the preliminary steps of the study. They may be encouraged to conduct a needs assessment: to identify problems, needs, and issues for ultimate presentation to the principal via the interview proce-dure. Since, in an effective change effort, three to five (or sometimes more) of these leaders are interviewed, canvassing of staff opinion on an informal basis can be quite thorough and highly productive.

Crucial Contributors

The contributions these informal leaders make are often of crucial importance. Without them, the staff questionnaire findings, per se, might be sterile and meaning-less. Their statements provide the detailed, qualitative information necessary for a more complete picture of conditions within the school, including attitudes, which are critically important to the change process. They also yield an accurate indication of the norms to which the various subgroups of the organization (e.g., guidance counselors, more experienced teachers, less experienced teachers, ninth grade team, tenth grade team) subscribe. Knowledge of such norms is invaluable if a program to improve relationships with teachers or to alter change strategy is to be instituted.

Independent Interview

Each of the informal leaders selected should be interviewed independently. After being assured that whatever is said will be held in complete confidence, the respondent may be shown a copy of the poll report for his or her grade, team, or unit and told that perhaps (s)he can help improve an understanding of some of these findings. For example, 15% of the special education teachers responding at Wheaton High School express dissatisfaction with the way that instructional supplies are delivered. The interviewee is shown the results and asked for his or her opinion of them. The key to this approach is its projective character. The subject is not asked to indicate his or her own likes, dislikes, or needs; (s)he is asked only about the responses of peers. Although the informal leader's personal opinions may be expressed within the open response, the approach allows the respondent to be more at ease and in a better position to give comprehensive and truthful answers.

The atmosphere of such an interview session is usually relaxed and permissive, further encouraging the informal leader to speak freely and at length. Most do, because the interviews are conducted individually and independently. If a specific grievance is mentioned by only one respondent, it is probably not significant. If it is volunteered by several, it is more important. If it is stressed by all, it is highly significant.

Realistic Overview

When the data from both sources (staff poll and informal leader interviews) have been assembled, collated, and interpreted, school leaders have, in unparalleled comprehensiveness, an overview of the true situation within the school regarding the dimensions measured. Among the principal findings are the answers to such questions as:

- What is the informal organization of the school?

- What are the major channels of informal communication within the school?

- What is the overall state of teacher opinion on various change and reform issues?

- Where are the groups who need time to be brought along with the school's restructuring?

- What are the roadblocks to reform within the school?

- What are the causes of lack of support for one or another change effort?

- Who are the informal leaders in each group and at every level?

- What schoolwide conditions, practices, and policies create legitimate, long-standing staff frustrations and antagonisms and impede the change process?

- What is the overall image of the principal and other members of the administrative and supervisory personnel in the eyes of staff members?

Some By-Products

In addition to the foregoing findings, such an organizational study provides additional valuable information for school leaders. It shows which teachers and other staff members, as informal leaders, have the potential for leadership. It also provides a basis for confirming or modifying the school's approach to its restructuring effort. It pinpoints the informal leaders who can subsequently be used as a channel for deepening communications with staff. If properly chosen, members of this group can be invaluable.

Using the Data

With these insights, it should no longer be necessary for the school's change leadership to grope blindly in guiding the school's reform effort. The principal will have a more clearly defined concept of relationships within the school; the leadership group will have better data with which interventions can be planned and implemented. At the same time, everyone will be able to see the administrative and supervisory personnel, and the school as a whole, through the eyes of the staff. What is seen may not be pleasing, but the picture will, at least, be comprehensive and objective and will provide the data on which corrective action can be based.

CONSTRUCTIVE STEPS

Once the previously described process is complete, there are a number of constructive steps that the principal can take in working with the school's leadership or decision-making body to better the functioning of the school. A clear understanding of staff needs and norms must exist before undertaking these effective, constructive steps in order to avoid the danger that messages from the principal or other leaders will conflict with existing beliefs and concepts.

First, the principal can begin to build greater staff support for the school's change efforts by reviewing existing conditions, policies, and practices in the light of staff attitudes toward them as revealed by the survey. In spite of the fact that some of these may be hallowed by age and usage, it is usually better for the principal, with the concurrence of the teacher leadership, to be ready to take prompt and drastic action to remedy what many people regard as legitimate grounds for dissatisfaction.

Second, (s)he can engage in a realistic program to build staff support. Such a program may include the elimination of the causes of legitimate staff grievances or, if this is impossible, the exploration of why it cannot be done. Most difficult, but also most urgent, in this area is the establishment of a program to bring disaffected groups into the mainstream of support for the school's new vision of itself.

Third, (s)he can facilitate communication from teachers to the school's leadership by supplementing conventional media (newsletters, the teachers union, the grapevine) through the use of additional channels, particularly those that facilitate the cross-checking and verification of the information produced. The best of these are biennial staff survey polls of the type described in this chapter, supplemented by periodic talks with informal leaders (who will have been identified previously during the latest poll) and frequent meetings with small groups of teachers, such as the teams or houses if this is the school's new organizational arrangement. This last strategy has the additional effect of strengthening the new school organization at a time of transition, when it can use all the help it can get.

Finally, the principal can expedite communication to teachers by depending less on conventional, one-way media (i.e., house organs, bulletin boards, letters to teachers) and more on sophisticated techniques that can be collaboratively planned and implemented, such as a series of schoolwide faculty forums.

COSTS OF PROCRASTINATION

The implementation of polling and internal communication techniques is time-consuming and can bring about a number of dislocations. These costs are often cited by some principals as a rationalization for doing nothing. It is this same kind of thinking, however, that often characterizes patients who suspect that they have a serious, possibly fatal disease such as cancer. They know that something is wrong but because of inertia or dread of what may be discovered, they procrastinate and seek plausible justifications for inaction. For a restructuring school, procrastination in dealing with internal communication problems and issues can scuttle the entire effort.

CONCLUSION

When a school's change leadership, whether it is the principal, teacher teams, or some other group, makes itself wholly dependent on sources of information of questionable authenticity, they place the entire restructuring effort in jeopardy. For the leader, the critical questions frequently are, "Can I face reality when it conflicts with long-held values or threatens my personal security?" and "Can I tolerate emotionally an intelligence system that will provide information that may conflict with cherished values and which reveals conditions that may signal a need to change my leadership style in working with staff?"

The leader who cannot face these risks will continue setting a blind course on the basis of incomplete or misleading information about the school's prime resource— its teaching personnel. In the short run, it is easier and less threatening to one's peace of mind to substitute wishful thinking for facts. In the long run, to function that way risks brutalizing the school's entire restructuring effort: the principal and the entire organization can go down together in disaster.

Good communication starts at the top. People follow a leader's actions more readily than they follow advice. If the school's chief executive and those charged with leading the faculty cannot face reality, it cannot be expected that management teams, assistant principals, or department chairs will wish to expose themselves either.

References

Beck, A.T. (1976). *Cognitive Therapy and Emotional Disturbance*. New York: New American Library.

Bransford, J.D. and Stein, B.S. (1984). *The Ideal Problem Solver*. New York: W.H. Freeman.

Fisher, R. and Ury, W. (1981). *Getting to Yes*. Boston: Houghton Mifflin.

French, J.R.P. and Raven, B.H. (1959). The basis of social power. In D. Cartwright (Ed.), *Studies in Social Power*. Ann Arbor: University of Michigan Press.

Glasser, W. (1986). *Control Theory in the Classroom*. New York: Harper and Row.

Johnson, D.W. (1990). *Reaching Out*. 4th ed., Englewood Cliffs, New Jersey: Prentice Hall.

Margolis, H. and Tewel, K. (1988). Resolving conflict with parents: A guide for administrators. *NASSP Bulletin*, 72, 1–8.

Napier, W. and Gershenfeld, M.K. (1989). *Groups: Theory and Experience*. 4th ed., Boston: Houghton Mifflin.

Raven, B.H. and Kruglanski, A.W. (1970). Conflict and power. In P. Swingle (Ed.), *The Structure of Conflict*. New York: Academic Press.

Rhenman, E., Stromberg, L. and Westerlund, G. (1970). *Conflict and Cooperation in Business Organizations*. London: Wiley-Interscience.

Walton, R.E. (1969). *Interpersonal Peacemaking: Confrontations and Third Party Consultation*. Boston: Addison-Wesley.

11

Putting It All Together: Provoking, Promoting, and Supporting Reform

Equipping school leaders to promote and sustain school-initiated change is the major focus of this book. If change is going to be the school's way of life, then becoming adept at tactics that will stimulate and nurture the change process and make those efforts long lasting is going to be an implicit part of every school leader's job. It will be a part of the leader's job every day that he or she is on duty.

Change of any sort in high schools is difficult to accomplish. Leading a school undergoing *fundamental and comprehensive* change is complicated, frenetic, almost always turbulent, and invariably messy. The school's internal dynamics are complex enough, not to mention the many problems and processes that originate outside the school, such as district requirements, state regulations, single-interest groups, and the breakdown of the pre-nuclear family. John Gardner once said that changing a school is like moving a cemetery. While Gardner's statement startles people at first, it is not much of an exaggeration. I remember the days when my own school was undergoing rapid and fundamental change. It felt as if the entire world had chosen sides; I was on one side, and everyone else in the world was on the other.

Change is especially difficult for those in leadership positions who have been at their current school for many years. There are always some people on the staff who expect them to behave in the future as they have in the past. Change is also hard for those who lead schools where students are doing well. In such places it is easier to become complacent. After all, in those schools, it is the old ways that produced success, making it hard for people to believe that there is now a need to change— sometimes radically—to remain current.

An additional complication is that motivational strategies are changing fast. The old bureaucratic incentives are disappearing. With the traditional bag of tricks gone, principals and other leaders need new and more effective incentives to keep people engaged in building the new school. Further, people tend to fear totally new situations. The advent of the computer is a perfect example. It took a long time for many principals and teachers to accept computers as an important part of the daily instructional and managerial life of the school. During the early days of the computer age, many principals and teachers were initially reluctant to take the plunge. Computers were expensive. Few people were "techies." Some were afraid to surrender the control over data represented by neatly organized rows of manually recorded information. Few on the faculty were comfortable with strange-looking printouts and a new language. Parents and students, however, placed high value on computer literacy and computer education programs. For a time, it almost seemed as if parents of prospective students had two primary concerns: whether or not it was safe for children to use the school bathroom and how many computer stations the school contained. Parents viewed schools in the forefront of computer technology more favorably than those without computers. Eventually, principals responded to parent demands. It should have been swifter and easier. One of the goals of this book is to equip school leaders with the skills needed for them to respond more quickly to changes when they appear in the future.

This chapter summarizes the information covered in preceding chapters by providing readers with a brief review of strategies they can employ to make schools responsive to change in five areas: (1) the thinking and planning process, (2) the capacity of the staff to sustain change, (3) the creation of a climate favorable to change, (4) managing the change process, and (5) organizational designs that facilitate the change process. This chapter is meant to summarize these strategies, as well as to stimulate the reader's appetite for further reading.

In order to show school leaders how it all comes together in real life, the chapter shows how a leader can move the reform agenda by taking advantage of heretofore routine procedures. It, and the book, concludes with an in-depth examination of the scheduling process and the ways in which it can be used to stimulate reflection and focused and mindful decision making among staff, parents, and community members. The thinking and planning processes described for scheduling can be applied to any other procedure as well.

THINKING AND PLANNING APPROACHES FOR SCHOOL RESTRUCTURING

Customer Focus Is Critical

High schools, with their single-minded focus on crisis management and short-term planning perspectives, are prone to tunnel vision. Many high schools, particularly those with declining student enrollment, are virtually putting themselves out of business because no one is asking if the programs they offer meet the needs and aspirations of the communities from which their students—their customers—come.

Typically, when school administrators confront the need for a customer orientation, they think about elaborate, time-consuming, and costly schemes. There are simple and easy ways of focusing on the needs and wishes of the school's customers: parents and students. There are two basic rules: (1) do not overlook the most obvious way to get to know customers: talk to them and (2) mine the data about customers that is already on hand. Parents volunteer a tremendous amount of information when they contact the school to file a complaint, make a suggestion, or request help. One high school developed a piece of software to collect information on parent interaction with the school.

In an effort to listen to parents, many schools are beginning to utilize focus groups. Focus groups, which have been around since the end of World War II, can make the job a little easier. However, new psychological techniques are competing with them, and new academic thinking indicates they may not be as effective as more traditional qualitative research. Given the way that focus groups work, it is easy to see why schools are enamored of them. It is easy to gather ten or so people to talk about a service or a problem and have them agree to their comments being taped or transcribed. While the ease is attractive to schools, there are problems with this approach. The sample of opinions in a focus group, far too small to be statistically representative, can shrink further owing to the *Twelve Angry Men* effect. Someone in the group—a vocal parent, student, or community member with a particular grievance—ends up acting like Henry Fonda in the classic movie, persuading the other jurors to change their minds. Focus group research should not be used for making decisions without further validation from other methods of research.

One school I know uses focus groups the right way. A team of teachers and administrators surveys the community using open-ended questions and then follows up by holding a series of focus groups to obtain parent and community input on priorities for change. The focus groups are used to validate survey findings and deepen staff understanding of the issues. One example is the career-related program to reduce the dropout rate. Each year the school checks up on how it is doing by polling parents about the efficacy of new instructional programs and the quality of administrative and support services.

At a second school, parents and teachers who previously had little opportunity to interact now arrange for monthly coffee and cake gatherings for each "family" of teacher teams. These gatherings, effectively facilitated, become forums to solicit parents' thoughts on current and planned curriculum and instruction efforts.

Mission Bay High School in San Diego involves both teachers and parents in an annual performance evaluation of the principal and other school administrators, thereby providing a systematic audit on the thoughts, opinions, and impressions among the school's customers.

Link All Improvements to Teaching and Learning

Starting a restructuring initiative inevitably requires an initial whirlwind of activity—holding facultywide thinking and planning sessions, organizing a new decision-making process, equipping people with problem-solving techniques—that can be terribly distracting. Some schools, regretfully, spend years on this first phase and never move to program implementation. One school spent three years deciding on a catchy acronym for a reform effort that never got off the ground.

Clear objectives can help make this start-up phase briefer. Additionally, a faculty commitment early on to the improvement of teaching and learning provides guidance and direction. At a high school in New York City, teachers have agreed that all change activities should answer three questions: Why are we making this change? What do we hope to achieve by the change? How and when will we know that we are making progress toward the goal?

Once up and running, planning teams and implementation task forces continue to need direction. At one sprawling high school in New Mexico, faculty committees have meandered into discussions on teacher restrooms and parking lot security because their efforts were not linked to the instructional mission of the school. Overall teaching and learning objectives were never fully agreed upon, making it easy to forget that all change efforts should rightfully be assessed for their impact on the education of students.

Link the Restructuring Efforts to a Few Strategic Goals

A well-planned overall approach with a few clearly defined goals is critical to an effective planning process. Unless it is linked to easily understandable strategic goals, however, even the most widely supported restructuring efforts flounder. Strategic goals provide focus for the school's restructuring. They force school planners, whether teachers or administrators, to do first things first—a very valuable discipline when they are inundated with myriad "important" details. A major concern about restructuring, as mentioned in Chapter 2, is that it overwhelms a school, since everything must be done concurrently. The risk, of course, is that people lose focus.

Focus is, frankly, one of the biggest benefits of restructuring. It forces the school to get back to basics. It helps a school develop a posture similar to that of a corporate raider and assists it to give up emotional attachments to old approaches and old ideas. School people get an opportunity to take a hard look, without blame placing, at everything going on in the building. If something has been tried, given a decent chance of success, and has not proven itself, it can be abandoned. Clear and widely understood strategies help school planning teams identify the essential activities to keep and the nonessential activities to eliminate.

It is important to ask regularly, "Just what am I attempting to achieve?" Capital High School in Santa Fe, New Mexico, trains its restructuring microscope on two issues: one is improving student achievement so that all students pass state competency tests on the first try; the other is increasing student engagement in the learning program as measured by school-developed quantitative indicators assessing oral expression, expository writing, and research skills. Teacher teams can organize classroom instruction in any way they like, as long as they focus on these two goals.

One high school in Louisiana with a depressingly high dropout rate developed a schoolwide objective of improving students' self-image by correlating content knowledge and skill development across the vocational/career and academic disciplines. Teachers at the school also agreed to modify the schedule to permit teachers from different, previously isolated, subject area departments to meet and develop joint projects. Achieving this required each subject area department to give up some turf.

The principal of the school and teachers attribute support for the curriculum and organizational changes to the overall focus of the school on lowering the dropout rate. One previously skeptical science teacher admits,

> We were about to be closed by the district. It was hardly worth keeping the building open since each year we had fewer students. We knew that we had to improve the school's holding power and we directed all our energy toward that goal. The goal made the difference. It allowed us to turn teacher resistance to support.

The Importance of Clear Goals

Explicit goals are needed for the *entire* organization. That is, the change endeavor needs to be looked at in the context of the total system (Senge, 1990). This requires defining the future *outside* of the short-term restructuring goals, such as the implementation of a specific curriculum pilot or a scheduling change. People will assume the worst when they are unclear or uncertain (e.g., unaffected people may assume the change applies to them).

There is a story about a traveler who in medieval times meets three stonecutters along a road and asks each of them what he is doing. The first says, "I am cutting stone." The second says, "I am shaping a cornerstone." The third answers, "I am building a cathedral." The strength of a restructuring effort lies in the fact that school staff become cathedral builders, not stonecutters.

It is important to tie all school change efforts together in a straightforward, easy-to-understand framework (Hunsaker and Alessandra, 1980). Contemporary concepts and practices such as site-based management, teaming, interdisciplinary courses, authentic assessment, mastery learning, outcome-based education, and the effective schools research, to name a few, can easily be understood within the framework of the whole school restructuring agenda. When the school's overall restructuring becomes a unifying factor, these different components become part of an ongoing philosophy of commitment to improvement, with roots that can grow deeper as time goes on.

People need a clear and simple "promised land" to which they can travel. People need to see the end to the ambiguities of the organization during the period after the change process begins and the reconstruction of a better school organization. This picture of the promised land becomes the pull for change. President Kennedy said, "We will land a man on the moon in this decade" (Belasco, 1990, p. 23), and it focused the nation's work for the next ten years. The easiest way to accomplish clarity of purpose is with an energizing, inspiring vision as the key to mobilizing support. This vision is the picture that drives all action. It includes both deeply felt values and a picture of the school's strategic focus.

Father Hesburgh built Notre Dame into a major American university during his 35 years as president. He infused his vision of a revitalized Notre Dame in students, alumni, faculty, and the general public. Talking about his role in changing the university, he said (Belasco, 1990, p. 24):

> The very essence of leadership is you have to have a vision. It's got to be a vision you articulate clearly and forcefully on every occasion. You can't blow an uncertain trumpet.

A vision is a certain trumpet. It identifies clearly for all concerned—teachers, students, community, and parents—exactly what the school stands for and precisely why they should support it, as seen in Chapter 7. A vision both enhances a school's focus and provides deep personal identification with the school's work. Vision directs attention to the critical factors that produce long-term success. It allows people to ask, "Is my action in keeping with the vision?" This focus, and inspiration, empowers people to change.

A vision also creates a sense of mission, helping people believe that their work is essential, particularly when other forms of security have evaporated. The principal can inspire other staff and give people a sense of purpose and pride in the value of their work. Pride is frequently a better source of motivation than the traditional promotion-based reward system.

BUILDING STAFF SUPPORT FOR CHANGE

Provide Opportunity for Professional Discretion

People generally value feeling some sense of control over their professional lives, i.e., over their own activities and direction. Principals and other leaders can provide this by encouraging people to develop their pet projects (within the parameters of the school's restructuring framework, of course) and then seeing that they have time to carry those forward. A second positive effect of this approach is a results-based orientation that involves working with teachers to develop outcomes and then giving staff the discretion about the procedures they will use to achieve them. Greater latitude in work assignment can be negotiated individually with staff and can be a reward for significant accomplishment.

Create Opportunities for Teacher Learning

The chance to learn new skills or apply them in new ways becomes important in a restructuring school. In a turbulent environment, learning enables people to create a niche for themselves in the new organization. In a climate where pay incentives are largely nonexistent, access to new training is a major inducement. At one Florida school, applicants for positions tripled when a new training and development program was put in place.

All restructuring efforts require intensive reeducation. Education facilitates the communication of new organizational values and provides a formal means to challenge the values and attitudes of the old organization: the high school everyone is working to change. It also demonstrates the leader's long-term commitment to the seriousness and importance of the change effort.

One must be cautious, since professional development, too, can quickly spin out of control. Many very expensive training efforts lead nowhere. Teachers are so starved for meaningful learning experiences that they can easily become unfocused in what they want and need. Moreover, they are presently accustomed to thinking exclusively of their individual learning needs rather than the needs of the school as a whole, i.e., the critical importance of viewing the achievement of teaching and learning goals as a schoolwide responsibility. Both are important.

One lesson of restructuring is that training teams, once they have achieved consensus about learning needs, are more likely to have follow-through. Staff training and education should be linked to some type of payback for the school. If the results are not there within two years, it is a good idea to rethink the school's approach to training.

Professional Visibility

Leaders can provide public recognition and visibility by crediting the authors of innovation at the school and by assisting people in connecting with professional networks outside the school.

CREATING A SCHOOL CLIMATE THAT NURTURES CHANGE

Help Staff Accept Uncertainty

An important element in the success of a restructuring effort is the staff's ability to become psychologically comfortable with uncertainty—an important ingredient in minimizing its negative impact on the change process. The question frequently arises of whether or not principals in particular can take the time, given their other responsibilities, to deal with the time-consuming task of handling staff problems related to coping with the ambiguity and uncertainty of the transition period (the period of time between the decision to change and the integration of the new organization and belief system into the minds and habits of staff). Some management experts argue that high schools are so complex and vulnerable to elusive internal and external influences, such as shared leadership issues, that principals' freedom to act is limited (Milone, 1990). Their argument is plausible, but my experience does not support it. By and large, the most successful principals I know are precisely those who strive to make a mark through creating a guiding vision, shaping shared values, and otherwise providing leadership for the entire school community.

Create an Environment Conducive to Mutual Trust and Risk Taking

Discussing ideas, discovering new ways of exploring and thinking, and experimenting under conditions of trust and respect enhance commitment and increase receptivity to new viewpoints. Restructuring will require significant risk taking and a radical shift in the way things get done within the organization. It is impossible in an environment in which open communication, mutual trust, and risk taking are not nourished and actively encouraged.

Be Focused and Consistent Over Time

Although it requires years to develop a new organizational form, it can take only a few weeks to erase years of progress through inconsistent behavior by the principal and other leaders. This is especially true during times of crisis. Staff members are always watching the principal and have long memories.

The change process must be ongoing and constantly renewed. Staff members are often more astute than they are given credit for. They can see through glossy programs and superficial "quasi-change" efforts. They will notice incompatible and inconsistent behavior by the principal or other leaders as the school moves toward its new organizational structure and the development of its new educational program. It will take twenty times as many positive examples of the desired management behavior to override just one example of incompatible behavior.

MANAGING CHANGE

The Principal Must Be Involved

The principal of a high school in Ohio learned this the hard way. On the opening day of school, he announced his support for a districtwide restructuring initiative and in effect said to the staff: "Go do it." The effect was zero. After a year, when he realized that nothing was happening, he designated a well-respected vice principal to coordinate the change process. This helped the effort gain some zip for a short while. However, before long, the principal realized that the vice principal could only work with staff on basic process issues. If he wanted to get beyond easy steps, such as setting up teacher teams or planning for increased parental involvement, "making it happen" required the principal's direct involvement. Since that time, this principal has been very visible at faculty staff development workshops and planning meetings and in promoting new instructional and managerial innovations. He has played a major role in facilitating implementation of change projects. He now participates at the weekly meetings of the teacher teams to hear concerns and problems, and he admits that his earlier policy of delegating responsibility for change, rather than sharing it, was a costly mistake.

A principal at a big-city high school in California agrees that her active and visible involvement in the school's restructuring has been a crucial factor in sustaining the momentum behind reform efforts. She has joined staff members in two week-long summer workshops on interdisciplinary curriculum. "I've had to visibly be part of it," she says. "People look to see if you just talk about things or actually do them."

This principal serves on two task forces involved in change. The first is investigating the establishment of a community service program to provide internships for students. The second is exploring ways in which new technology can support the school's new student grouping, grading, and assessment procedures. She helps the task forces by scanning the reform literature for useful information, doing some basic research, making arrangements for on-site demonstrations by software developers, and securing the financial resources so that teachers can attend professional conferences and visit other restructuring schools.

The lessons are clear. To achieve a fundamental change in school culture and practice, principals must use a hands-on approach. They must be physically present at important events, must repeatedly state their support for change, and must reward those who respond to the challenge.

Some, like the Ohio principal, have trouble understanding that change by fiat or policy pronouncement is only the first and easiest step in the change process. Such a statement sets a process in motion. When the change is consistent with the school's mode of conducting business, a subordinate, such as an assistant principal, can manage the process.

Restructuring, however, involves a fundamental change in the school's orientation toward reaching its goals. It contravenes the traditional belief system and customary posture. Thus, it creates anxiety, doubt, and skepticism. New ways of doing and thinking require the utmost attention from sensitive, responsible leadership at the highest level. The principal must be an active participant in urging, persuading, and making it clear how important the changes are to those affected, as well as to the administration. It is important not to confuse change in policy with change in practice. Aligning practice with policy takes hard work. It creates opportunities for miscommunication because those most important to the change effort—the teachers—are not accustomed to focusing on what is occurring outside of their own classrooms or do not talk directly with each other regularly about change issues.

In the first of Deming's well-known fourteen points for quality management, he establishes the preeminent need for management to create constancy of purpose for the improvement of products and service. Quality, insists Deming, cannot and must not be delegated. Responsibility for quality processes, systems, and outcomes rests with management; in the case of schools, it rests with the principal and members of the administrative team. Teachers, acting by themselves, cannot create the optimum schoolwide conditions under which change processes can take place. That is the job of management. It is entrusted with the responsibility of fully adapting any new philosophy throughout the organization by building relationships of trust from the top down and by empowering and enabling teachers to make ongoing reflection and continual improvement the new way of working. By removing the barriers to change and garnering the necessary resources to provide ongoing training, principals can keep the engine of change moving in the right direction.

Finally, and most importantly, principals must use a hands-on approach in their effort to drive fear out of the school. The old fear-based system of compliance, control, and command has no place in a school where teachers are the key to successful change and where people must think creatively, work in self-directed teams, and build cultures of mutual support for everyone's continuous improvement.

Leading is helping, coaching, and supporting; it is not threatening and punishing. Because of this, administrators and other school leaders play essential roles in initiating and maintaining the transformation process required to build new schools. Because the journey is never-ending, school leaders must be enabled and supported by all of the school's stakeholders in their continuous efforts to make the school better and better, day by day, year by year.

Communication Is Key

There needs to be a strong two-way communication system, as described in Chapter 10, to minimize distortions (Little, 1982). Every opportunity to spread information about ongoing activities, meetings, and accomplishments should be used. That also includes establishing an ongoing relationship with the media. Instead of providing the media with symbolic numbers to demonstrate student progress, the school might provide local newspapers and television stations with opportunities to observe and interview teachers and students. If the community has cable television, use the public access channel to broadcast programs describing the change process and efforts that are at the heart of the school's transformation. It is much more effective for people to see with their own eyes the good things happening in the school than to read canned press releases.

Communication can take many forms. Develop opportunities for firsthand discussions with other people at different levels of the organization. Communication in too many schools is characterized by one-way communication, from principals to staff. In many schools, the memos and reports and suggestions made by staff disappear into a void. Staff never receive a response. As a result, principals have no idea how effective they are until someone blames them for something. Lack of feedback forces teachers to focus on how they do something, not what they do.

A key communication strategy is to celebrate all successes, even small ones. Successful whole school transformation efforts invariably recognize incremental improvements, especially by teams, and celebrate them in collaborative, noncompetitive environments. Teacher teams should be recognized by their peers, administrators, and parents for their ongoing success.

Checkpoints and Milestones

There need to be specific checkpoints and milestones along the way—benchmark processes and outcomes. Benchmarking should be done in collaboration with the shared decision-making group, with the consensus of the others in the school community. One approach is to search for standard-bearer restructuring schools in other districts, learn from their experiences, and then apply their lessons. The redesign committees at Lane visited and learned from other restructuring schools. At Beacon High School in Chapter 7, Dr. Forrest and the members of the SPC collected information from other restructuring schools through on-site visits. They also collected information by phone and mail, through a search of the literature, and from outside consultants.

Adapt Anything from Outside the School to the School's Own Needs

A school restructuring effort can be energizing. It brings together people who have long been apart. Its immediate result is to release a huge amount of creative energy—some positive, some negative—into the school environment. The energy can turn into zealotry: grabbing poorly thought-out programs from other schools just to get something into place. School personnel must always question what is offered by other schools' approaches to education; merely learning their slogans by rote is of no use. The school's reform leaders should constantly check to make sure the other schools' approaches work for their own school. It is a mistake to negate the uniqueness of a school by adopting an off-the-shelf program that may be succeeding elsewhere. Although it is not necessary to reinvent the wheel, it is important to make sure that someone else's wheel fits the particular school's wagon.

CREATING AN ORGANIZATION THAT PROMOTES CHANGE

Eliminate Barriers to Change

Barriers to change can be individual and organizational. Organizational barriers include narrow, formal rules for accomplishing work, rigid job definitions, and lack of a common language for articulating the goals of the restructuring effort. Individual barriers include lack of awareness of the need for change and lack of critical skills required for the success of the change effort (e.g., problem-solving skills, participatory management style, etc.). Hence, focused education and training are vitally important. Education is one of the most effective vehicles to reduce individual fears and concerns and gain the support and commitment of staff.

Develop Flexible Management Systems

All management systems must be flexible and geared to embrace change, rather than to obstruct it. Questions that every principal and leadership group should ask early on in the change process are, "Are our school's management systems flexible?" and "Are our consultative processes able to adjust to new situations and opportunities as they occur?"

The essence of flexibility is the ability of the entire school community to adjust quickly to new circumstances. Schools can usually better meet the challenge of change with a form of management that allows the faculty to face change and to gain experience in dealing with it. This means providing teachers with the opportunity to plan together and to work collaboratively. It also means helping teachers gain experience in solving the educational problems facing the school. As stated earlier, it means building lines of communication that ease the direct transmission of information among the school's constituent groups. Traditionally, normal procedure in schools is to funnel all matters through the principal's office, inhibiting free thinking and planning. This practice stifles the change process and reduces the willingness of teachers and others to offer suggestions. If school staff members are to be equipped to think deeply about solutions to students' learning problems, then school management systems must be planned accordingly.

Decentralize Authority and Responsibility

How can principals meet their responsibility to keep the school running smoothly without inhibiting the ability of teachers to respond to change? One way is to create maximum opportunity for the organization's instructional units, e.g., mini-school clusters responsible for a group of students, teachers teaming with a particular grade, and members of subject area departments taking group responsibility to develop procedures that are most conducive to accomplishing the unit's job. This, of course, must be done within the framework of the school's instructional mission. In this way, educators can design programs that meet the specific needs of youngsters.

Principals are trained to exercise a leadership role. Many feel that they are relinquishing this responsibility when they allow groups of teachers to plan new initiatives on their own. Some feel an overwhelming compulsion to inject their opinions into teacher planning conversations. Although offering a menu of ideas shows interest and support, this approach, however well-intentioned, has its shortcomings. Even though principals offer ideas as suggestions or options, many teachers will still act on them as if they were mandatory. Even when teachers believe that the principal would like them to use their own judgment, they still have the "internalized principal" to contend with: that is, the conscious proclivity to behave in ways they think the principal wants them to.

Convincing staff that the principal's suggestions are really just suggestions takes hard work. It may mean withholding suggestions, at least until teachers actually know from experience that the principal's invitation to share in decision making is genuine. It can also mean shifting the school's reward system to value teacher independence and creativity. In other circumstances, the principal's presentation of a menu of ideas is helpful to the change process. It can provide the principal with the information he or she needs to build greater flexibility into management structures that meet the different faculty concerns.

One district shifted the responsibility for assessing the effectiveness of the instructional program from the central office to the schools. The district no longer relied on districtwide examinations, but invited each school to develop its own assessment instruments based on broad district standards issued by the local Board of Education. The district backed up this responsibility with a budget for experimentation. The district's schools, which once suffered from success complacency, no longer do.

A flexible management system is helpful in keeping people current with new research and trends. One neighborhood high school in San Diego had declining student enrollment. The city had many magnet programs that attracted youngsters away from the local high school. The principal was adept at public and community relations and could have developed a major student recruitment drive on his own. He realized, however, that such a shortsighted approach would not promote faculty ownership of schoolwide problems beyond the walls of the classroom. The principal confronted this problem by including the staff in discussions on schoolwide issues. Staff members agreed to assume responsibility for the development of new career-focused programs to attract additional students. They also took charge of budget and staffing decisions. Decisions about which staff members would lose their jobs if student enrollment fell short of projections became staff decisions.

The approach at this San Diego school had two outcomes: (1) student enrollment rose dramatically and (2) the management system helped staff members detect changing trends and customer requirements more quickly. They established an ongoing feedback mechanism, so that this information was given to teacher leaders and school administrators. Thus, policies and programs became more customer oriented and responsive to student and parent wishes and aspirations.

Attack Change Problems Through Decentralization

Principals of large high schools find it difficult to know all the implications of changes occurring within the school. No one can keep up with new developments in bilingual education, special education, vocational and technical education, instructional technology, guidance, curriculum, custodial operations, labor negotiations, and finance. Staff members at every level, therefore, should have the authority to deal with change as it occurs. The business community is increasingly using this approach, allowing decentralized management to empower lower-level employees with a great deal of freedom and flexibility to respond to changing conditions. Flexible, decentralized management requires that authority be pushed downward as far as possible so that those closest to the environmental changes can observe, analyze, and react to the change. Should the initial conclusions prove incorrect, or the charted response ineffective, front-line decentralized management will be the first to spot the warning signals. This will allow them to reevaluate and respond, rather than perpetuate an ineffective system (DePree, 1989).

Every broadening of authority, however, must also have an accountability system to make it practical: whoever decides must be accountable for producing results. The process leads to more realistic control than does rigid regulation.

Consider the experience of one school in Miami that had a serious problem with student tardiness. Each year the school administration would try to solve the problem with a new and different approach. The principal would announce the new initiative with a great deal of hype. It would usually involve incentives and penalties. Parents would receive notices informing them of the importance of regular attendance, administrators would lecture teachers about their responsibilities, teachers would receive memoranda about the importance of following the new regulations, financial and personnel resources would be reallocated to managing the new system, and so on. It would become a major add-on. Other efforts would stop to focus on attendance; it was a campaign, rather than part of the school's organization.

Each year the new effort would begin with a bang. By October teachers would tire; the press of other business would intrude. By Halloween, the new tardiness policy was forgotten; by November is was back to business as usual. Between 500 and 700, a third of the school population, could be seen outside the building as late as 11:00 A.M. as some loitered and others straggled into the building.

Two years ago, the school district started a school-based management/shared decision-making initiative. Only when the school administration made each "house" unit of five teachers responsible and accountable for student tardiness did the school begin to focus on the real issues and to develop more flexible and effective plans. The approach to handling tardiness problems differed from one house to another.

Large organizations resist decentralization. This often causes them to change slowly. Smaller units can respond more aggressively (Hickman and Silva, 1984) to diverse needs. In fairness to large organizations, the effects of any change for them may seem complex and overwhelming.

In a school context, it is uncomfortable, if not frightening, to permit many people to decide on school issues. In addition, many principals have a love affair with central planning, through which policies and procedures are uniform for all. They homogenize teachers and students the way dairy workers homogenize milk.

The failure of some schools to maintain instructional effectiveness in the classroom can be attributed to a lack of opportunity for individualization. For example, one school's overall plan for individualized instruction did not differentiate its approach for *all* students from its approach for *each* student. Each unit in the organization must be allowed to plan and operate to suit its own needs.

Decentralization of decision making sometimes runs into another problem. A principal may promote decentralized decision making only to find that heads of smaller units, such as subject area departments, set up small centralized regimes, as in the Lane case study. Middle managers, such as assistant principals, program coordinators, department heads, or lead teachers, need assistance to equip them to work within a decentralized system and to share decisions with those around them. For example, at one high school in California, the principal responded to a faculty request to decentralize curriculum decisions by giving planning and scheduling authority to each subject department. Unfortunately, the department coordinators had not been taught how they should share the authority of their own operation. Until this was done, the decentralized plan could not work, as demonstrated in Chapter 9, which dealt with strategies for gaining the support of middle managers.

Free and creative thinking is not possible in the presence of rigid authority that attempts to control people's thinking and free expression. Strict adherence to procedure is antagonistic to change. It focuses on regulating activity instead of encouraging people to take risks by experimentation. For example, in the typical large high school using a centralized scheduling system, the master scheduler can in fact hold the entire school hostage. He or she is usually convinced that the system is ideal. It does work fine from the scheduler's vantage point. It provides school administrators with a neat picture of where every adult and student is at each moment during the day. It provides a sense of neatness and order creating the aura of a smooth and efficiently run organization. It causes problems, however, among teachers. A schedule for the entire building is usually complex and cumbersome. It occupies the school's administrative energy for weeks at a time. It requires a great deal of time to put together, thereby limiting teacher creativity. It cannot accommodate last-minute ideas, no matter how useful. Most important, a schoolwide master schedule is not user friendly. It is difficult to incorporate new courses that require different meeting times than the rest of the school, it is difficult to meet the particular needs of one department without altering the entire program, and the needs of individual students become subordinate to the schools' overall efficiency.

There are alternatives to such a rigid, schoolwide schedule. More important than the alternative scheduling models are the thinking and planning processes that must undergird the schedule—or, for that matter, any other organizational or programmatic decision. Each need for a decision—any decision on any topic—can also become an opportunity to advance the school's change agenda and build capacity for further change and innovation, as explained in the final portion of this chapter.

USING SCHEDULING TO FACILITATE CHANGE

The school schedule is only a tool to carry out the school's educational vision. It is not an end in itself, and it should not be allowed to dominate curriculum decisions or school staffing patterns. How can the scheduling process be used to ease the flow of new ideas into the school? How does a school develop scheduling practices that stimulate innovation and creativity? This section of the chapter concludes the book by bringing together the lessons of previous chapters in order to describe an approach that involves staff in the creation of a high school schedule that is truly based on student needs.

Examining the Status Quo

First, it is wise to borrow an idea used by corporations to stimulate thinking about how time, resources, and personnel can be used to greatest advantage: zero-based budgeting. Zero-based budgeting is a process designed to promote accountability. Instead of using an add-on or incremental approach, zero-based budgeting assumes that all budgeted items should be justified each year from zero. It also assumes that those at the operational level of the corporation will choose the most cost-effective option when they have the authority and the resources needed to meet the general goals of their unit. When applied to the process of creating an instructional program for high schools, this approach provides an opportunity to base scheduling decisions upon changing learning priorities, instead of the status quo.

Zero-based scheduling means that school people must forget last year's schedule. Forget all the schedules the school has ever put together. Forget previous deadlines and cumbersome programming procedures. Erase the mental tape about what the schedule is *supposed* to look like. Throw out all the preconceived notions about course titles, number of periods per day, and the number of days per week. Get rid of course codes and programming charts. Start fresh.

Second, principals should ask themselves and the staff members some very important questions about the school's purpose, student learning, and curriculum and instruction. Each question should be posed to the members of the school staff, primarily teachers but also to custodial, food service, and clerical workers. Why, the reader might ask, should custodial, food service, and clerical workers be involved? What contribution can they make to discussions about education? I remember one occasion in a New Jersey district when a custodial assistant—Jim— provoked high school teachers to rethink the school's approach to educating emotionally handicapped youngsters. At that time the New Jersey district separated most emotionally handicapped students from other youngsters for the entire school day. Jim stood before the large group of staff members. He recalled his experiences as a teacher's aide in a rural Ohio district that integrated all special needs students into the regular school program. As Jim told the group, "When you think about what's good for the school, think about what's good for the students...always begin with the students." No one could have said it better.

Three basic questions should be posed to the school staff.

Who Are the Students?

There is more to students than the traditional terms used to define them, such as age, grade, family background, ethnic group, and achievement scores. They can, and should, be described by their learning styles, competency in all curricular areas, responsibility and commitment to learning, physical abilities and emotional health, interests and aptitudes, special talents, and their futures as reflected in their career and educational goals. Once the staff has spent time looking carefully at the many indicators of the strengths and characteristics of the students, they should have a greater understanding of the young people for whom an educational program must be created.

What Should the Students Learn?

A statement of educational outcomes with a description of what must happen educationally to qualify a student for graduation should be drawn up. It ought to contain a series of measurable goals from which the curriculum and instructional strategies must flow. It is important that there be consensus about these outcomes among faculty before proceeding to the next question.

How Can the School Best Provide for
the Learning that Will Produce the Desired Outcomes?

If school colleagues answer this question by listing the current course offerings and curriculum arrangements, they are on the wrong track. Most schools steeped in the tradition of past practice reflect common expectations about how schooling should be conducted, as evidenced by nearly standardized buildings, scheduling, and curricula. Teachers and administrators find it difficult to think "outside the box" about how to adapt to students' varied skills, interests, and needs—or even to see the need to do so (Fullan, 1988). The gap between the standard forms of schools and optimum learning conditions is seen most dramatically in schools that serve the lowest socioeconomic groups (Firestone and Rosenblum, 1988; Metz, 1990). Most tradition-bound secondary schools, however, do not provide young people with the skills and experiences to equip them for a society driven by the transmission of information.

If current research is not convincing enough, then the staff might be asked another series of questions:

- How many students are actually thriving on the school's learning program?

- How many of them excel?

- How many of them are hanging around the fringes of the legal system committing crimes?

- How many parents have confidence in the school?

- How many teachers have satisfying and productive professional lives and how many voice frustrations after each workday?

If the answers to these questions indicate that all is well, then that school is an exception. If, however, the answers elicit unmet needs, and staff members are willing to seek some new and creative answers to one of the original questions—what students should learn—then the school should continue with a process by which people in the school community have an opportunity to link their original statement of desired outcomes to the experiences and content knowledge to which each student should be exposed. The document that results from this process can be called the school's program goals.

The answers to the last group of questions should focus the school on the specific steps to be taken to translate goals and objectives into actual practice. The answers also lead to additional questions:

- How will the school organize the curriculum?

- Will learning be available through independent research or tutorial experiences?

- Will students show competence by examination or performance?

- Will there be small-group seminars, traditional class settings, and large-group presentations?

- Will provision be made for hands-on experiences, work/study, or career education?

- Will learning be interdisciplinary, thematic, or project centered?

- Will variable-length courses be offered or will all courses last a full term or year?

- Will all students move from one learning experience to another at the same rate, or will there be flexibility based on individual need? (For example, how will the school define physical education outcomes? Will the school build a physical education program based on achievement of physical skills alone, or will the school include competitive and noncompetitive activities? What about health development? Will illness or physical disability be considered failure? How will mastery be assessed?)

- Will the school allow students to enter and exit programs only at specified times, such as the beginning of a new school term, or will it be possible to start a new course or lesson module when a student is ready to do so?

By this point in the process, the group has started to define learning outcomes, consider curriculum arrangements, and weigh instructional strategies. Learning, however, does not occur in a vacuum; school climate and faculty morale play a key role. Thought must be given to the options for organizing the school to create a nurturing atmosphere for students. Thus, consideration must be given to student grouping and the arrangement of support services. The school must be set up so that each youngster feels well taken care of and has an equal chance to succeed.

Improving the School Climate

Take Good Care of Students

Taking good care of each student requires a structuring of the school to make it *easy* for a student to succeed and *hard* for him or her to fail. In most regulation-driven schools today, the opposite is true. A growing body of literature shows that the traditional organization of high schools damages students' emotional and intellectual development and encourages failure (Sizer, 1984; Firestone and Rosenblum, 1988). Curriculum is organized in unrelated, compartmentalized, and trivialized courses that often have no connection to students' lives (Lightfoot, 1983). For the most part, they are places in which students become anonymous and drop out.

I remember one pathetic illustration of anonymity at a large Florida high school with a 50% dropout rate. A despondent young lady exiting the building informed me that she was dropping out. When I asked her why, she responded, "Well, there are lots of reasons but, for one, you're the first person to ask me that question."

At this Florida high school, in a procedure reminiscent of Kafka's *Castle*, students who drop out must first get a pass from a teacher they never met to see a guidance counselor they do not know to drop out of a school they rarely attended. One way to prevent student anonymity is to give teachers the opportunity to work with a common group of students and to be able to assess student progress during the workday.

Foster Teacher Collaboration

Students are not the only victims of outdated scheduling practices. Scheduling can also contribute to the creation of a school that does not take good care of teachers. Long hours in self-contained classrooms, with little relief or revitalization through professional development, contributes to deepening demoralization (Rosenholtz, 1989) and makes it difficult for teachers to view themselves as members of a professional community (Sirotnik, 1983; Wilson and Corcoran, 1988). At most traditionally organized high schools, as we know, teachers see 150 students during 45-minute periods. They rarely have an opportunity to discuss a particular student with others because they rarely share common planning periods with a child's other teachers. Are these circumstances attributable to the inflexibility of a schoolwide 45-minute period schedule? They most certainly are.

Is it sensible to schedule teachers individually if doing so constrains their ability to meet and plan collaboratively? Teachers must have an opportunity to meet regularly to share knowledge about new instructional strategies and to explore new techniques that may work with students with special learning problems. This is not anything new. After all, most teacher contracts make provision for individual planning time. Teachers complain, however, that they are unable to make good use of this time. Teaching should not be a solitary task. Teachers need to share ideas, trade theories, reinforce each other, test their beliefs, and share knowledge. Collaborative work with peers increases a teacher's sense of affiliation with the school, along with a sense of mutual support and responsibility for the effectiveness of instruction (Rosenholtz, 1989). Collaboration leads to a sense of community and an increased commitment to carry out more substantial (and difficult) innovations. Teachers should not have to struggle against an inflexible schedule to find time to work with colleagues.

Prepare the New Schedule

Once the staff has decided on the type of learning program they want and the strategies they will use to implement the program, it is time to turn to the schedule itself. In essence, scheduling is the management of time: finding the best possible way to bring together the students, staff, and program of instruction in sensible, organized, and feasible time segments. These time segments should be compatible with the answers to the following three questions: (1) How many hours will be required to present this learning experience to that individual or group of students? (2) What will be the most appropriate way to divide those hours so that maximum learning experiences can be offered to the students? (3) How can choices be presented to students with a minimum of conflict and maximum of opportunities? To deal with these three basic questions, the school staff needs to arrange the school program in a format that will explain each defined group of learning experiences (course, module) in terms of the following:

- Clearly stated outcomes in content, attitudes, values, and behaviors

- Student learning styles and ability levels

- Learning experiences in and out of school

- Groupings (individual, tutorial, seminar, class, large-group presentation)

- Instructional techniques and strategies

- Materials, equipment, source books, and resources

- Assessment of performance

- Credits earned toward graduation and content areas to be applied

- Rough estimates of time needed for course in total hours; division of hours into segments, such as two hours, one half day, full day, etc.

Consider the following example of how this approach is carried out. A curricular theme that focuses on the steel industry is chosen. This topic is part of a combined practical and theoretical interdisciplinary look at the development of industry in America. Activities will include doing the background research and primary source readings in the school's media center; learning to understand computer applications such as charting inventories, production reports, and employment statistics; seeing and discussing films such as *The Valley of Decision*; conducting interviews with businesspeople and economists; listening to audiotapes made during the Depression; and attending seminars, meetings, and lectures. Perhaps resource personnel such as curriculum specialists or executives from a nearby steel distributor will work along with groups of teachers. At least twenty school days of seven hours each will be necessary to complete the work.

If teachers agree that all students at a particular grade level will be exposed to such varied experiences in the steel industry, the unit might be offered at different times of the year, thereby optimizing the use of resource personnel and school facilities such as the media center. A second option might be to have different groups of teachers present the unit concurrently. There are additional options: a block program that allows students to spend three consecutive periods in a single subject, a cluster program or media program that offers an interdisciplinary approach to learning, or an integrated curriculum program in which two subjects are taught together, such as English and social studies or industrial arts and math. It also might make sense to rearrange rooms to provide a network of media centers and labs where teachers and students can work when not in class.

How can teachers arrange for these interdisciplinary units in a traditional six-, seven-, or eight-period day, meeting students for 45-minute time segments, five times a week? Simply put, they cannot. Feeding the information into the computer has become the easiest part of the scheduling process. The technical support provided by the actual computer program is getting more varied each year. If a school is still tied into a purchased, computerized data-processing firm that offers an option of two, three, or four different scheduling models from which to choose and a series of deadlines that restrict flexibility, the school would be well advised to get rid of it and for the same money hire some part-time clerical help to do the sorting and cataloging that will be needed. The school will never obtain a creative schedule if the district's data-processing company is allowed to dictate a school schedule from limited choices. It will not be the school's schedule; it will be theirs. The odds are that it will not be compatible with the learning program designed—with much thought—by the school's staff for the school's own students. A schedule, like the entire restructuring effort, must be homegrown. My intention in this portion of the chapter has been to describe the thinking process that must accompany the preparation of a school schedule. This same process can be used to make any policy, programmatic, or organization decision.

It is still too early in the educational restructuring movement to draw conclusions about the impact of specific school structures on student learning. Not enough schools have established significant alternatives to study the effects of different structures alone or in combination. One thing is clear: to be effective, alternate structures must nurture and reflect broader changes in values and human relationships in schools. When teachers and students believe that they are working in a caring and stimulating environment, change can evolve to fit specific needs and preferences of the school community (Conley, 1989).

Until now, schools have been too busy trying to fit new curriculum and instructional innovations into their current schedules or, for that matter, into current school practice in every area. If schools are serious about improving education, they must break loose from the straitjacket imposed by many current practices. Aligning educational goals and the school policy and practice, such as the schedule, should be an exciting and intellectually stimulating experience. Having all the pieces fit neatly together in a lovely, geometric design is not an indicator of a successful school. Scheduling, for example, is only a mechanical tool that arranges time to serve students, staff, and the instructional program. It needs to be used wisely and creatively.

What will the thinking process described above do for a school? By increasing staff participation in school decisions, particularly those involving teaching and learning, incentives are created for teachers to experiment with and develop new instructional programs (Newmann et al., 1988; Little, 1982). A considerable body of research suggests that where workers are given genuine opportunities to make decisions about how to organize and carry out their work, their increased sense of control contributes to increased satisfaction, engagement, and productivity. This greater involvement helps teachers to develop competence in their work and builds both the *will* and the *skill* needed to create a new generation of effective high schools.

References

Belasco, J. (1990). *Teaching the Elephant to Dance.* New York: Crown.

Conley, S.C. (1989). Who's on first? School reform, teacher participation and the decision-making process. *Education and Urban Society,* 21(4), 366–379.

Deal, T.E. and Kennedy, A.A. (1982). *Corporate Cultures.* Reading, Massachusetts: Addison-Wesley.

DePree, M. (1989). *Leadership as an Art.* New York: Doubleday.

Firestone, W. and Rosenblum, S. (1988). The alienation and commitment of students and teachers in urban high schools: A conceptual framework. *Educational Evaluation and Policy Quarterly,* 10, 285–300.

Fullan, M. (1988). *Change Processes in Secondary Schools: Towards a More Fundamental Agenda.* Toronto: University of Toronto.

Hickman, C. and Silva, M.A. (1984). *Creating Excellence.* New York: New American Library.

Hunsaker, P.L. and Alessandra, A.J. (1980). *The Art of Managing People.* New York: Simon & Schuster.

Lightfoot, S. (1983). *The Good High School.* New York: Basic Books.

Little, J. (1982). Norms of collegiality and experimentation: Workplace conditions of school success. *American Educational Research Journal,* 19(3), 325–340.

Metz, M.H. (1990). How social class differences shape teachers' work. In M.W. McLaughlin, J.E. Talbert, and N. Bascia (Eds.), *The Concepts of Teaching in Secondary Schools: Teachers' Realities.* New York: Teachers' College.

Milone, M. (1990). Handling the heat. *Technology and Learning,* 2(2), 56–60.

Mitchell, W. (1985). *The Power of Positive Students.* New York: Bantam Books,

Newmann, F.M., Rutter, R.A., and Smith, M. (1988). *Organizational Factors Affecting School Sense of Efficacy, Community and Expectation.* Madison, Wisconsin: National Center on Effective Secondary Schools.

Rosenholtz, S.J. (1989). *Teachers' Workplace: The Social Organization of Schools.* New York: Longman.

Senge, P. (1990). *The Fifth Discipline: The Art and Practice of the Learning Organization.* New York: Doubleday.

Sirotnik, K. (1983). What you see is what you get: Consistency, persistency, and mediocrity in classrooms. *Harvard Educational Review,* 53, 16–31.

Sizer, T. (1984). *Horace's Compromise: The Dilemma of the American High School.* Boston: Houghton Mifflin.

Sizer, T. (1987). His trumpet was never uncertain. *Time,* May 18, p. 68.

Wilson, B. and Corcoran, T. (1988). *Successful Secondary Schools: Visions of Excellence in American Public Schools.* East Sussex, England: Falmer Press.

Index